Greek Tragedy and the Digital

Related Titles

A Cultural History of Tragedy in Antiquity
Edited by Emily Wilson
ISBN 978-1-4742-8789-0

A Cultural History of Tragedy in the Modern Age
Edited by Jennifer Wallace
ISBN 978-1-4742-8809-5

*Avatars, Activism and Postdigital Performance:
Precarious Intermedial Identities*
Edited by Liam Jarvis and Karen Savage
ISBN 978-1-3501-5931-0

Classical Greek Tragedy
Judith Fletcher
ISBN 978-1-3501-4456-9

*Contemporary Adaptations of Greek Tragedy:
Auteurship and Directorial Visions*
Edited by George Rodosthenous
ISBN 978-1-4725-9152-4

The Bloomsbury Handbook to the Digital Humanities
Edited by James O'Sullivan
ISBN 978-1-3502-3211-2

Greek Tragedy and the Digital

Edited by George Rodosthenous and
Angeliki Poulou

methuen | drama

METHUEN DRAMA
Bloomsbury Publishing Plc
50 Bedford Square, London, WC1B 3DP, UK
1385 Broadway, New York, NY 10018, USA
29 Earlsfort Terrace, Dublin 2, Ireland

BLOOMSBURY, METHUEN DRAMA and the Methuen Drama logo are trademarks
of Bloomsbury Publishing Plc

First published in Great Britain 2023
This paperback edition published 2024

Copyright © George Rodosthenous, Angeliki Poulou and contributors, 2023

George Rodosthenous and Angeliki Poulou have asserted
their right under the Copyright, Designs and Patents Act, 1988, to be
identified as Editors of this work.

For legal purposes the Acknowledgements on p.ix constitute an extension
of this copyright page.

Cover design: Ben Anslow
Cover image: *THE AGE OF RAGE*; Based on 6 plays by Euripides and Aeschylus ;
Directed by Ivo Van Hove ; Adapted by Koen Tachelet and Ivo Van Hove.
Barbican Theatre, London, UK ; 5th May 2022. (© Jan Versweyveld / ArenaPAL)

All rights reserved. No part of this publication may be reproduced or transmitted
in any form or by any means, electronic or mechanical, including photocopying,
recording, or any information storage or retrieval system, without prior
permission in writing from the publishers.

Bloomsbury Publishing Plc does not have any control over, or responsibility
for, any third-party websites referred to or in this book. All internet addresses given in
this book were correct at the time of going to press. The author and publisher regret
any inconvenience caused if addresses have changed or sites have ceased to exist,
but can accept no responsibility for any such changes.

A catalogue record for this book is available from the British Library.

Library of Congress Cataloging-in-Publication Data
Names: Rodosthenous, George, 1973– editor. | Poulou, Angeliki, editor.
Title: Greek tragedy and the digital / edited by George Rodosthenous and
Angeliki Poulou. Description: London ; New York : Methuen Drama, 2022. |
Includes bibliographical references and index. | Identifiers: LCCN 2022014169
(print) | LCCN 2022014170 (ebook) | ISBN 9781350185852 (hardback) |
ISBN 9781350185951 (paperback) | ISBN 9781350185869 (epub) |
ISBN 9781350185876 (ebook) Subjects: LCSH: Greek drama–Modern presentation. |
Greek drama (Tragedy)—Adaptations–History and criticism. | Theater—Technological
innovations. | Technology and the arts. | Digital media. Classification: LCC PA3238 .
G746 2022 (print) | LCC PA3238 (ebook) | DDC 792.1/2—dc23/eng/20220523
LC record available at https://lccn.loc.gov/2022014169 LC ebook record available
at https://lccn.loc.gov/2022014170

ISBN: HB: 978-1-3501-8585-2
PB: 978-1-3501-8595-1
ePDF: 978-1-3501-8587-6
eBook: 978-1-3501-8586-9

Typeset by RefineCatch Limited, Bungay, Suffolk

To find out more about our authors and books visit www.bloomsbury.com
and sign up for our newsletters.

Contents

List of illustrations	vii
Notes on contributors	viii
Acknowledgements	ix

Introduction *George Rodosthenous and Angeliki Poulou* 1

Prelude   The digital in ruins: Greek tragedy and the postdigital
  David M. Berry 26

Part 1 The presence of the digital in Greek tragedy: Developments and encounters with technology 39

1. From the *Ekkyklema* to Ivo van Hove: The technology of presence in multimedia theatre and the presence of the digital in performance *George Sampatakakis* 41
2. Digital media and Greek tragedy: A rhizomatic dramaturgy *Angeliki Poulou* 64
3. Digitizing the canon: Mediated lives and purloined realities in Jay Scheib's *The Medea*, Wooster Group's *To You, the Birdie!* and Persona Theatre Company's *Phaedra I—* *Avra Sidiropoulou* 81

Part 2 The chorus and the digital: Rediscovering the politics 97

4. 'Inventing' the ancient tragic chorus: Communality and the digital in the 1999 *Oresteia*s by Katie Mitchell (NT, London) and Georges Lavaudant (Odéon, Paris) *Estelle Baudou* 99
5. Augmented vocal chorus: Sounds of digital chorus in Euripides' *Bacchae* *Chloé Larmet and Ana Wegner* 114
6. Tragedy and the digital environment: Ancient desiring machines, choruses and Oedipus *Sebastian Kirsch* 130

Part 3   Avatars, masks and cyborgs: Augmenting the reality   147

7   Digital masks for ancient Greek drama: Artificiality, constraint and metamorphosis   *Giulia Filacanapa and Erica Magris*   149
8   Cassandra in *PythiaDelphine21*: Oracles, cyborgs and the tragedy of Cassandra and temporalities within the digital   *Julie Wilson-Bokowiec*   163
9   Colonial convulsions: Akram Khan's *Xen(os)* and the digital Prometheus   *Mario Telò*   182

Postlude   Pre- and post-human(-ist) confluences in contemporary productions of Greek tragedy: The complete eradication of the live actor from the tragic stage   *Paul Monaghan*   199

In Memoriam – Michael Cacoyannis   Technological triumph and Greek tragedy: Digitizing Michael Cacoyannis' Trojan *Trilogy*   *Marianne McDonald*   213

Index   224

Illustrations

8.1	Performance Schematic: *PythiaDelphine21*	169
8.2	Oracle mediation loop	172
8.3	Cassandra mediation loop	175
8.4	Wonderment mediation/encounter loop	180

Contributors

Estelle Baudou is Postdoctoral Researcher and Marie Curie Postdoctoral Fellow at APGRD, University of Oxford, UK.

David M. Berry is Professor of Digital Humanities (Media and Film) at the School of Media, Arts and Humanities of the University of Sussex, UK.

Giulia Filacanapa is Associate Professor at the Departments of Theatre Studies and Italian of the University Paris 8, France.

Sebastian Kirsch is a theatre and literature scholar who most recently was affiliated as a Feodor Lynen research fellow at the Department of German Studies at New York University, USA (2019/2020) and the Leibniz-Zentrum für Literatur- und Kulturforschung, Berlin (2021).

Chloé Larmet is Post-Doctoral Researcher at the School ArTeC-EUR ArTeC, University of Nanterre, France.

Erica Magris is Associate Professor at the Department of Theatre Studies of the University Paris 8, France.

Marianne McDonald is Emeritus Professor of the Department of Theatre, UCSD, USA.

Paul Monaghan is Assistant Professor, Department of Classical Studies and Modern Languages, Faculty of Arts and Science, Nipissing University, Canada.

Angeliki Poulou is Adjunct Professor at the Department of Digital Arts & Cinema of the National and Kapodistrian University of Athens, Greece.

George Rodosthenous is Professor of Theatre Directing at the School of Performance and Cultural Industries of the University of Leeds, UK.

George Sampatakakis is Associate Professor at the Department of Theatre Studies of the University of Patras, Greece.

Avra Sidiropoulou is Associate Professor at the MA Programme in Theatre Studies, Open University of Cyprus, Cyprus.

Mario Telò is Professor in the Departments of Rhetoric, Classics and Comparative Literature of the University of California Berkeley, USA.

Ana Wegner is Adjunct Professor at the University of Poitiers, France.

Julie Wilson-Bokowiec is Honorary Visiting Research Fellow at the University of Huddersfield, UK.

Acknowledgements

We would like to thank Mark Dudgeon at Methuen Drama for his continuing support and interest in our research on Greek Tragedy following the volume *Contemporary Adaptations of Greek Tragedy: Auteurship and Directorial Visions* (2017). Also thanks to Ella Wilson and the editorial team at Methuen Drama, the anonymous reader for constructive feedback, Merv Honeywood and our copy-editor for their hard work.

Sincere thanks to the Michael Cacoyannis Foundation and their *Ancient Drama: Influences and Modern Approaches* initiative (2013) funded by the European Union which initiated the editors' first collaboration and the forum *Ancient Drama & Digital Era* (2018). Special thanks to Xenia Kaldara, Alexandra Georgopoulou and Olga Gratsaniti for this invaluable experience.

Additional thanks to Arthur Pritchard, Varnavas Kyriazis, Nikos Charalambous for their guidance, Dr Duška Radosavljević for her constant support, Dr Maria Kapsali, Dr George Sampatatakis and Dr Demetris Zavros for their feedback on the Introduction; also Dr Manolis Manousakis and Medea Electronique Art Collective, Dr Irene Moundraki, Dr Scott Palmer, Ms Susan Daniels, Professor Jonathan Pitches, Dr Leila Jancovich, Mrs Linda Watson, Dr Kelli Zezulka and all the colleagues, technical and support staff, stage@leeds and students at the School of Performance and Cultural Industries for their constant and invaluable brilliance.

We are grateful to all the excellent contributors of the volume for their superb contributions and working ethos during the production of this volume.

This book is dedicated in the loving memory of Dimitris Yolassis, an inspirational and innovative mind.

George Rodosthenous and Angeliki Poulou

Introduction

In *Contemporary Adaptations of Greek Tragedy: Auteurship and Directorial Visions* (2017), George Rodosthenous suggests that directors are now more eager to incorporate technological and posthuman representations, and in this way '[i]nnovations with technology will unfold new ways of representation, audience perception and engagement, perhaps involving a new interactive element, which will engage the audience in a new dimension and at a much deeper intensity' (Rodosthenous 2017). *Greek Tragedy and the Digital* builds on and integrates Rodosthenous' 2017 book by focusing on renderings of Greek tragedy in the digital era. The volume's objective is to explore the encounter between digital culture and Greek tragedy in the way this is developing within the contemporary performing arts. The volume introduces an innovative, artistic and theoretical approach to Greek tragedy at its intersection with digital media art (mixed media performances, augmented reality art events and immersive environments). It deals with new textualities in the performing arts and with the rhizomatic fragmentation of content in the digital age, which provides experiences in augmented realities, environments and immersion. When speaking of the presence of digital technology in the theatre, we imply image technology (digital video, real-time video, cameras and reproduction devices: surveillance cameras, webcams, TV screens, monitors, miniature cameras, giant screens, hologram projections), sound technology (microphones, speakers, recording devices, Musical Instrument Digital Interface systems) and the construction of an interactive/immersive environment, interactive design and animation.

The volume presents a critical account of the encounter of Greek tragedy and the digital. Directors and theatrical groups experiment with new media, with new structures of interpretation, perception and experience of art. Greek tragedy and digital media are products of different eras and cultures, and of cognitive as well as perceptual models. This new perspective – chronological, stylistic and aesthetic – reveals the dynamics and deadlocks of technology (and of the world), and acknowledges the contradictions in the performing arts. Apart from a philological or archaeological approach to the past, an attempt to understand the material, social and political terms and frameworks of ancient theatre arises in the present. Through staging tragedy, directors and their creative teams attempt to define a series of concepts about the present, placing modern civilization in a confrontation with itself and its historicity.

The encounter between ancient drama, on the one hand, and digital culture on the other has proven to be extremely inspiring for a scientist or an artist: it rejuvenates the political standards (conventional, religious, ritual, tragic aspects of theatre) of the fifth century through the contemporary art forms. It is important to remember that this oldest genre of Western theatre used sophisticated technologies to present myth. Art has always relied on elementary or more evolved levels of technological innovation, or rather, has always been in constant dialogue with technology, science and other human activities. The mixing of colours by the painter, the use of the pulley by the architect and builder of temples, palaces or tombs are also important technical steps. So, thinking about art and technology is a diachronic reality. This dialogue is undoubtedly necessary and dictated by life, but, still more fundamental, is the interrogation of the terms of this relationship and the revealing moments in their history, such as the interaction of performances of Greek tragedy with digital technology, which is the main research question of this book. Our focus in this collection remains on ancient Greek tragedy; in particular, we do not expand on Greek comedy, since there have been more 'tragic' engagements with the digital. As Berry explains, '[t]ragedy might, therefore, speak vividly to a digital audience reflecting the feelings of a fragmentary and contradictory life within computational societies' (see page 29 below).

The pandemic or better the 'syndemic' (Stiegler 2021) entered our lives at the time of the anthology's completion, bringing to the fore the debate on theatre ontology, as well as the limits of our culture and policies. Major theatrical organisations adopted live streaming. So, the debate over online and remote performance attendance, as well as digital communities and remote co-presence, were revived. At the same time, companies such as Theater of War turned to the Ancient Greek tragedies (*Oedipus the King*) in order to speak symbolically about the virus and the city. Ivo van Hove has created his *Age of Rage* (2021) based on six Greek tragedies and using digital screens in an impressive way, while Punchdrunk have embarked on an epic immersive journey *The Burnt City* (2022) capturing the fall of Troy. There has also been hybridisation between live and mediated in various cultural spheres as well as a wider acceptance of online forms of education and communication. The performing arts, after the pandemic, have brought to the fore the issue of presence rather than representation, building on the Auslander-Phelan debate, Zarrilli's work on the presence of the actor and the emphasis on live performance in the 1960s. The performing arts undertook a compensatory function in relation to the growing importance of technical models in our lives: the importance of physical presence is reinstated in the theatre; it carries an aura that no image can have, even when interactive (see Davis (1995) on digital reproduction). Physical presence is, therefore, the new horizon of the performing arts and *performativity* is its new grammar. Thus, a misconception has also been cultivated: the digital has become synonymous with the online. These two are often used interchangeably, but while something that is online is digital by definition, the reverse is not necessarily true. Things can be digital but take place entirely offline (see Blake 2014, Gere 2008, Dixon 2007). Interestingly, Dixon (2007) maps the different kinds of digital performance in a succinct way.

Increasingly, digital theatre directors have managed to converse creatively with the digital media (see Chatzichristodoulou and Jefferies (2016) and Broadhurst and Machon (2006)), and see in them more than their technical qualities: immediacy, intimacy, realism, illusion and remote communication (see Kozel 2007). In contrast, the historical artistic avant-garde was not focused only on aesthetic formalities or new tools of expression, but on articulating a new story for humanity, attempting to answer the question of 'how one should live in the world'. What are the narratives about the world presented by Greek tragedy in a digital era? Does it challenge existing relations with the public? Does it re-politicize art or does it opt for a de-signification and aesthetic experimentation?

In this collection, the contributors envision Greek tragedy as a performative phenomenon and as a *dromenon*. The authors theorize the digital and its technology as a new era that affects the reception, the theatre experience, dramaturgy/*logos*, the ideas, the thought, and our connection to the Cosmos, while introducing theoretical tools and concepts, as well as a new useful typology in 'reading' the performances. We aim to shed light on contemporary transformations of myths, revisit and further adapt the myths and try to revitalize the debate concerning the adaptation of Greek tragedy. Finally, we challenge ancient theatre conventions through the contemporary arsenal of sound masks, avatars, live code poetry, new media art, and digital cognitive experimentations. In summary, through a range of contributions, the edited collection raises the following artistic, philosophical and anthropological research questions which have not been raised before in an extensive collection:

- In what ways does augmented reality (digital fragmentation/hybridity) work within the mythical landscape?
- How are productions of Greek tragedy representing the digital body using the sound mask and avatars?

- In what ways are mythology, classics and tradition being transformed/re-appropriated/revisited?
- How can we investigate the tragic (the myth, the tragic idea and performative phenomenon) in the digital era?

Navigating the encounter between the digital and Greek tragedy

What is the digital?

Digital literary is a representation of data, of physical quantities in the form of numbers (as opposed to the analogue), and the processes that use this way of representation. The digital is a computing principle that reduces content to a blind combination of points devoid of meaning.

When referring to the term digital we mean, first, the era. The cognitive state, the digital condition (see the Prelude by David M. Berry), the way we communicate, the way we produce and consume content are important considerations in understanding the digital. The digital is the space in which we live. It is no longer a question of tools at the service of ancient practices, but of an environment in which we are immersed, which determines and shapes our world and our culture. In the digital era, there is not only a change of technological model (from analogue to digital) but, first and foremost, a sensory one (see the work of Castells (1999), Kittler, (1999), Latour (1996), Manovich (2001), Stiegler (2014) and Virilio (2006)). This requires a change in the way of perception, and observation: a change of study, of experiencing the real, which also leads to rearrangements in artistic creation and practice. After all, techniques are not just tools, but 'perception structures'; they determine how the world looks to us and how phenomena are presented to us. As a result, techniques also change the way art is produced and understood. André-Georges Haudricourt stated that technology belongs to the humanities, as a real human creativity and intellect. It is the 'science of human activity' (Sigaut 1987).

Secondly, we will refer to the tools used: the media. The term 'media' denotes first a number of technologies that offer the possibility of communication, and second the protocols and socio-cultural practices that have been developed around these technologies (Giesekam 2007). The main principle of digital media is the rendering of the elements of the material world as binary numerical sequences that form a unified whole, a process, the 'digitization' (Manovich 2001: 28), in which digital media are distinguished by the preservation of the autonomy of their individual elements, since each digital whole can be seen as a synthesis of independent self-managing units. New media are characterized by variability and convertibility while their open architecture allows their constant modification.

Thirdly, we will discuss the techniques available; digital art is the new way of communication which leads to connectivity. Digital technology is changing our practices and their meaning. Techniques, according to Mauss (2012), are the object, together with its organic and material practices, while technology is the *logos* regarding them, that is, the object of study, the field devoted to these practices. Technology is used to describe the subject and its practices. Techniques differentiate human from non-human while there is a two-way causality between human and techniques: humans make them and they allow humans to make them. Mauss also stressed that techniques are social in their function and are presented as creators and mediators of social relations (Mauss 2012: 73). Technique here is related to the will, and specifically to consciousness. Non-human entities act as agents performing skills, but not with intention (Bennett 2010).

The term *technology* primarily means tools and machines that help solve problems. Secondly, it means techniques or knowledge including methods, materials, information and procedures for resolving a situation. And thirdly, the activity that shapes culture such as construction technology, infrastructure technology or even space travel technology. Technologies emerge not only as a remarkable aesthetic phenomenon, but also, as a key to understanding the modern spectacle. Just as the term technology has a dual content, so is the digital both the technical means and the *logos* produced regarding them. The digital is a cognitive state, a trend, a condition (as noted by Berry, 2014, 2015 and in his Prelude here), as well as a tool.

Greek tragedy and the digital as semantic and performative tool

Digital technology calls into question embedded ideas about the nature of the theatre. The application of new media in the theatre is proving to be extremely diverse: the internet has clearly played a key role in their development, not only as an interactive immersive database, but also as a means of distribution and collaboration. New media and digital technology have been colonizing the theatrical scene since the 1970s, and of course throughout the twentieth century there have been experiments with technology (Meyerhold, Piscator, Appia, Svoboda etc.).

De Kerckhove shows, in his thought-provoking but highly speculative study, that the ancient Greek theatre was a product of the phonetic alphabet, which decisively influenced the sensory life of the Athenian community. This transition influenced the way the writers composed the drama, as they could not compose the tragedies as we know them if they were not first literate:

> Greek tragedy was probably not an artform primarily. It is more likely that it was a technology of change which arose at the point of conjunction of several previously unrelated strains: the practice of sport competition, the cultural policies of a prestige oriented bureaucracy, the growth of literacy, the bardic tradition and, as Gerald Else pointed out in his essay on The Origins and the Early Forms of Greek Tragedy, the need for Athens to develop a mark of distinction among other Greek states, and efface the memory of a previously unremarkable cultural background. (De Kerckhove 1980: 23–6)

In the history of culture, theatre has played an important role at any turning point in media technology. This was true both in the introduction of the phonetic alphabet and in the invention of perspective, typography and, more recently, the 'mechanization' and 'computation' of society. Theatre becomes a new medium every time new media technologies (communication and information) become dominant, and in addition it adapts and spreads new cognitive strategies, just as it did in ancient Greece (Chapple & Kattenbelt 2006: 146 and Havelock 1981: 59).

The use of alphabetic writing has greatly contributed to the transformation of worldview and standpoint, the first exemplary revolution in Western history to occur in antiquity. As its use became popularized, humans had to practise recognizing or reading symbols. It was then that visual perception, intent on the activity of reading (as well as theatre arts), began to acquire importance, along with the acoustic perception that prevailed until then. In this way, there was a gradual transition or crossing from oral to written communication (cf. Walter J. Ong's and Havelock's writings about orality amongst others).

Addressing the ears and the eyes, theatrical activity has been, ever since its advent, an early manifestation of what we will call 'audiovisual' (Garbagati and Morelli 2006: 41) two millennia later. The wide availability of printed text or paper and pencil has helped to transform authority, beliefs, attitudes and values. We have every reason to believe that the widespread use of personal computers will transform attitudes to and perceptions of the world (Hébert and Perelli-Contos 2001: 174). A similar revolution in modern theatre has been the introduction of digital writing, algorithm writing and programming.

For ancient Greek culture, the concept of the machine and its significance that includes concepts such as art, *metis* (practical wisdom), creation, etc. are characterized by a fundamental ambiguity: they offer humanity the time, the opportunity for a better life or even for salvation, but sometimes they function as divine or as human swindles and traps, leading to destruction. It was as if the Greeks identified the machine with the god because of the enormous power of the machine, a god they had to be reckoned with because its reckless treatment could lead to disaster, since it was *hubris* (as in the Prometheus myth). Identifying this very ambiguity and ambivalence of technology, Bernard Stiegler called modern technologies φάρμακα 'remedies'. Technique, finally, relays to the background the ultimate subject of modernity (Stiegler 1994) who sets out to conquer the earth and the sky. In *La Technique et le Temps 1: La faute d'Épimethée*, Stiegler argues that contrary to the traditional metaphysical view of the relationship between human and technique, according to which technique complements re-existing human nature, the human is structured through his relation to technique.

Technology emerges as a myth equivalent to its ability to be transformed and transform, to visualize imaginary worlds. In a similar way, the directors of digital theatre with the special stage writing that they develop, beyond and above that of the text, appear like present-day poets. The ancient poet did not reproduce myths, but recreated them, first through speech, and then through the performance. In a similar way, our modern directors transform myths, not only through speech, but also through the technology of image and sound. For the public of ancient Athens, myths were performances – there was no sacred text that proclaimed the truth about the gods. There was no final version of a Greek myth that irrevocably consolidated a story in writing. In an oral culture, myth-makers were free to recreate their material in response to new audiences and new situations. Poets who, like the tragic Athenians, paraphrase the already known myth, provide it with new versions, while directing the creation of the performance. Creators become *auteurs*, in the sense that they do not simply aim at a successful representation of the text but 'write' on stage, a practice that Taplin calls 'interpolation' (Taplin 2005: 133), using additional tools, altering the tragedies, offering new versions. Digital technology drives new dramaturgical interpretation by bringing the archaic universe to the imagination of contemporary audiences while preserving its alterity and distance.

This volume offers a panorama of digital practices within the performance of Greek tragedy. As the volume unfolds, we will witness that digital media function as a compositional, dramaturgical and performative tool. They are used not only as mere scenographic tools, but mainly as structural dramaturgical tools for the construction of the stage narrative. They emerge as a myth equivalent, through their ability to transform, to visualize imaginary worlds and to serve in the hands of directors as tools of interpretation of the classical world, activating tragedy in the present. With these, contemporary directors approach a series of notions regarded as 'tragedy conventions', for example, the digital as a way to re-invent the ancient chorus and free it from the clichés accumulated in its performance and reception history, offering new possibilities regarding the synthesis and formalization of the spatiotemporal.

While digital technologies can unleash unexplored potential in memory by externalizing it, they can also do the opposite, that is, block hidden possibilities in memory – especially today. Human memory is constituted by its exteriorization. Georges Canguilhem (Canguilhem 2013) also sees human life in this way. However, contrary to what Michel Serres (2012) writes, Canguilhem asserts that this externalization is not inherently positive; Plato, just like Leroi-Gourhan and Canguilhem, presents this externalization as a problem (Stiegler 2014).

We do not encounter the discourse about 'technology' in antiquity, nor in the Middle Ages; it only appears in modern times, in the context of industrial capital. Without the development of machines, without 'big industry', 'technology' has no meaning. Technology has to do not only with a specific materiality but also with speech (with an ideology), which structures it historically. 'Technology' literally means 'reason for art', it is the primary reason for the equivalence of industrial/mechanical arts. Technology in origin is the science of classifying the industrial arts (Tympas 2018 : 221).

The machine is different from the tool. Some call a simple machine a tool and a complex tool a machine. Unfortunately, they do not see any significant difference between the two and even call simple mechanical aids, such as the lever, the inclined plane, the screw and the wedge, machines. Every machine is really a combination of simple aids or power sources, no matter how differentiated they are. But the historical element is absent from such an explanation (Marx 1977: 492–3). The difference between a machine and a tool is not just in the way power is provided: humans activate the tool, while for the machine an animal, water, wind or some other physical force independent of humans is used. The machine is 'a mechanism which, after being set in motion, performs with its tools the same functions previously performed by anyone who worked with the same tools' (Marx 1977: 495).

So, if ancient Greek theatre utilized the revolving stage, the crane, the *periaktos* or the *ceraunoscopium* (Arnott 1978), digital theatre uses the automated technical stage systems, real-time video, sound design, microphones and speakers. Of course, digital media are not simply tools, they are machines that organize the word.

Data and poiesis, time and space

Ancient Greek tragedy incorporates many of the elements that make up the 'spiritual world' of its time, but in a distinctive way: through intensity and confrontation. Thus, every era, every society projects on the body of ancient drama its own values, anxieties, hopes and concerns. Myth, and its connection with the transcendental, fuel and force the dynamics of the restoration to start, or to repeat these questions through and across time. While the digital media can also contribute in this direction, presenting on stage the multiplicity and complexity of our lives, as well as its construction, digital technologies can create nuclei of intensity on the stage (live/mediated, absence/presence, natural/artificial, over-accumulation/scarcity).

Ancient Greek tragedy in its encounter with new and older digital technologies highlights exactly these antinomies of our culture, offering the necessary distance – through the myth – for critical reflection. Poetry, according to the beautiful definition of Franco Berardi, is an 'excess of the fields of dominant significance, a premonition of a possible harmony inscribed in the present chaos' (Berardi 2019: 8). The expiring digital civilization has failed to dispel inequalities, it has not liberated art from the market, it has not created strong organized avant-gardes; on the contrary, it has created a new hyperconcentration: the big data are here. Data, and their multiple arborizations, have become new epistemic landscapes. They have also become new existential terrains.

Greek tragedy could reinforce the re-poetization of our dataficated and digitized world. The poetical act is the emanation of a semiotic flow that sheds a light of non-conventional meaning on the existing world. The poetical act is a semiotic excess hinting beyond the limit of conventional meaning, and simultaneously it is a revelation of a possible sphere of experience not yet experienced. 'Only the self-organization of cognitive cyber-workers, only an alliance between the engineer and the poet, might reverse humanity's slide toward self-annihilation' (Berardi 2018: 10).

The timeless quality of myths, captured in ancient drama, is presented in synchrony with history. Historical events and myth are performed at the same time. History no longer operates in an environment of vertical time (past-present), but manifests itself in the present time, operating horizontally. This notion of time becomes a reality using on-stage technology, image capture and real-time projection, providing space with a distinctive horizontal form: the dimensions of the stage allow many dramatic actions to take place at the same time.

The introduction of new technologies on stage stems from the need for the theatre to further strengthen its connection with the real world, ultimately calling into question ways of life, communication and thinking. Undoubtedly, this is one of the reasons why the use of real-time video in the theatre is rewarding, as it maintains a temporal dimension of the shared experience. In this way, the widely dominant real-time video image allows a dramatic act to be viewed from a different angle, which at the same time is directly visible to the naked eye (Plassard 1992: 46-7).

In the twentieth century an attempt was made to provide a sense of community through the use of space, e.g. the spectacles of Reinhardt. Now, however, the construction of a community is attempted not through the creation of new spaces, but through the use of new media. The screen functions as a palimpsest of the stage. The amplification of the voice with microphones helps extend the gaze, while diffusing the sound in the room embraces the spectators in the same way as if they were present in the action, on the stage, among the heroes. Therefore, the spectators are practically immersed in this constructed atmosphere, through the video, lighting and sound, as if it were an environment specially designed to merge the auditorium and the stage. It is really insightful to note that the video as used by Mitchell (Chapters 1 and 4 below), van Hove (Chapter 1) or Warlikowski (Chapter 2) in their artistic practice, shows the viewers that the ability to see everything really reveals the responsibility they have to choose what they will see, but much more the task of choosing a viewing mode and a viewing angle.

To show what we cannot see also means to show that we cannot see everything. Viewers are obliged to make choices. The directors show the viewers at the same time, that they are the ones who choose where to look; they invite them, if they do not force them, to act as actors. As Perrot observes, they transform the theatre, which etymologically is the place where we see, into a place where we see what we do not see, a place where we see that we cannot see everything (Perrot 2013: 195). What remains uncontested is the ability of the digital media to ultimately examine live performance itself, the theatre as the art of direct and physical presence, as art that mimics reality.

Contextualizing Greek tragedy: Reception and digital media

Directors' work in relation to Greek tragedy has been extensively archived and analysed within contemporary performance adaptations (Rodosthenous 2017; Taplin 2005; Sidiropoulou 2014 amongst others). Sidiropoulou states that

[w]hether iconoclastic and irreverent, deconstructive or formalist, a strong mise-en-scène is ultimately a mise-en-scène that remains in love with its stable, unfaltering companion, even as it betrays it. (Sidiropoulou 2021: 153)

These studies of recent adaptations demonstrated explicit links between Greek tragedy and contemporary theoretical and artistic movements such as cultural/subcultural adaptations (in the impressive work of Melinda Powers, 2020) and the stranger effect, documentary theatre, archaeo-mythological dramaturgy, performance art, reception of foreign dramaturgies and postdramatic tragedies (Cole, 2019). Demory (2019) critiques our engagement with adaptation and reminds us that, '[t]o adapt is to modify, to evolve, to transform, to repeat, imitate, parody, make new' (Demory, 2019:1).

Intriguingly, there has not yet been explicit research literature on the interaction of digital technology with Greek tragedy. As Campbell (2021) discusses, absence and intimacy offer a unique mediation within the use of the digital:

The intimacy and shared space and time of live theatrical performance, ironically, become less 'real' because they are less familiar than the hegemonic media to which many of us are now accustomed. The mediated world, in this construction, makes us desire absence in order to feel intimacy. (in Liapis and Sidiropoulou (eds) 2021, 229–30)

This encounter between Greek tragedy and the digital era is still to be explored in depth. This volume aims to explore Greek tragedy's reception within the digital and postdigital era, charting and systematizing our position in relation to the digital, activating the debate of what will follow. It is about the use of digital technologies in performances of Greek tragedy, the function of performances of Greek tragedy within a digital culture (even if digital technologies are not used as such) and about how key aspects of Greek tragedy and key aspects of the digital relate to one another.

The novelty of the anthology lies in the fact that it participates creatively in the discussion concerning contemporary performance, drama and the *poetization* of technology (Berardi 2018; Lewis & Poulou 2022). Digital media could also act in a poetic way, offering to the public and the theatre productions 'virtualizations' of life. The theatre productions under investigation are indicative of the transformations that emerge when new media encounters long-established concepts, conventions and methodologies. A new poetics emerges, the poetics of the digital era, rendered via augmented realities, new spatialities and temporalities.

Scholars have already extensively studied performer training and technology (Kapsali 2020), the question of the body in acting, training and staging, the public's aesthetic transformative experience, the shifts of theatre's ontology and the historicity of the encounter between theatre and technology. Philip Auslander (2008) discusses the ontology of the media and of the live performance, challenges the view that the physical body on stage is more real and direct than the technological. Therefore, according to his reasoning, 'pure' representation is no more true or privileged than representation mediated by modern technologies. This discussion was reactivated during the coronavirus quarantine, where live spectacle was affected as art spaces, as places of mass gathering, were closed. The dialogue brought to the fore stereotypes about the nature of the theatrical event and the 'threat of the digitization of living art'.

There were those who considered that the remote viewing of a performance through a digital channel threatens the viewer's experience, distorting it as the theatre focuses on live presence and immediacy. The above approaches insist on the ontological differences between live performance and live transmission, not realizing that digital theatre in its hybrid form is at their intersection. Digital theatre is both a live and a mediated performance. It is the set of its diverse elements; on stage, theatrical, cinematic, electronic and digital elements work together, with the result that the performance emerges through the reciprocity of the constant communication between the body and the technological means. As we aim to show through the volume's chapters and analysis of performances, the extensive use of new media does not invalidate the live character of the show. 'Live' has nothing to do with the form of the medium, but at its core is related to temporality: for the viewer, 'living' means 'being there', regardless of the form of the performance.

New Dramaturgy: International Perspectives on Theory and Practice by Trencsényi & Cochrane (2014) is the first book to explore new dramaturgy in depth, and considers how our thinking about dramaturgy and the role of the dramaturge has been transformed. They deal with the stage and the text as well, with the material terms of the performance in a mediatized environment and with the dramaturgy as well. Eckersall, Grehan and Scheer (2014) explored new media dramaturgy, addressing drama theory and new media. Their work focuses on the tranformations of dramaturgy in the digital era, exploring contemporary productions. It gives an excellent overview from multimedia performance and hybrid projects of contemporary art, but does not have any overlap with the case studies of theatre productions suggested in our volume.

Our work deals with the stage and the text as well, with the material terms of the performance in a mediatized environment and with the dramaturgy as well. In the digital era, new media become equivalent to *Logos*. Artists, create and re-create current mythologies and ancient myths, using the dominant technology of the era: digital image and digital sound, immersive tools. Renowned dramaturgs and institutions, as well as smaller-scale efforts, are dealing with the potentialities of digital technology regarding the performative. As Poulou points out (Chapter 2), new media act as text-makers, developing a script, a dramaturgy, creating and re-creating current mythologies and ancient myths. Digital performance functions as myth, and artists as contemporary versions of the ancient tragic poet, transforming and visualizing fantasy worlds. Theatre directors, experimenting within their productions with the digital, modify the mythological 'megatext' in their artworks. Digital technology may also satisfy the need for narration, acting as a rhapsode, resolving and rewriting dissimilar dramatic elements. In addition to mimesis and illusion, the digital media act as performers on stage, in the words of Pierre Sarrazac (2012) as 'rhapsodes'. Thus technology acts as a performer.

Janet Murray's book *Hamlet on the Holodeck* is crucial in the discussion about new forms of the performative, the adaptation of poetic texts in digital theatre, in other terms about new media dramaturgies. It addresses the possible perspectives that emerge from the meeting of traditional storytelling and digital technology, explores how computers affect and reshape the way we experience, enjoy and communicate our stories. Murray discusses the unique qualities and pleasures that digital offers in dialogue with the traditional pleasures of storytelling, stating that 'I wrote this book to explore my belief that the computer, like the camera or the typography, has unique expressive possibilities for narrative' (Murray 1998: 15). She focuses on the idea that all successful narrative technologies become transparent, that the public loses the sense of the medium (whether it is a book or a movie) and is absorbed in the story. Once digital arts reach the same level of expressiveness as the older media we will not be interested in how we receive information. We will only think about what truth taught us about ourselves. The unique ability of computers to store vast amounts of information, especially in relation to other media, offers interesting prospects for the future of storytelling. Hypertext, artificial intelligence, 3D environments, simulations and video games offer the viewer-player unprecedented experiences and possibilities. The stories and the ways we narrate them on stage evolve through the inevitable process of moving away from the old media and creating new rules in order to satisfy the desires stimulated by digital environments. All of the above enable the artist to create a wealth of detail with scope, but also with precision: playwrights to write stories from different angles or create stories in large complex worlds. It allows more freedom of 'navigation', more detail and more direct handling of the elements of the story. Finally, Murray insists on the concept of 'transformation', the experience offered by 'digital environments'. Through kaleidoscopic narrative, as she characteristically calls it, the multifaceted ability of digital environments to mutate is exploited. The parallel narration of the same event from many perspectives, the freedom of the one who interacts to create his own stories or the creation of narrative worlds that support many possible stories, are some examples of exploiting diversity. Additionally, academics have written on artistic creation in outer space (Cern Collide residency) and on the materiality and performativity of materials and objects (Bennett 2010; Fischer-Lichte 2008; Maurin 2014) and have also explored the disruption of boundaries between art and technology, artificial and live, human and machine (Santorinaios 2020).

The issue of transformation concerns not only the adaptation of the text or the sensory impact on the viewer but also the theatre itself: the theatre is transformed through its encounter with the cutting-edge technology of its time, while each new medium embraces and surpasses the previous one; it incorporates it. Bolter and Grusin (1998) argue that new media are gaining cultural significance precisely by paying tribute to competing media and reshaping the past, such as painting and its perspective, photography, the cinema and television. They call this process of regeneration 'remediation' and point out that the previous media have also transformed some predecessor: photography replaced painting, the cinema replaced stage production and photography, television replaced the cinema, variety shows and the radio. They argue that remediation is a defining characteristic of the new digital media (Bolter & Grusin 1998 : 2–19). Steve Dixon, who back in 2007 authored the most complete study on digital performance to date, addressed not only image technology, but sound and interaction technology as well; he argues that digital theatre is an extension of the on-going history of adopting and adapting technologies in order to increase the effectiveness, the sensory and emotional impact of a performance and its symbolic and mental power (Dixon 2007: 40). Furthermore, it is also useful to note the work of Rydberg-Cox in 2011 in relation to the digital and the language of Greek tragedy. His visualization of the characters in Greek tragedy and social networks can bring new insights to the reader/director. The project used linguistic dependency treebanks and digitized texts to create 'social networks for a collection of Greek tragedies that allow users to visualize the interactions between characters in the plays' (2011: 1).

Chapple & Kattenbelt (2006) and Giesekam (2007) are amongst the first to systematize the discussion about digital theatre, dealing not only with study cases but also trying to describe trends and to see the transformations of theatre. They engage with cutting-edge productions and debates on performance and the digital and the reception of the classics, elaborating on notions of performativity, liveness, immersion, intermediality, the theatre as hypermedia, rhizomatic technological fragmentation, chorality and rhapsodization. Their analysis of 'intermedial' and 'multimedial' played a crucial role in the understanding of digital theatre. The hypermedial theatre engages the viewer in the awareness of the interaction of different media, and hence in the presence of the media themselves. In this way, the construction of the event requires from the viewer a sensorium based on the flow, interconnection, interaction and synchronicity, reminiscent of modern culture, offering a direct confluence with the form and texture of this culture.

Béatrice Picon-Vallin (1998), Josette Féral (2012) and Edwige Perrot (2017) have delivered powerful panoramas on the intersection of performing arts and digital media, from the very beginning (screens on stage) to the most sophisticated experimentations of today (robots on stage). Their works offer an overview of emblematic artists of the field, discussing the dramaturgical and directorial issues that emerge. They discuss digital media in their historicity, registering them in the history of theatre. Both of them pay attention in the question of the 'body' and of 'presence'. Their fruitful dedication to this theme led them to introduce new concepts about the performative, such as 'effets de présence'. Picon-Vallin and Perrot focused on image technology, leaving aside the sound dimension. Marie-Madeleine Mervant-Roux (2014) contributed crucially in the discussion especially of the question of sound in performances.

All the above had inaugurated the discussion about theatre and digital media, from a directorial point of view, insisting more on directors' and performers' practices, registering their analysis in the history of '*mise-en-scène*' than on dramaturgy. Consequently, even if they analysed adaptations of classical plays in digital theatre, they had not explored this encounter between classic forms of theatre with emerging media and methodologies. That is to say, *Greek Tragedy and the Digital* aims to enlighten the use of digital media not only through a director's oeuvre, but mostly to discuss the encounter between two different genres.

Contextualising intermediality, remediation and performativity

Greek Tragedy and the Digital deals with cutting edge productions and debates on performance and the digital and the reception of the classics: performativity, liveness, immersion, intermediality, the theatre as hypermedia, rhizomatic technological fragmentation, chorality and rhapsodization. In addition, the collection discusses the relationship of Greek tragedy with the past through the analysis of performances. The volume explicitly dissects the analysis of the performance and the philosophy and anthropology of art and technique.

In hypermedial theatre, the construction of the event requires from the viewer a sensorium based on flow, interconnection, interaction and synchronicity, reminiscent of modern culture, offering a direct confluence with the form and texture of this culture. A characteristic of this new form of theatre is intermediality which

> is an effect performed in-between mediality, supplying multiple perspectives and foregrounding the making of meaning by the receivers of the performance, the new theoretical base of modularity, inter-activity and a self-reflexive process, appropriate to postmodern theatre and visual performance culture. (Lavender 2006: 63)

Intermedial and multimedial performances can also be characterized as 'dialogic media productions' (Bell 2000), while there is also the term 'mixed media performances' (Auslander 2008), suitable for performances and artistic events, mainly from the 1970s onwards, in which artists combined many varied artistic practices, methods and tools (Crossley 2019).

In the performances under study, we will see techniques such as motion capture, real time processing, diffusion of the voice though kinaesonic means, immersive environments, devices, software and hardware, digital environments (platforms), mapping, encoding, multi-channel loudspeakers and human and non-human interaction. In this collection, performances of ancient Greek tragedies which are both 'intermedial' and 'multimedial' (Giesekam 2007: 8) are studied in depth. Artists discussed range from Kzryztof Warlikowski, Jan Fabre, Romeo Castellucci, Katie Mitchell, Georges Lavaudant, the Wooster Group, Labex Arts-H2H, Akram Khan, Urland and Crew, Medea Electronique, Robert Wilson, Michael Cacoyannis, Klaus Obermaier, Guy Cassiers, Luca De Fusco, Ivo van Hove, Avra Sidiropoulou, Jay Scheib, Georgia Spiropoulos and Andy Lavender. In other words, the reader will encounter directors who are milestones in the performance of the classics, but also directors of contemporary hybrid art considered as 'digital artists'. Specific productions, for example Mitchell's *Oresteia* and the work of Castellucci and the Wooster Group, recur and re-appear in these chapters and remind us of the above common thematic threads.

In the performances under study, the means of mimesis have changed greatly, while the creators seek the 'transformation' of the spectator, through his participation in an 'encircling' theatrical experience. It could be said that the performances balance imitating an act (representation of a reality, illusion, identification of the spectator with the actors) with performance. The technologies of sound, image, interaction and immersion (construction of immersive environments) prove helpful in this. Consequently, new technologies are not only used for representational purposes, but often operate independently of the text and the performance of the actors, allowing us to speak of 'audio' and 'visual' drama, which in turn act as performers or even further, narrate another parallel story as context or subtext.

Digital theatre offers cinema, television and digital video on stage, in a *performative condition,* in which they function first and foremost as theatrical symbols/signs. They act and bring about changes, sensorially affecting the viewer. To put it another way, film, television and digital video are not only screened, but also 'directed' and presented, as theatre is the art of performance (*mise-en-scène*/staging). They create first and foremost *a sense of presence*, through the virtual figures, the *disembodied voices* and the digital images of the actors on the screen. They have been invested with another role, decisive for the development of the play: the role of the partner, which completes one or more acts and guides the development of the narrative or the stage acts. In this connection, these *senses* play a role that transcends the narrow field of representation. They act and interact. Maria Kapsali in her insightful *Performer Training and Technology: Preparing Our Selves* re-affirms that according to Scott and Barton

> technologies are no longer 'merely tools' (2019: 78) which might compete with the performer for status and attention. They rather propose that the performer's 'presence' and 'agency' are constituted in relation to the behaviour and performance of technological devices through a range of 'actions, interactions, and relationships'. Involving both human and technological counterparts (Scott and Barton 2019: 63). (Kapsali 2020: 15)

Digital heroes are performative, to the extent that they stop representing and establish a new reality, that is, to the extent that they enact a presence as actors or as partners in the performance. The potential body transcends the imitation of things, moving towards performativity, through the sense of presence and reality that it creates. Finally, they are useful for the establishment of language levels and meta-levels (narration mechanisms, flashback, appearance of a thought like a comics bubble etc.). The flow of information on stage is a factor that shapes the experience of the performance; it is performed in a lasting continuum between the living presence and the live transmission, the material and the incorporeal dimension.

Structure of the book

The volume is divided into three Parts: The Presence of the Digital in Greek Tragedy: Developments and Encounters with Technology; The Chorus and the Digital: Re-Discovering the Politics; and Avatars, Masks and Cyborgs: Augmenting Reality. It also includes a Prelude and Postlude which focus on the journey from the digital to the posthuman and an in-memoriam essay on Michael Cacoyannis' Trojan *Trilogy*. The reader is free to navigate this anthology in their own preferred order without losing the overall unity of the discussion.

Prelude

In the Prelude, David M. Berry wonders how Greek tragedy can be read differently under conditions of computational analysis and distant-reading techniques. Equally, can we seek to understand the digital using the idea of the tragic? Do the notions of myth, stage or ruins offer a useful way to think about the digital and how does a collision between the ancient form of tragedy and the contemporary milieu of the postdigital assist in thinking about these questions? He investigates these questions and especially the extent to which the ontology of the digital is indeed tragic and whether this understanding can help diagnose our current situation.

Part One – The presence of the digital in Greek tragedy: Developments and encounters with technology

The first Part discusses the intertextuality of Greek tragedy and the intermediality of our era, the ways that myth is being transformed through the digital. Digital media is emerging as a compositional-dramaturgical tool. A substantial theoretical discussion is developed for basic concepts that define this encounter of the tragic with the digital. We see, then, the digital media being used both as simple scenographic tools, but mainly as structural dramaturgical tools for the construction of stage narration.

George Sampatakakis inaugurates the volume, offering an in-depth overview of the uses of digital in the context of a representation of ancient Greek tragedy on the modern stage. He provides a typology of media uses in modern productions of Greek tragedy, where 'the material body and its subjectivity are extended, challenged and reconfigured through technology' (Causey 2006 : 16).

Poulou (Chapter 2) insists on the possibilities provided by the digital media – with their rhizome logic – to activate the intertextuality of tragedy.

Thus, artists, experimenting within their productions with the digital, modify the mythological 'megatext' in their artworks. In other words: digital technology, with its ability to construct worlds and atmospheres, functions as the myth and directors become a contemporary version of the ancient tragic poet.

Avra Sidiropoulou (Chapter 3) considers digital media as tools of interpretation of the classical world. She examines the function of technology in contemporary adaptations of Greek tragedy, highlighting a few of the multiple interpretative levels that are generated upon the collision of the ancient text and the digitally semiotized performance. She argues that the remediation of the classical text produces a kind of turbulence that is both risky and necessary to our twenty-first-century spectator sensibilities and discusses a number of ways in which the new hegemony of the mediated image has radically affected the ways in which directors can read and audiences can appreciate the dramatic canon.

Part Two – The chorus and the digital: Rediscovering the politics

Part Two expounds on the discussion about how the digital activates chorus, chorality and polyphony. A question is raised here of the collective and the community as well as the political, concepts that have colonized ancient Greek tragedy. The performances reflect the change that has taken place in the city–citizen, individual–group relationship, while new forms of communities appear. Real-time video, audio and video technology and the environments/atmospheres contribute significantly to the creation of a theatre community that is a 'sustainable dialectic between loneliness and coexistence with others (Fischer-Lichte 2008: 250). In addition to their role in building the fleeting sense of community, digital media are presented in the performances as equivalents of the chorus, replacing some of its functions, while at the same time, with their ability to build environments and atmospheres, they satisfy the need of the directors for experimentation with the space of the performance.

Throughout the twentieth century, directors projected on the body of ancient drama the utopia of the reconstruction of the 'community of citizens'. There is a lot of experimentation on what community/communality means today. At the same time, the difficulty which artists have in approaching the issue of the chorus is remarkable, while many talk about the unperformability of the ancient tragic chorus. In this volume, Estelle Baudou (Chapter 4) tackles this very tricky issue. Through a comparative analysis of performances staged by important European directors, she examines the question of whether real-time video can create communality effects. Can modern image technologies replace dance functions? In her view, the aim is no longer to invent communality but rather to perform the fragmentation of the postmodern world and individual. She shows how the digital is a way to invent the ancient chorus and free it from the clichés accumulated in its performance and reception history.

Chloé Larmet and Ana Wegner (Chapter 5) explore sound, sonority and voice: both ancient Greek tragedy and the digital media open up a privileged field for the investigation of sound and otherness. With Euripides' *Bacchae* as a point of reference, they explore the other-digital and non-digital, focusing on the actor and acting. In search of a 'modern ritualization', they discuss the concepts of the augmented actor, augmented voice, augmented environment. They explore how these forms of alterity (augmented voices) could possibly give a contemporary twist to mythical characters and create original encounters. The emphasis on the voice (and therefore on the actor) strengthens the presence of the body on stage while the imaging technologies eliminate (or replace) it; the voice re-introduces the text on the stage, dissolved in the sonorities of speech that penetrates the sounds and meanings to find the language of feeling.

Sebastien Kirsch (Chapter 6) enriches the volume with a philosophical approach – a parallel discussion of tragedy and the digital. In what ways does tragedy – as a landmark of a total worldview – converse with another cognitive model, that of digital culture? What does ancient Greek tragedy have in common with modern networks? How do the non-protagonists of the tragedy relate to the digital world? In his analysis, he relies on *Oedipus Rex* and the work of Michel Foucault, arguing that the logic of digital media liberates the perception that ancient Greek tragedy had of the world and the human. He argues that the chorus in ancient Greek tragedy is activated in the digital world, as the chorus did not fit into the dualistic frame of the picture/stage and its optical/mirroring framework. In the digital age, the chorus is related to all the cosmic forces which lie beyond the public/oikos.

Part Three – Avatars, masks and cyborgs: Augmenting reality

Part Three deals with immersive/interactive technologies on the theatre stage, which re-activate Greek tragedy as a performative phenomenon, as a *dromenon*. It develops the discussion beyond imitation and performance: the new horizon is immersion and virtual reality. Immersion is now a possibility of hybridization, regeneration, magnification with artificial prefixes, improvement, with the installation of technical assistance inside and on the body. The immersive experience produces pleasure, which blends the body with its environment and disrupts the knowledge of the familiar boundaries.

Belting speaks of 'unreal consciousness' (Belting 2004: 114), noting that there is in this experience a revival of the old feeling of ecstasy: this feeling of immersion, of diving into a new 'I', in a universe of unlimited transformation.

The three chapters of this section study ancient Greek tragedy performances made with interactive technologies, bringing avatars and cyborgs on 'stage'. The means of *mimesis* have changed greatly, while the creators seek the 'transformation' of the spectators, through their participation in a 'circular' theatrical experience. Virtual environments invite the spectators, instead of identifying with the heroes of the action, to enter this world, not merely observe it from a distance. Theatre has always been a *virtual reality*, where the actors conspired imaginarily with the audience in order to create a common faith.

Giulia Fillacanapa and Erica Magris (Chapter 7) study the multiple variations of the actor's relationship to analogue and digital technologies, formulating the hypothesis that the mask can help to understand the actor's response to new technologies and augmented stages. They discuss the way in which the mask-avatar device is a 'technological mask', a dramaturgical and acting tool. Thanks to new technology, the audience is invited to live a collective experience and to take part in this attempt to build a polis for the twenty-first century through theatre.

Julie Wilson-Bokowiec (Chapter 8) explores ancient oracular practices and cyber-art performance, the spatiotemporal abilities of oracles and cyborgs, so as to foreground the dialectics between visible and invisible, exterior and interior, procedure (or tension) inherent in ancient Greek tragedy and digital media. She is interested in the issue of space and time, the technologies of synthesis and formalization of the spatiotemporal, as well as the digital and online environments that are being used for the making and presentation of new theatre work (Zoom, Streamyard etc.). She suggests that the connection between ancient analogue forms embodied in myth linked to landscape/nature, are reinvigorated by the specificities of digital mediation where past, present and an imagined future become malleable and dynamic.

Mario Telo (Chapter 9) considers how the digital medium may not just disseminate but inhabit – despite itself – the aesthetics of Greek tragedy. Inspired by the dancer Akram Khan, Aeschylus' *Prometheus* and the philosophical view of the aesthetics of Jacques Rancière (2015), Telo looks for ways to connect the somatic 'infinitude' of kinetic spinning with modes of recalcitrant expansion, continuity and infinitude in tragic language as well as in the digital medium per se. He suggests that the digital could be seen as an archival medium, 'embedded in software architectures and in the political economy of social media platforms' (Ibrus and Ojamaa 2020: 66).

Postlude

In the Postlude, Paul Monaghan focuses on a series of attempts to minimize and depersonalize, and eventually to eradicate, the presence of the live human actor in the performance of Greek tragedy. Discussing the topic in its historical context, he shows how the modern subject and its counterpart, the modern dramatic character, can be seen to have been an aberrant interloper. The chapter asks to what extent such virtual performances, in which the 'sullying corporeality' of the live human actor is extracted from the performance of Greek tragedy, serve the inherent aim of the genre to reflect on what it is to be human.

In Memoriam - Michael Cacoyannis

Marianne McDonald is a pioneer in the reception of Greek tragedy: her *Euripides in Cinema: The Heart Made Visible* (1983) was one of the first books about Greek tragedy in film; her *Ancient Sun, Modern Light: Greek Drama on the Modern Stage* (1992) traced modern stage versions; and *Living Art of Greek Tragedy* (2003) continued to document this technological progress. In the final section of this book she presents a retrospective about the relationship of technology and Greek tragedy, with special reference to Michael Cacoyannis' film adaptations of *Iphigenia*, *The Trojan Women* and *Electra*. In her own distinct style, McDonald offers a valuable overview of the works and the impact of their cinematic counterparts in order to offer a moving in memoriam to Michael Cacoyannis and his contribution to Greek tragedy.

Tragedy in the digital age can be led in a postdigital direction, showing not how we can live with the digital media or how they help our lives but more reminiscent of the concept of 'sympoiesis' (Haraway 2016); of 'inhabiting the world together', new ways of thinking and becoming together with other species in an on-going process of sympoiesis or co-creation, which is crucial in order to think with both human and non-human agents and ecologies (2016: 61). It can show this new cosmological and terrestrial architecture and its horizon can be the environment: nature, universe and ecology. Greek tragedy speaks about the place of humans in the world and about their eternal agony in setting order and boundaries to chaos.

References

Arnott, P. (1978), *Greek Scenic Conventions in the Fifth Century*, Westport, CT: Greenwood Press.

Auslander, P. (2008), *Liveness: Performance in a Mediatized Culture*, London and New York: Routledge.
Bell, P. (2000), 'Dialogic Media Productions and Inter-media Exchange', *Journal of Dramatic Theory and Criticism*, 14(2): 41–55.
Belting, H. (2004), *Pour une anthropologie des images*, Paris: Gallimard.
Bennett, J. (2010), *Vibrant Matter: A Political Ecology of Things*, Durham, NC: Duke University Press.
Berardi, F. (2019), *Breathing, Chaos and Poetry*, Cambridge, MA: MIT Press.
Berry, D. M. (2014), *Critical Theory and the Digital*, New York: Bloomsbury.
Berry, D. M. (2015), 'The Postdigital Constellation', in D. M. Berry and M. Dieter (eds), *Postdigital Aesthetics: Art, Computation and Design*, London: Palgrave.
Blake, Bill (2014), *Theatre and the Digital*, London: Bloomsbury.
Bolter, J. D., and R. Grusin (1998), *Remediation: Understanding New Media*, Cambridge, MA: MIT Press.
Broadhurst, S., and J. Machon (eds) (2006), *Performance and Technology: Practices of Virtual Embodiment and Interactivity*, Basingstoke: Palgrave Macmillan, 2006.
Campbell, Peter A. (2012), 'Technology, Media and Intermediality in Contemporary Adaptations of Greek Tragedy', in V. Liapis and A. Sidiropoulou (eds), *Adapting Greek Tragedy: Contemporary Contexts for Ancient Texts*, 227–46, Cambridge: Cambridge University Press.
Canguilhem, G. (2013), *Le Normal et le Pathologique*, Paris: Puf.
Castells, M., (1999), *The Information Age*, 3 vols., Cambridge, MA and Oxford: Blackwell, 1999.
Causey, M. (2006), *Theatre and Performance in Digital Culture: From Simulation to Embeddedness*, London and New York: Routledge.
Chapple, F., and C. Kattenbelt (2006), *Intermediality in Theatre and Performance*, Amsterdam and New York: Rodopi.
Chatzichristodoulou, M., and J. Jefferies (2016), *Interfaces of Performance: Digital Research in the Arts and Humanities*, London New York: Routledge.
Cole, E. (2019), *Postdramatic Tragedies*, Cambridge: Cambridge University Press.
Crossley, M. (ed.) (2019), *Intermedial Theatre*. London: Springer.
De Kerckhove, D. (1980), 'A Theory of Greek Tragedy', *SubStance*, 9 (29): 23–36.
Demory, P. (2019), '*Queer/Adaptation: An Introduction*' in Pamela Demory (ed.), *Queer/Adaptation: A Collection of Critical Essays*, 1–13, Cham: Palgrave Macmillan.
Dixon, S. (2007), *Digital Performance, A History of New Media in Theater, Dance, Performance Art, and Installation*, Cambridge, MA: MIT Press.
Eckersall, P., H. Grehan and E. Scheer (2017), *New Media Dramaturgy Performance, Media and New-Materialism*, London: Palgrave Macmillan.
Féral, J. (2012), *Performatives Body Remix*, Quebec: Presses de l'Université du Quebec.
Fischer-Lichte, E. (2008), *Theatre, Sacrifice, Ritual, Exploring Forms of Political Theatre*, London and New York: Routledge.

Fischer-Lichte, E. (2008), *The Transformative Power of Performance: a New Aesthetics*, London and New York: Routledge.
Garbagati, L., and P. Morelli (2006), *Théâtre et nouvelles technologies*, Dijon: Presses Universitaires de Dijon.
Gere, Charlie (2008), *Digital culture*, London: Reaktion Books.
Giesekam, G. (2007), *Staging the Screen: The Use of Film and Video in Theatre*, New York: Palgrave Macmillan.
Haraway, D. (2016), *Staying with the Trouble, Making Kin in the Chthulucene*, Durham, NC, and London: Duke University Press.
Havelock, E. A. (1981), *The Literate Revolution in Greece and its Cultural Consequences*, Princeton: Princeton University Press.
Hébert, C., and L. Perelli-Contos (2001), *La Face cachée du théâtre de l'image*, Paris: L'Harmattan.
Kapsali, M. (2020), *Performer Training and Technology: Preparing Our Selves. Perspectives on Performer Training*. London and New York: Routledge.
Kittler, F. A. (1999), *Gramophone, Film, Typewriter*, Stanford, CA: Stanford University Press.
Latour, B. (1996), *Aramis, or, The Love of Technology*, Cambridge, MA: Harvard University Press.
Lewis, E., and A. Poulou (2022), *From Fruit to Root: Medea Electronique's Interactive Archive of New Media Art*, Athens: Onassis Foundation.
Liapis, V., and A. Sidiropoulou (eds) (2021), *Adapting Greek Tragedy: Contemporary Contexts for Ancient Texts*, Cambridge: Cambridge University Press.
Manovich, L. (2001), *The Language of New Media*, Cambridge, MA: MIT Press.
Maurin, F. (2014), *Ivo van Hove*, Arles: Actes sud.
Marx, K. (1977), *Capital: A Critique of Political Economy*, vol.1, transl. B. Fowkes, New York: Vintage Books.
Mauss, M. (2012), *Techniques, technologie et civilisation*, Paris: Presses Universitaires de France.
McDonald, M. (1983), *Euripides in Cinema*, Philadelphia: Centrum Philadelphia.
McDonald, M. (1992), *Ancient Sun, Modern Light: Greek Drama on the Modern Stage*, New York and London: Columbia University Press.
McDonald, M. (1993), *The Living Art of Greek Tragedy*, Bloomington, IN: Indiana University Press; Chesham: Combined Academic.
Mervant-Roux, M.-M. et al. (2014), *Soundspaces: espaces, experiences at politiques du sonore*, Rennes: Presses universitaires de Rennes.
Murray, J. (1998), *Hamlet on the Holodeck: The Future of Narrative in Cyberspace*, Cambridge, MA: MIT Press.
Perrot, E. (2013), *Les usages de la vidéo en direct au théâtre chez Ivo van Hove et chez Guy Cassiers*, PhD thesis, Paris-Montréal: Université de la Sorbonne Nouvelle & Université du Québec à Montréal.
Perrot, E. (ed.) (2017), *Guy Cassiers*, Arles: Actes sud.

Picon-Vallin, B. (1998), *Les écrans sur la scène: Tentations et résistances de la scène face aux images,* Lausanne: L'Age d'Homme.
Plassard, D. (1992), *L'acteur en effigie,* Lausanne: L'Age d'homme.
Powers, M. (2020), *Reclaiming Greek Drama for Diverse Audiences: An Anthology of Adaptations and Interviews,* London and New York: Routledge.
Rancière, J. (2015), *Dissensus, On Politics and Aesthetics,* trans. S. Corcoran, London: Bloomsbury.
Rodosthenous, G. (2017), *Contemporary Adaptations of Greek Tragedy, Auteurship and Directorial Visions,* London: Bloomsbury.
Rydberg-Cox, J. (2011), 'Social Networks and the Language of Greek Tragedy', *Journal of the Chicago Colloquium on Digital Humanities and Computer Science* 1(3).
Santorinaios, M. (2020), 'The *Keyword* against *–isms*: The Conditions for the Completion of a Quiet Reovlution', *Krisi Biannual Scientific Review 8,* Athens: Topos editions.
Sarrazac, J. P. (2012), *Poétique du drame moderne,* Paris: Editions du Seuil.
Scott, J., and B. Barton (2019), 'The Performer in Intermedial Theatre' in Mark Crossley (ed.), *Intermedial Theatre,* London: Springer.
Serres, M. (2012), *Petite Poucette,* Paris: Éditions Le Pommier.
Sidiropoulou, A. (2014), 'Adaptation, Re-contextualisation, and Metaphor: Auteur Directors and the Staging of Greek Tragedy', *Oxford Journals, Adaptation* 8: 31–49.
Sigaut, F. (1987), Preface to André-Georges Haudricourt, *La technologie, science humaine,* 9–34, Paris: Editions de la maison des sciences de l'homme.
Stiegler, B. (1994), *La Technique et le Temps 1: La faute d'Épiméthée,* Paris: Éditions Galilée.
Stiegler, B. (2014), *Digital Studies, humanités numériques et technologies de la connaissance,* Limoges: Fyp Éditions.
Stiegler, B. (2021), *De la démocratie en Pandémie ; Santé, recherche, éducation,* Paris: Gallimard.
Taplin, O. (2005), *Greek Tragedy in Action,* London and New York: Routledge.
Trencsényi, K., and B. Cochrane (2014), *New Dramaturgy: International Perspectives on Theory and Practice,* London and New York: Bloomsbury.
Tympas, T. (2018), 'Marxism, Technology and Science, History: Notes on a footnote about an unwritten book', *KRISI Biannual Scientific Review* 4 (2): 215–31.
Virilio, P. (2006), *The Information Bomb,* London: Verso.

PRELUDE

The digital in ruins

Greek tragedy and the postdigital

David M. Berry

Introduction

Digital transformations from the widespread use of computational technology have had a huge effect across societies, economies and cultures. This has brought new challenges, such as digital computers that replace the factories and offices of yesterday, and networks and satellites that transform the kinds of social ontologies possible under digital conditions. These transformations place new pressures on the human subject, some of which increase a sense of division and inner turmoil in relation to new modes of being-in-the-world. Indeed, lives are lived and culture is understood and accessed through digital forms mediated through technology. The subject of the digital condition is seen as already always divided and constantly caught in the contradictions of experience. We see new attempts to rethink the human self as a multiplicity, often represented as a fragmented subject distributed across digital media, creating what Deleuze calls 'dividuals' rather than individuals, and masses that become 'samples, data, markets, or "'banks"'' (Deleuze 1995: 180). With the advent of a comprehensively digital society, the older distinctions between the physical and the digital, online and offline, no longer make sense, and society can be said to be postdigital (see Berry 2015: 50). Similarly, people's lives are increasingly affected by algorithms which they do not fully understand, subject to the seeming whims of an alien intelligence whose force is evident across all levels of society.

Algorithmic thinking pervades digital life, substituting human action for the programmed calculations of computers and making algorithms the *doxa*, or common-sense, of contemporary life. For example, a simple application like the spreadsheet has transformed how groups and institutions work. It can be used to suggest pathways for action via the operation of the rows and columns of the document.[1] The spreadsheet thus dictates the horizon of possibility for many decisions by concretizing and reinforcing an operationalization of instrumental rationality. It uses techiques from accountancy hidden within algorithms that are often only partially intelligible to human agency. Decisions that previously might have been simply creative now tend to be pushed through a spreadsheet meat-grinder for it to spit out the reality of the idea as expressed in monetary terms. This means that computation becomes hegemonic, and entangled with everyday life and experience to the extent that we use it without thinking about it. All that remains is to actualize the reality that the algorithm has uncovered. The means determine the ends.[2]

The effects of computation are wide-ranging and threaten notions of individual liberty, undermining a sense of individual autonomy, and weakening even that bulwark of the neoliberal system, consumer sovereignty. Profit from computation also often appears to require the mobilization of persuasive technologies that cynically but very successfully create addictive human behaviour, further breaking the link between individual autonomy and choice. This highlights the tragic register of digital society with its notion of the individual as a rational monad, but in reality it is shattered into component pieces and distributed across multiple systems and algorithms. As such the notion of autonomy, in the Kantian sense, is under constant stress from an environment that is constructed to overwhelm and shape its behaviours. Here, there are echoes of interpretations of tragedy that provide a shared sense of the order of things even as they fall apart. For example, we might note that even as computation destabilizes the moral economy of capitalism, creating vast profits from exchange and production processes that might be considered pre-capitalistic or obscenely inegalitarian, such as intensive micro-work or fragmented labour in the gig economy, the ideology of computation promotes self-reliance, freedom and agency for the individual.[3] This has created new feelings of alienation and disorientation from society and from the self. The social might be said to be in ruins. In which case, the question becomes how should we dwell in the ruins?

To examine this, in the first section I look at how we might read the digital through tragedy that is to ask how theorizations of tragedy might give us concepts and ideas for thinking about the digital. In the second section, I turn to look at how tragedy might be read using the resources and tools which digital technology makes available to transform readings of tragedy – that is, the idea of 'distant reading' or the use of computation to augment our understanding of tragedy. Lastly, I turn to bring these together to consider how the notion of the postdigital itself can change the way we think about tragedy and ways forward for a research programme that might address some of these questions.

Reading the digital through tragedy

Around the 1800s, idealist thinkers like Hegel and Hölderlin used Greek tragedy to creatively reflect on the ways in which distinctive forms of human freedom might be manifested historically, but also how notions of agency and subjectivity might be represented and discursively constructed at particular historical moments. The nineteenth century was a time of new translations and readings of classical authors and as such sparked new creative ideas and new ways of thinking philosophically and historically in a culture that was on the cusp of the industrial revolution. This was important for idealist thinkers regarding the growing tensions experienced by the individual within industrial society, and with it notions of alienation and inner conflict which could be explored through the tragic form. Antigone's struggle against the laws of Creon, for example, are seen as representative of an important concept of freedom between the particular and the universal, where Antigone represents the conflict between the family, as the natural source of ethical life, and ethical life itself in its social universality in the *polis* (Mills 1998).[4] Billings (2014) argues that it was the possibility of parallelisms in thought, and through the comparison and critique of culture that these generated, a space of reflection was opened up for thinking about differences and similarities between cultural moments.

As Eagleton argues, tragedy has a double role, 'both validating social institutions and calling them into question' (Eagleton 2020: 13). Similarly, Goldhill observes that 'tragedy was perceived to be literature to inform and form the imagination'; from the beginning, ancient Greeks 'believed that tragedy was somehow offering them insights into the human condition' (Goldhill 2008: 56). Perhaps as cultures react to the new digital transformation of the wider economy and society, Greek tragedy might again be a useful way to reflect on the human condition. For example, Felski argues that tragedy tends to involve conflict within a single protagonist who has divided desires (2008: 7). Within the context of social media this description echoes the experience of life in the stream of data, the individual caught in a forest of dividing paths through clicks and likes. The idea of the tragic, or a collision between the ancient form of tragedy and the contemporary milieu of the digital might offer new ways of seeing the human condition today. But rather than insinuating the 'Christianized' notions of tragedy which seeks a sense of a redemptive ending that Goldhill (2014: 638) observes in the interpretations of Schelling and Hegel, the subject of digital society embodies tension, ambiguity and conflict but no necessary implicit redemption. Tragedy might, therefore, speak vividly to a digital audience reflecting the feelings of a fragmentary and contradictory life within computational societies.

Similarly, in cultural life, computation has had and continues to have a revolutionary effect on the production, dissemination and reception of culture. Indeed, in a Hegelian sense, computation may be seen as a medium for world-historical forces, causing a revaluation of values and a dramatic transformation of our sense of recognition and social and ethical life. As computation has been distributed across society it becomes spirit and an important part of culture itself. But it is not just the medium of cultural life that is changed, and not just for the worse. The very process of writing and thinking is reshaped when word-processing replaces the typewriter and zoom transforms script-writing meetings. As Nietzsche observed of his use of a typewriter for writing philosophy, 'our writing tools are also working on our thoughts' (quoted in Kittler 1999: 200). Many a musician (and record label) watched in horror as the internet swallowed the political economy of music writing and performing in the early 2000s whilst enjoying new freedoms from digital technology for writing and recording music.

A similar process is now underway in relation to film and television, as streaming services challenge the previous distribution channels of the film and television industries undercutting previous economic models, whilst simultaneously making available new digital camera techniques, editing processes and ways of watching and enjoying visual forms. We see also that previous cultural formations, such as dramatic theatre, can be radically changed under postdigital conditions. Elements of a residual culture in decline can be reversed through the new distribution and storage capacities of digital media by making it more widely accessible to a larger number of people. But the effects of digital media go far beyond the revolutionary aspects of new storage and distribution techniques, and change the ways in which cultural artefacts might be experienced and understood more generally, even how they might be translated, performed or critically appreciated, such as by National Theatre Live in the UK which presents their productions via YouTube and as an app.

This can result in cultural transformation, where the possibilities of the new medium opens up new ways of working with culture, potentially democratising access, widening reception or creating new communities around cultural forms. Indeed, through the internet, new collectivities have formed around elected affinities of shared cultural interests and often forgotten cultural objects, from obscure Japanese Manga comics to obsolete media technologies. Witness the changing nature of film and television under digital conditions, or the form of the album under streaming services. Similarly, the theatre itself potentially becomes a theatre without walls where live-stream technologies allow an audience from the internet to watch a performance across time and space, changing what is performed and how actors stand, speak and move within the narrow lenses of the live-stream cameras.[5] A good example of this is given by *Medea* performed by the National Theatre in which the use of wide-angle lenses and close up camera techniques bring an internet-based audience right into the action of the play whilst preserving the sense of a theatre production.[6] The Archive of Performances of Greek and Roman Drama similarly utilizes new media forms made possible by Zoom and video streaming platforms to perform plays, interpretations and artistic collaborations online (see APGRD 2021).[7]

As digital systems can automatically classify even very large datasets, we see a growing use of computational systems to abstract, simplify and visualize complex cultural 'Big Data'. Many of these systems allow researchers to analyse data without a hypothesis so they can 'play' with the data until a preferred result is found. This is what Ramsay has called 'the hermeneutics of screwing around' and involves the ability to undertake 'what if' experiments with humanities data (Ramsay 2014). This ability to analyse large cultural data sets can be combined with the desire to deepen or widen the corpus from which data is being extracted, meaning that often the entire set of texts on which the data set rests is never read in total, or even partially, by a researcher. This is the 'computational turn', the move towards what has been called 'distant reading' and assumes the automation of the reading process to locate themes and concepts from within a set of texts (Berry 2011; see Underwood 2019). They are very powerful methods for working with cultural objects;[8] however, a note of caution is required – a researcher might naively trust the output of the algorithm without understanding how the results were calculated or their significance (see Da 2019; Eccles 2020 has an excellent summary of this debate).

Humanists can seemingly throw their data into large-scale computing clusters and let machine learning algorithms find patterns that might have evaded human capacities – but a 'hermeneutics of screwing around' may also encourage a carelessness with the data and what it may mean to specific communities (Johnson 2018: 61).[9] The digital therefore generates questions about how humanists should undertake their practices and the ethical considerations that might guide their work (Berry 2022). For example, how should humanists approach the resources they draw upon, how can they respond sensitively to the underlying materials that might inform their work? What issues are raised when encoding textual materials that may unwittingly introduce unconscious biases into the metadata or codings that enclose the text but which are often unseen by humans but relied upon by computers to calculate and manipulate the texts? Indeed, with regard to encoding itself, questions also arise as to is doing the encoding, what is their subject position and what is their relationship to the research project? This becomes very pertinent in relation to crowd-sourcing unpaid labour in a humanities project, for example.

Reading tragedy through the digital

The postdigital brings, therefore, methodological innovations for studying and understanding texts, whether dramatic or otherwise, represented most clearly in the discipline of digital humanities which is often associated with approaches such as distant reading, computational analysis, and topic modelling. Digital humanities emerged as a term in 2001 to capture a field with an early focus on database collections of texts, artworks, scholarly works, dictionaries and lexicographic corpora.[10] We tend to group digital humanities work into the divisions of digital tools and digital archives. Digital tools are software methods for working with textual data, such as the 'word cloud' which provides a visualization based on the frequency of words in a text so that words that have greater frequency are visually represented in a larger size. For example, Niedzielski (2018) presents an interesting comparative word cloud analysis that shows how in A. S. Kline's translation of Homer's *Odyssey* the main characters are particularly prominent – Odysseus, his son Telemachus, his wife Penelope, and the gods Zeus and Athene. However, when compared to the Odyssey in its original ancient Greek, no single word is nearly as large as Odysseus was in the English word cloud because, unlike in English, 'Ancient Greek is a language where the endings of nouns change based on how they are used in a sentence. A good comparison in English is how "he", "him", and "his" are all used in different ways – you wouldn't say "Him went to the store". So, while the word "Odysseus" can be used in English no matter where in the sentence it goes, Greek has to use different forms, such as ὀδυσσεύς (subject form) and ὀδυσσῆος (possessive form)' (Niedzielski 2018). These word clouds might be used in teaching to quickly show to students how translations can change how a play might be read and understood, or indeed to give a rapid visual overview of different textual resources, but they require scholarly care in their use.[11]

Digital tools augment the humanist's ability to select and manipulate datasets so that they can be grouped and re-sorted to look for patterns. Digital humanists have introduced methods that are new to the humanities, such as computer statistical analysis, search and retrieval, or data visualization, and applied these techniques to archives and collections that are vastly larger than any researcher or research group can individually handle comfortably. These digital methods allow us to explore how to negotiate between close and distant readings of texts and how micro-analysis and macro-analysis can be usefully reconciled in humanist work.

In contrast, the creation of digital archives tend to be image-based or transcriptions of physical textual archives, often with diplomatic versions for reading and searching. In the case of digital archives, automation is embedded in databases that collect corpora together and allow various searches and filters to be applied. Some archives have attempted to use OCR (optical character recognition) to change the text-based images into searchable text, but generally the quality of automated OCR output has remained relatively unsatisfactory for unsupervised use and actually generated a requirement for a lot of human labour to correct the mistakes that it inevitably created. This drove a need for what has come to be called 'crowd-sourcing' through the use of internet technologies to mediate a relationship between a researcher and a purported public (Terras 2016: 420-439). This has also raised the interesting idea of 'slow digitisation' that foregrounds the difficulty of producing digital archives (Prescott and Hughes 2018).

These approaches augment the capacities of humanists to work with larger data sets, corpora and image archives and also to move between them with greater ease. As the use of these digital tools increases across the humanities, it tends to be at different speeds depending on the discipline. Nonetheless, the rise in convenience and the ease of access to both digitised and born-digital content in online databases strongly creates affordances towards using these techniques (see Posner 2016, 2018). The digital humanities can therefore be understood as a set of interlocking and interdependent parts that, whilst made up of researchers in distinct disciplines, nonetheless adds up to make the whole greater than the sum of its parts. In other words, digital humanities is a coherent, if nonetheless still contested, discipline that offers great potential for studying cultural forms like tragedy (Berry and Fagerjord 2017).

By changing the way in which texts and traditions are stored and represented, from the encoding of plays in XML, a digital annotation language, to the possibility of multiple variation representation within a single critical edition of a play or text, the digital makes the multiplicity of interpretations and context manifest to readers. Using 'knowledge representation' and the careful encoding of textual materials, new ways of manipulating and transforming texts create new ways of seeing and understanding them. These techniques offer a great deal of potential for studies of tragedy, particularly as they allow the refinement of methods in terms of comparative and experimental humanities due to the ease of movement between multiple translations, versions and representations of the texts under analysis. For example, we might imagine that Greek tragedy might be read differently under conditions of computational analysis and distant-reading techniques which help present simultaneous multiple version variation in translations to aid the scholar by creating what are called 'treebanks'.[12] Additionally, works can be treated as a single corpus and through computational manipulation hidden patterns and relationships might be uncovered, such as the possible correlation between the degree of variance that a passage shows in editions and the number of citations to it in the scholarly literature (see Mambrini 2017). Additionally, by bringing together the contextual and historical information about a work, what is called its metadata, the movement of ideas, concepts and interpretations can be mapped and studied with these new methods, such as network analysis (see Concept Lab 2017; de Bolla et al. 2019). This can potentially open new avenues for research and performance (see APGRD 2020; National Theatre 2021; Out of Chaos Theatre 2021).

As such, exciting possibilities are opened up within a postdigital milieu. However, whether applied to tragedy or other cultural forms, the technologies do not thereby replace or make redundant the humanist. It remains crucial for the scholar to be critically oriented and reflexive of the way in which computation is no longer merely a tool for thought, but an infrastructure or milieu. This requires that social, cultural, political and economic questions raised by digital technology be part of this understanding.

Conclusions

In this chapter I have sought to outline at least two aspects of the digital in relation to tragedy. First, I considered the way in which the digital itself might be read as, in some senses, tragic due to the way in which it creates a relationship between freedom and determinism, through the 'laws' that the digital brings into our lives. This brings home the ways in which tragedy itself allows us to rethink the digital using the tragic form as a tool for thought. Second, I examined how the digital might be applied to tragedy itself through a methodological turn which is particularly associated with the digital humanities. These digital tools have tended to emphasize the 'distant reading' of textual or image collections, but used with care a new hermeneutics of reading is possible by moving between the close and distant reading modes that digital technology makes possible. In both these cases tragedy is unique as a site of thinking about the digital and for its richness and depth for developing digital tools for the analysis of textual data.

This points, I think, to the possibility that we begin to think of our scholarly practice as becoming increasingly *postdigital*. That is, that we will reach for the 'right' methodological tool for the right job without necessarily worrying about whether it is digital or not. Rather we will mix and match our methods for our research practices as appropriate. However, this means that we as humanists must continue to be aware what these powerful new digital tools can do, and how they do it. This requires us to be critical of the tools we use, and to make their use in research explicit. This is part of a wider practice in relation to digital humanities and being critical of postdigital culture requires that we continue to develop a programme of critique with respect to the computational and particularly its application to and transformation of cultural forms more generally. This is to be open to the possibilities of freedom that technology makes possible, but also cognisant of the limits imposed by the new 'laws' of the computational milieu we are entering. Perhaps the tragic, through its call to contemplate the dialectic between the particular and the universal and which Eagleton (2020: 37) notes 'may only manifest itself artistically at certain key historical moments', may indeed contribute towards preserving the task of thinking and dwelling in the ruins of the postdigital.

Notes

1 This also has implications for classification and identity in relation to the modal logic of computation and the ways in which the postdigital both enforces certain categories, such as gender or race, but also opens the possibility of their recognition and co-option into the technologies of digital media (see, for example, Eubanks 2019; Noble 2018).
2 If, as Eagleton observes, 'one does not need to do anything in particular to qualify as a tragic protagonist. One simply has to be a human being at the end of one's tether,' then the experience of being subject to the whims of an inflexible Excel spreadsheet surely suffices (Eagleton 2020: 46).
3 The contradictions generated by this new system can also be observed in discourse. This might be most clearly seen in the way in which computation is described simultaneously as both creative and deterministic, transparent and opaque, open and closed, augmented and automated, creating freedom and control, resistance and hegemonic power, the future of the economy and its destruction. Concepts are borrowed from the computational industries and used as explanatory ideas across society by so-called thought leaders, the sophists of the digital age. Principles from software engineering are offered up to facilitate social engineering, with, for example, 'open source' or 'open access' identified as an exemplar principle of organization and practice, platforms are given as future models for governance, calculation is substituted for thought, and social media networks are used to replace community and face-to-face interaction.

4   Although limited in space in this short chapter, the issues of gender, race, class and identity in relation to Hegel's reading of *Antigone* are discussed in Mills (1998).
5   See for example, National Theatre Live https://www.ntlive.com or Glyndebourne Open House https://www.glyndebourne.com/on-screen/ or indeed Tate Modern Live, https://www.tate.org.uk/whats-on/tate-modern/performance/bmw-tate-live.
6   https://www.ntathome.com/products/medea (accessed 25 March 2022).
7   In particular see the 'Greek Tragedy: Masterclass on Film: Antigone' which 'explores different interpretations of scenes from Antigone with director Paul O'Mahony through discussion and in rehearsal, alongside talking heads from the creative industries and academia' (TORCH 2021).
8   See also Rydberg-Cox 2011.
9   As Ramsay himself notes, 'if everyone is screwing around, one might legitimately wonder whether we can achieve a shared experience of culture sufficient to the tasks we have traditionally set for education' (Ramsay 2014: 118).
10 John Unsworth outlined a proposal for a master's degree in digital humanities in 2001, noting, 'the name of the program ("Digital Humanities") is a concession to the fact that "Humanities Informatics" (which would probably be a more accurate name) sounds excessively technocratic, at least to American ears. The other obvious alternative – "Humanities Computing" – sounded too much like a computer support function' (Unsworth 2001). This is one of the earliest uses of the term 'digital humanities' in relation to this field of study that I am aware of; see also Clement 2012; Kirschenbaum 2010.
11 It also highlights the importance of bringing together both the distant and the close readings of texts, rather than treating them as independent (Niedzielski 2018).
12 Treebanking is 'the activity of annotating texts syntactically. It is part of a relatively new field of research exploring the potential of linguistic annotation for a great variety of purposes, ranging from natural language processing tasks, such as machine translation or summarization, to linguistic research, where computational treatment of data has been significantly impacting method and results in linguistics' (Celano n.d.).

References

APGRD (2020), *Episode 5: Reading Greek Tragedy Online,* Archive of Performances of Greek and Roman Drama, http://www.apgrd.ox.ac.uk/digital-resources/podcast/episode-5 (accessed 24 March 2022).
Berry, D. M. (2011), 'The Computational Turn: Thinking about the Digital Humanities', *Culture Machine* 12.

Berry, D. M. (2015), 'The Postdigital Constellation', in *Postdigital Aesthetics: Art, Computation and Design*, edited by D. M. Berry and M. Dieter, London: Palgrave.
Berry, D. M. (2022), 'AI, Ethics and Digital Humanities', in J. O'Sullivan (ed.), *The Bloomsbury Handbook to the Digital Humanities*, London: Bloomsbury.
Berry, D. M., and A. Fagerford (2017), *Digital Humanities: Knowledge and Critique in a Digital Age*, Cambridge: Polity Press.
Billings, J. (2014), *Genealogy of the Tragic: Greek Tragedy and German Philosophy*, Princeton University Press.
Celano (n.d.), Ancient Greek and Latin Dependency Treebank 2.0, Digital Humanities Universität Leipzig, https://www.dh.uni-leipzig.de/wo/projects/ancient-greek-and-latin-dependency-treebank-2-0/ (accessed 25 March 2022).
Clement, T. (2012), 'Multiliteracies in the Undergraduate Digital Humanities Curriculum: Skills, Principles, and Habits of Mind', in *Digital Humanities Pedagogy: Practices, Principles and Politics*, edited by B. Hirsch, Open Book Publishers.
Concept Lab (2017), 'About', *The Concept Lab*, https://ccdkconceptlab.wordpress.com (accessed 24 March 2022).
Da, N. Z. (2019), 'The Computational Case against Computational Literary Studies', *Critical Inquiry* 45 (3).
De Bolla, P., E. Jones, P. Nulty, G. Recchia and J. Regan (2019), 'Distributional Concept Analysis', *Contributions to the History of Concepts* 14 (1): 66–92, https://doi.org/10.3167/choc.2019.140104
Deleuze, G. (1995), *Negotiations, 1972–1990,* New York and Chichester: Columbia University Press.
Eagleton, T. (2020), *Tragedy*, New Haven, CT: Yale University Press.
Eccles, K. (2020), 'Digital Humanities', *The Year's Work in Critical and Cultural Theory* 28 (1): 86–101.
Eubanks, V. (2017), *Automating Inequality: How High-Tech Tools Profile, Police, and Punish the Poor*, New York: St. Martin's Press.
Felski, R. (2008), *Rethinking Tragedy*, Baltimore, MD: Johns Hopkins University Press.
Goldhill, S. (2008), 'Generalizing about Tragedy', in R. Felski, *Rethinking Tragedy*, 45–65, Baltimore, MD: Johns Hopkins University Press.
Goldhill, S. (2014), 'The Ends of Tragedy: Schelling, Hegel, and Oedipus', *PMLA* 129 (4): 634–48.
Johnson, J. M. (2018), 'Markup Bodies: Black [Life] Studies and Slavery [Death] Studies at the Digital Crossroads', *Social Text 137* 36 (4).
Kirschenbaum, M. G. (2010), 'What is Digital Humanities and What's It doing in English Departments?' *ADE Bulletin* 150: 55–61.
Kittler, F. A. (1999), *Gramophone, Film, Typewriter*, Stanford, CA: Stanford University Press.
Mambrini, F. (2017), 'From Breadth to Depth. A digital collection of editions of Greek Tragedies', http://www.dh.uni-leipzig.de/wo/from-breadth-to-depth/

Mills, P. J. (1998), 'Hegel's Antigone', in John Stewart (ed.), *The Phenomenology of Spirit Reader: Critical and Interpretive Essays*, New York: State University of New York Press.

National Theatre (2021), 'Greek Tragedy at the National Theatre', https://artsandculture.google.com/exhibit/greek-tragedy-at-the-national-theatre%C2%A0/wRnC0fJ0 (accessed 25 March 2022).

Niedzielski, B. (2018), 'Textual analysis and word clouds', https://humtech.ucla.edu/news/textual-analysis-and-word-clouds/ (accessed 25 March 2022).

Noble, S. U. (2018), *Algorithms of Oppression: How search engines reinforce racism*, New York: New York University Press.

Posner, M. (2016), *What's Next: The Radical, Unrealized Potential of Digital Humanities*, Debates in the Digital Humanities, Minneapolis: University of Minnesota.

Posner, M. (2018), 'Digital Humanities', in M. C. Kearney and M. Kackman (eds), *The Craft of Criticism: Critical Media Studies in Practice*, 331–46, New York: Routledge.

Prescott, A., and L. Hughes (2018), 'Why do we digitize? The case for slow digitization', *Archive Journal*, http://www.archivejournal.net/essays/why-do-we-digitize-the-case-for-slow-digitization/ (accessed 25 March 2022).

Ramsay, S. (2014), 'The Hermeneutics of Screwing Around; or What You Do with a Million Books', in K. Kee (ed.), *Pastplay: Teaching and Learning History with Technology*, 111–20, Ann Arbor: University of Michigan Press, doi:10.2307/j.ctv65swr0.9.

Out of Chaos Theatre (2021), *Reading Greek Tragedy Online*, https://www.out-of-chaos.co.uk/greek-tragedy (accessed 25 March 2022).

Rydberg-Cox, J. (2011), 'Social Networks and the Language of Greek Tragedy', *Journal of the Chicago Colloquium on Digital Humanities and Computer Science* 1 (3).

Terras, M. (2016), 'Crowdsourcing in the Digital Humanities', in S. Schreibman, R. Siemens and J. Unsworth (eds), *A New Companion to Digital Humanities*, 420–39, Chichester: Wiley-Blackwell.

TORCH (2021), *Greek Tragedy: Masterclasses on Film*, https://www.torch.ox.ac.uk/greek-tragedy-masterclasses-on-film#/ (accessed 25 March 2022).

Underwood, E. (2019), *Distant Horizons: Digital Evidence and Literary Change*, Chicago: University of Chicago Press.

Unsworth, J. (2001), 'A Master's Degree in Digital Humanities: Part of the Media Studies Program at the University of Virginia', https://johnunsworth.name/laval.html (accessed 25 March 2022).

Part One

The presence of the digital in Greek tragedy: Developments and encounters with technology

1

From the *Ekkyklema* to Ivo van Hove

The technology of presence in multimedia theatre and the presence of the digital in performance

George Sampatakakis

Theatre from ancient times has always been a virtual field of mediation and multimedial imagery. Yet much of the contemporary discussion surrounding the use of new technologies in theatre overlooks the fact that technologies of enhancement were originally used in Greek theatre (*ekkyklema, mechane*) and authentically belongs to the actual genre. For example, the *mechane* consisted of a counterweighted pole with a pulley-operated rope on the end and the *ekkyklema* would have been little more than a wheeled 'rolling platform' (Ley 2007: 269). In tragedy, the *ekkyklema* wheeled out disturbing scenes of slaughter, the effect being that the audience was allowed to see 'the unspeakable acts committed behind the *skene* [i.e. the stage building behind the orchestra]' (Pollux 1967: 4.127–8.) by means of an enhanced reality. Moreover, the *periaktoi* were the 'prismatic scenic units which could revolve to give different indications of stage location' in rotating proto-digital 'screens', and were certainly used in Roman, if not in ancient Greek, theatres (McDonald & Walton 2007: 5).

This type of noble artificiality, to use Craig's (2009[1911]: 17) term, complied with a *theatrical theatre*[1] of antirealist stylization, and a virtual space that seeks to embrace synthetic audiovisual structures with synergistical mediated effects. The fusion of the human and the material was then achieved in certain climactic moments, enhancing the visual reality and the ethics of the tragic action, proving thereby that he roots of digital performance practices can be traced back through even centuries of performance history:

> Theatre has always used the cutting edge technology of the time to enhance the 'spectacle' of productions. From the early *Deus ex machina*, to the guild-produced Medieval pageant wagons, to the innovation of perspective painting and mechanical devices on Italian 16th Century

stage sets, to the introduction of gas, and later electric, lighting effects, to the modern use of computer to control lighting, sound and set changes, technology has been used in ways that have created incredible visual and auditory effects. (Arndt 1999: 66)

After presenting a prehistory of multimedial techniques and landmark developments, the aim of this chapter is to propose a working typology of mainstream media uses in performances of Greek tragedy, drawing on the work of major European directors and landmark performances.[2] It seems to be the case that the unpretentiousness and clearness of technological means call for a precision in the visualization of the subject matter, especially when it comes to the contemporization/modernization of Greek tragedy and its aesthetic relocation in modern environments, which in most cases require historical accuracy and factuality, if not digital 'naturalness'.

A prehistory

While writers like Michael Arndt (1999) and Oliver Grau (2003) have traced the precedents of digital arts back to antiquity, some historians of new media theatre place the ancestry of digital performance in the nineteenth century (Dixon 2007: 41–3) and Richard Wagner's perception of the *Gesamtkunstwerk* (total artwork which unites every branch of Art into a common artifact). Wagner's Romantic vision, expressed in writings such as *The Artwork of the Future* (1849), called for the creative unification of multiple artforms (theatre, music, singing, dance, dramatic poetry, design, lighting, and visual art) into a total multimedial structure 'with often beautiful – sometimes even sublime – effects, but also with enhanced meaning' (Brown 2016: 35). More significantly,

> Wagner suggested that the arts had once been unified, but had become undone under certain historical pressures. An 'organic' unity of the arts—that is to say, one that was more than just a wanton combination of discrete parts—depended on an 'organic' state. Modernity had effected a compartmentalization and atomization of different, largely autonomous spheres of life (one of them being art). In such a 'mechanical' state, the 'organic' unity of the arts had to come asunder. (Daub 2014: 13)

Moreover, Wagner attempted to engineer a wholly immersive audience experience through a variety of well-known technical and artistic strategies (hiding the orchestra out of view to remove alienation effects, dark auditorium, use of hypnotically repetitive musical leitmotifs and sonorous chords), sometimes referring directly to the conditions and the sublime emotional experience of ancient Greek tragedy as lived in the Greek polis, the ideal state:

> This people ... came they, in this Titanic masterpiece to see the image of themselves, ... to fuse their own being and their own communion with that of their god; and thus in noblest, stillest peace to live own communion with that of their god; and thus in noblest, stillest peace to live again the life which a brief space of time before, they had lived in restless activity and accentuated individuality. ('Art and Revolution', in Wagner 1892: 34)

Tragedy for Wagner was regarded as the perfect artwork of multimedial harmony, unifying the 'three chief artistic faculties' of man, that are brought out for display as 'the arts of Dance, of Tone, and Poetry' (Fischer-Lichte 2018: 72).[3]

At the beginnings of the twentieth century the ideal of the unification of the arts corresponded – not quite equivalently – with the idea of the synthesis of the arts in the new artform of the future. Although Italian Futurists heralded film as the new theatrical zone (Marinetti et al. 2009 [1916]: 230), they also called for a hybrid synthetic theatre that will gain the capacity to incorporate the newest visual media, such as film, into the sequence of numbers that made up a performance as early as 1913:

> The Variety Theater is unique today in making use of film, which enriches it with an incalculable number of visions and spectacles that couldn't otherwise be performed (battles, riots, horse races, automobile and airplane meets, travels, transatlantic steamers, the recesses of the city, of the countryside, of the oceans and the skies). (Marinetti 2009 [1913]: 159)

> Put onstage all the discoveries (no matter how unrealistic, strange, or antitheatrical) that our talent is discovering in the subconscious, in ill-defined forces, in pure abstraction, in pure conceptualism, the purely fantastic, in record-setting, and body-madness. (Marinetti, Settimelli & Corra 2009 [1915]: 208)

Thus, the multimedial synthesis of contradictive 'materials' coming from the technological arts was the only adequate way for Italian Futurists to emit the new dynamic Weltanschauung in performance. But this was not a development with solely visual performative results.

Within what was called sonic modernity, experiencing 'sound as an invasive, affective force', 'crystallized long-standing processes of modernization relating to sound and hearing' in performance (Curtin 2014: 9-10). The Dadaists' interest in performing sound and the failure of language to communicate a meaning was manifested, for example, in the performance of the poem 'The Admiral Looks for a House to Rent' composed and performed by Tristan Tzara in collaboration with Richard Huelsenbeck and Marcel Janco at the renowned *Cabaret Voltaire* in 1916. As we read in Huelsenbeck's (1974: 23) *Memoirs of a Dada Drummer*, originally written in 1969:

> Tzara, Janco, and I recited a 'simultaneous poem'. We came out on stage, bowed like a yodeling band about to celebrate lakes and forests in song, pulled out our 'scores', and, throwing all restraint to the wind, each of us shouted his text at the bewildered spectators. This was the first simultaneous poem ever performed on a European stage.

The vocal lines in French, German and English were all delivered or sung at the same time and were accompanied by 'a large drum, a wooden rattle (a cliquette), and a whistle' (Curtin 2014: 118), creating a multimedial chaos with heightened emotional effects.

Following post-Futurism and Dada modernism, The Ballets Suédois in Paris was one of the first companies to explore intermediality in performance. The company employed artists who were especially fond of combining media, such as Francis Picabia who used a film within and around the ballet *Entr'acte* (Théâtre des Champs-Élysées, Paris, 1924), showing motifs drawn from his painting, poetry and polemical writings.[4] Nonetheless, a similar interest in producing dynamic sensations was historically evident in the provocative and situative artistic happenings ranging from the Futurists' *Grande Serate* (1910 onward) to the Dadaists' *Cabaret Voltaire* and the events staged by neo-Dada and Fluxus artists in the future.

Despite the peripheral advances, the major performative turn occurred with Erwin Piscator in the twenties. Within the Bauhaus enthusiasm, artists in Weimar were calling for 'a new synthesis of art and modern technology' (Gropius 1961:7) as a 'synthesis of the elements of presentation: SOUND, COLOR (LIGHT), MOTION, SPACE, FORM (OBJECTS AND PERSONS)' (Moholy-Nagy 1961 [1924]: 49). Given the historical circumstances, Piscator's obsession with technological innovation conveyed a newly articulated experience of media synthesis in theatre, linking the stage to the realm of film and mass culture. More than any other theater artist of the time, Piscator's perception of a political documentary theater was essentially related to the use of film projections on stage as part of a 'new mode of representation-one based essentially on the spectacle. performance, and image' (Bathrick 1989: 77), therefore employing either existent pieces of film or motion pictures filmed specifically for a performance with the cast of the actual production.

For the first time motion picture film accompanied a Piscator production in *Trotz Alledem* (*In Spite of it All*) at the Großes Schauspielhaus, Berlin in 1925 (previously Piscator had only used projected slides). He obtained his film from government archives in Berlin, which retained film documents of World War I, showing the German demobilization, various troop parades and similar authentic footage of the events between 1914 and 1919 in newsreel fashion. The film served to document the action depicted on stage (Piscator 1980: 65), augmenting the stage image and the emotional impact of the actual play, thereby offering a comment on historical events:

> Everyone in the house had, for the most part, lived through this epoch; it was truly their fate, their own tragedy which played before their eyes. The theater became reality for them and soon it was no longer a stage and audience, but one large assembly hall, a great battlefield, a great demonstration. The unity achieved on this evening supplied the final argument for the agitation-power of political theater. (Piscator 1980: 69)

Sturmflut (*Tidal Wave*) at the Hamburg's Kammerspiele in 1926 stands as the first Piscator's production where film was shot for a specific production. Although *Trotz Alledem* used film footage linked to the themes of the actual script, *Sturmflut* used film made specifically for the production. Piscator hired professional movie director Johann Hiibla-Kala and the Filmhaus Mischke film company to shoot film sequences simulating the real historical locations of the play (St Petersburg) and using actors who appeared in the performance. In any case, between 1925 and 1926 all the possible advances in theatrical film projections (from either existing or specially made film footage) were achieved, waiting only for liveness to emerge in the distant future, although the actors in *Sturmflut* appeared simultaneously 'live' on stage and in the film. Bertolt Brecht himself welcomed the introduction of film in performance as a 'far reaching innovation', precisely because 'the setting was thus awakened to life and began to play on its own, so to speak; the film was a *new, gigantic actor* that helped to *narrate events*. By means of it, documents could be shown as part of the scenic background, figures and statistics. *Simultaneous events* in different places could be seen together' (Brecht 1964 [1935]: 77–8; my emphasis). And if 'real time/simulated time simultaneity ... displac[es] the human figure into different media' (Causey

2006: 37), Piscator's and Brecht's political theatre was interested in presenting the suffering social subject exploited and suppressed in any given historical circumstances (visualized by different means on stage).

The mediated theatre of the future spread throughout the world during the coming decades, although 'little multimedia theater actually took place during the 1940s and early 1950s' (Dixon 2007: 80). The fusion of theatre and cinema in 'the simultaneous use of the living actor and the talking picture' offered 'a wholly new theatrical art, an art whose possibilities are as infinite as those of speech itself', as Robert Edmond Jones (1992 [1941]: 106), one of America's leading theatre designers, envisioned it his 'Theatre of the Future'. In the style of a neo-romantic idealism Jones reimagined the fusion of theatre and motion pictures as an aesthetic way to 'bridge reality and dreams' (Hostetter & Hostetter 2011: 26) and unify the two 'existent' worlds of human experience.

During the sixties, the old call for the unification of the arts rendered into a new cultural demand for 'simultaneity' and intermediality of the artistic media in the dawn of a new era. Marshal McLuhan (1967: 8) argued that the 'alphabet and print technology fostered and encouraged a fragmenting process, a process of specialism and detachment. Electronic technology fosters and encourages unification and involvement'. These new media, in some sense, promoted a return to an earlier era, one inclined toward a unified 'global village' of global aesthetics. McLuhan (1967: 91) writes, 'our age translates itself back into the oral and auditory modes because of the electronic pressure of simultaneity', precisely because 'the electric is total and inclusive' (McLuhan 1964: 57) as an extension of Man. Still, the performance events of the sixties and seventies under the genre of kinetic theatre were a particular development of the Happening and Fluxus movements, which welcomed 'literal dimensionality and varied media in radical juxtaposition' (Green 2014: 140), rejecting the strategies of unification in favour of anti-art[5] intermediality and the pursuit of a provocative political spectacle. Wolf Vostell's happening in a dog kennel at Wantang Long Island (21 May 1966, 7.30–9.30) is a good example on how the intermediality of the seventies used film projections as documentary comments on contemporary events in order to poltically alert and provoke the audience:

7.30–7.37 lying on the ground DOGS BARKING
7.38–7.44 walking around projecting a film about the war in Vietnam in his [Vostell's] tongue with an 8-mm mobile projector DOGS BARKING.
(Friedman et al. 2002: 110)

The developments in multimedia performance were immediate after the release of the first portable video recorder in late sixties. The explosion of the media arts followed, 'when video finally entered the privileged domain of High Art' and came to be used in certain 'production set-ups', as Günter Berghaus (2005: 179–80) notes. The most performative of Berghaus' set-ups which continue to be extremely popular in contemporary *mise-en-scène* and performance art, are the following:

- Real-time, *closed-circuit* situations, where the artist engaged in an interactive dialogue with the video camera and recorded this on tape for future distribution.
- Video performance, where in a live event the artist *confronted physical* presence with mediated presence, and encouraged the audience to reflect on the representational qualities of the electronic medium.
- *Interactive or participatory events*, where the electronic media of video and television were manipulated and transformed by the audience, following scores or instructions provided by the artist.

Such artistic practices invoke a plurality of artistic and cultural references through all available resources, juxtaposing live actors with visual images by interlinking technology and live performance. Still, in the eighties performance artists like Laurie Anderson 'interpreted the old cry to break down the barriers between life and art to be a matter of breaking down the barriers between art and the media, also expressed as a conflict between high and low art' (Goldberg 1988: 190), using photographs or clips taken from television shows, slideshows with pictures or paintings, abridged film footages and live music, all of which 'disturbed the boundaries between media and real life' (1988: 195) in performance. But 'it was not until the 1980s with the advent of digital sound that sound-reproduction technology was effectively integrated into production practice as part of a *complete design*', inviting integrated technology to act like a 'figurative co-performer' (Curtin 2014: 64–5), that is, a total co-maker of the meaning of the performance with highly 'affective force' (2014: 146). And through the integration of media and digital screens within the performance 'artists experiment with techniques that at times fragment and dislocate bodies, time, and space, and at others unify physical, spatial, and temporal significations' (Dixon 2007: 336). This clear distinction is not only practically performative, but defines the poetics and hermeneutics of the genre Digital Theater where 'performances sometimes utilize the screen space to highlight a marked separation between the relative times and spaces of stage and screen, and at others attempt to combine them to create (the illusion of) an integrated time and space' (2007: 336).

In any case, digital projections and installations are used to intensify the visual meaning of a performance and, when it comes to a classical text, offer a new interpretation or, even, reinvent the text. An excellent example is the work of Robert Lepage who often rewrites 'an extant work by offering spectators an embodied and uncommon (albeit not unique) reading.... Robert Lepage's scenic writing defines his affective adaptations, allowing him to visually adapt canonical texts and revive other lesser-known works through his distinctly twenty-first-century version of *écriture scénique*' (Poll 2018: 2). Not rarely, the digital adaptation is so dichotomic in terms of time and space that the canonical classical text is seen in double distance from authenticity, as in the case of the Wooster Group's *Hamlet* (2009), where the live performers strived 'to replicate the famous 1964 televised production of *Hamlet* starring Richard Burton, which was projected behind the performers in human-scale' (Saltz 2015: 110). Such directorial attitudes re-author the classical text and put the digital medium in the core of the staging process as a meaning regulator beyond its aesthetic functionality and eloquent presence.

From Piscator to van Hove: Same strategies, different aesthetics

The use of video technologies in contemporary theatre can be understood as a symptom of a new mediatized culture historically equivalent to the one which triggered the introduction of film in the theatre of the twenties. But even if digital modernism today 'aligns with strategies of the avant-garde, it challenges traditional expectations about what art is and does. It illuminates and interrogates the cultural infrastructures, technological networks, and critical practices that support and enable these judgments' (Pressman 2014: 10). Even so, the productions of Greek tragedy that use audiovisual technologies (video projections, live cameras, digital screens), follow the inevitability and marketability of a popular aesthetic trend in contemporary theatre. Patrice Pavis (2013: 132–57) in like manner observes the dominance of audiovisual technologies in theatre and the work of many contemporary directors, rejecting the old idea of the synthesis of arts in support of the integration of media (137; my emphasis):

> Multimedia performance is not simply an accumulation of arts (theatre, dance, music, projections and so on); it is in its true sense the *merging of technologies* in the space–time of representation. Cybertheatre, created with the help of the new media and computer technologies, is the use of media in theatrical performance, and is also particularly concerned with the internet's capacity to produce virtual spaces.

Despite the recent advances in technological theatre and the clichés of live cameras and digital scenography, Piscator's (1980: 236–40) basic taxonomy of filmic possibilities in theatre is still useful, if we are to outline the scenic function of electronic media in contemporary theatre and specifically in productions of Greek tragedy. These possibilities were applied to the genre by the director himself (in his so-called *Oresteia*, as we will see below) and, not only that. In inventing the function of film in theatre, Piscator was inspired by the Greek chorus, thereby transforming the moving pictures on the stage into a *chorus filmicus*,[6] which 'levels criticisms, makes accusations, provides important facts, indeed at times it carries direct agitation. When it [is] superimposed on a picture, new contrasts, pathetic or satirical, [are] produced' (Piscator 1980: 239). Accordingly, three basic dramatic functions for film are applicable according to Piscator (1980: 239–41):

1. Didactic: film supplements the onstage drama by presenting facts and information that broaden the subject.
2. Dramatic: film carries the action forward and becomes a substitute for the live scene.
3. Choric: film commentates the action in the manner of a visual chorus.

In the programme notes of Gerhart Hauptmann's *Atrides Tetralogy* (1941–48) presented at the Volksbühne (Theater am Kurfürstendamm, Haus der Freien) in 1962, Piscator (quoted and translated in Fischer-Lichte 2018: 222–3) maintained that Hauptmann wrote the *Atrides* 'in an act of inner liberation as a coded indictment of the Nazi regime ... Just exchange the Greeks for Germans and Hellas for Germany: it takes no further demonstration to recognize that we have a very clear stance here. How could one utter the word "barbarism" in the Third Reich without being reminded of that of the Nazis?' The play was revived in an attempt to level criticism, make accusation and remind important facts and images repressed in the common cultural memory; or, as Fischer-Lichte (2018: 222) writes, 'Piscator staged Hauptmann's tetralogy in order to make a clear statement ... concerning the "loud" silence on the Third Reich, the war, and the Holocaust'. The best available way for Piscator to document the past and make a political comment on present-day issues was the *chorus filmicus*, that vividly linked the mythic atrocities of the Atreids to Europe's recent history, employing an iconography from the modern technological archive:

> The drone of bomb squadrons. Dive bombers howl. Aerial mines explode. All recorded. – Accompanied by an image of Dresden in ruins and the projection of Hauptmann's lament for the bombed city. Spotlights find writings in the dark, which are set up on both sides of the stage like

a political-biographical chronology: Summer 1940 'Iphigenia in Delphi', France capitulates. Autumn 1942 'Agamemnon's Death', Stalingrad. Spring 1943 ninth draft of 'Iphigenia in Aulis', total war, German cities bombed. Autumn 1944 'Electra', allied troops on the Rhine. Then the curtain rises. (From Rolf Michaelis' review in *Theater heute*, quoted and translated in Fischer-Lichte 2018: 223)

Appealing to film, it is historically evident that Piscator imagined his political theatre and the revival of the classics 'as part of a new mode of representation – one based essentially on the spectacle, performance, and image' (Bathrick 1989: 77), beyond the formal conventions of the stage and the basics of new technology. In the case of the *Atrides*, the film was used to document history and create the 'general atmosphere' for the individual drama' to emerge: The filmic 'chorus of the masses speaks as a collective and a Destiny', while 'the powers of the times are first addressed in general, before the single fate of the individual speaker is enacted against the background of a fate', the backdrop being the film depicting war atrocities (Bernhard Diebold's review in *Die Skene* quoted and translated in Piscator 1980: 240). Not surprisingly, this was a technological theatre of *instruction* exactly as Brecht (1964 [1957]: 71–2) defined it some years earlier:

> Oil, inflation, war, social struggles, the family, religion, wheat, the meat market, all became subjects for theatrical representation. Choruses enlightened the spectator about facts unknown to him. Films showed a montage of events from all over the world. Projections added statistical material. And as the 'background' came to the front of the stage so people's activity was subjected to criticism.

The unpretentiousness and factual realism of the technological means called for a new 'epic' acting with 'precision in movement and character representation which was essential both for the portraying of the subject matter ... and for manipulating the emotions of the audience' (Innes 1972: 120). This, in my view, was one of the most crucial contributions, precisely because in the years to come the issue of duplication and amplification (of either the image or the emotion) of the actor will become essential for digital theatre and its factual iconography. As the pioneer of video installations Carolee Schneemann (1996: 27) admits: 'When there's an accumulation of images, I'm forced to make those images "actual"'. In that sense, the actor in mediated contexts assumes a new subjectivity through technological means, in as much as 'culturally specific images of bodies mediate in this process' (Bleeker 2008: 147), without however discarding the possibility of radical transformation. The assuming of a new radical form effects, on the other hand, the attentional reversal of appearances and expectations that introduce the option of undoing the 'real' physical image and its perception. Historically, the major and most popular acts of undoing the 'traditionally' human, that suspended the ableness of humanhood in theatre (by technological means or not), were committed by Romeo Castellucci:[7]

> Technology is present on the stage as metaphor and spirit. Technology and machines are bearers of phantoms who inhabit the set, the stage – the concept is animistic. So, a machine has an entrance and an exit, it lights up, it takes up a chunk of the world; in short, it creates its own world. So, it's quite clear that it's not merely a gadget, a decoration, because it is energized and it is triggered by argument with the actor, and thus it has in some way a dehumanizing function. It dehumanizes the actor, puts him in danger, places him in the paradoxical position of deuteragonist, so that finally it creates an inhuman tension. (Castellucci 2004: 17)

In like manner, Castellucci's new 'factual' iconography of the difference documented humanhood as a cruel and nightmarish condition (or at least as a technologically altered condition), using media and medicalized fictions which offer a new assuming of the human (see also Poulou, Chapter 2 below). This is another indication that the use of digital and other media in performance is primarily related to the *mise-en-scène* and the conceptual contemporization of a play, supporting thereby a 'newer development of art and theatre forms, which seek to depart from the Gestalt as totality, mimesis and model' (Lehmann 2006: 45).

Digital relocation of tragedy and a typology of tropes

Despite the pressing funding conditions throughout Europe, media performance forms are highly fashionable and recognizable due to their *auteur* status in re-authoring a classical play. Many artists, striving to attract a place in the cultural market, resort to this 'new' theatre aesthetics, making their performances look strikingly similar, although the issue of cultural diversity[8] remains critically significant for European theatre. Instead of reclaiming a text and 'transform[ing] the material into an expression of [one's] own personality' (Buscombe 1981: 23), many directors 'learn' a prevalent canon in order to fit in an established tradition and a feasible market.

Accordingly, this section is interested in presenting a typology of mainstream media uses in performances of Greek tragedy, drawing from the work of major European directors and celebrated productions that formed a sub-canon in progress concerning the directing of Greek tragedy in the twenty-first century. This functional typology can fairly be regarded as new, if we are to compare it to Piscator's landmark contributions and the performance experimentations of the seventies. Moreover, the American director and academic David S. Saltz (2001: 124–6) has already outlined a taxonomy of media usages and effects which define the relationship between performance and media: (1) virtual scenery (backdrop); (2) interactive costumes; (3) alternate perspective (another visual perspective); (4) subjective perspective (on the dramatic character); (5) illustration; (6) commentary; (7) diegetic media; (8) affective media (which produce an emotional effect); (9) synesthesia; (10) instrumental media (which create new kinds of instruments); (11) virtual puppetry (which creates a performer's double); (12) dramatic media.

My typology aims to combine Saltz's and Piscator's taxonomic models into a classifying list of digital tropes, which transformed Piscator's documentarism into a digital naturalism of new 'facts' and audiovisual tactics imported in the performance of Greek tragedy by certain means (that is, visual and sonic *ekkyklemata*, digital *periaktoi*, and digital enhancements in general). These tropes concur with the aesthetic contemporization and historical relocation of Greek tragedy from the past to the present as a theatrical genre that celebrates the freedom to redirect a play, although my list is neither exhaustive nor mutually exclusive.

Digital naturalism (affective commentary)

For Causey (2006: 16), the televisual 'is the primary modality of contemporary technological representation', which also connects theatre with a plurality of mediated presences and meanings in the form of a new aesthetic naturalism (if the televisual is the socially natural). The unpretentiousness and clearness of technological means call for a precision in the portraying of the subject matter, especially when it comes to the *historicization* of Greek tragedy and its aesthetic relocation to contemporary environments, which in most cases require historical coherence, if not digital 'naturalness'. And despite the hundred or so years of multimedia performances, most critics associate the use of media with the modernization of Greek tragedy. For example, the Almeida *Oresteia* (directed by Robert Icke) was heralded as 'Aeschylus for the modern age' (Billington 2015) not only due to the contemporization of the myth and the modern costumes, but also because the 'clean minimal design with its translucent screens and its digital display' (Tripney 2015) was used as a 'contrast between private and public utterance, with video and mics being used ... to exceptionally good effect' (Clapp 2015). In the previous years, Billington had already defined his idea of the modern age as the 'directorial adventurism' of the 'auteur in a continental European tradition' (Billington 2007: 405–6), at the same time when British 'traditionalists' were annoyed by the emergence of digital media and 'new visual motifs' in British theatre (Rebellato 2010: 333).

Similarly, in the older case of Katie Mitchell's *Oresteia* (National Theatre at Cottesloe Theatre, London, 1999) the critics connected again the dramatic meaning of the production with the use of video cameras and videated close-ups which intensified the dramatic atmosphere and offered a more eloquent characterization of the dramatis personae, indicating the modernizing aims of a *mise-en-scène* that transformed Aeschylus visually into either Beckett or a morality play due to the use of live cameras:

> Past actions echo and reverberate in the present: Even the accompanying sound, reminiscent of childhood piano practice, intensifies the emotional force. The past is also eternally present in the way Agamemnon watches over proceedings: Mitchell even puts a camera inside his tomb with extraordinary results. As the onstage screen gives us a worms-eye-view of Electra with her feet straddling his resting place, we are inescapably reminded of Beckett's 'They give birth astride of a grave.' (Billington 1999)

Moreover, in Mitchell's *Oresteia* Agamemnon (the guilty male) was dressed like a Bosnian warlord, and Clytemnestra (the eternal Mother) 'had an Eva Peron hairstyle and New Look full-skirted summer cocktail dress, patterned with poppies', announcing 'the victorious ending of the war to the background of projections showing "national" jubilations' (Maurice 2017: 52). Similarly, in Ivo van Hove's 'clinical, cold and hypnotic' *Antigone* (Toneelgroep, Amsterdam, 2015), in which 'naturalism prevailed within an atmospheric and domesticated setting' (Rodosthenous 2018: 75), a shadowlike crowd of citizens was projected onto a wide screen above the main stage area, when Creon (Patrick O' Kane) was talking about 'his city', and Antigone (Juliette Binoche) was burying her brother on stage to the background of projections showing a red sandstorm outside the walls of Thebes. Still, this mechanism of 'naturalism' is also functional for subcultural visibilities and the transposition of a mythical hero.

In Latina playwright Caridad Svich's *Iphigenia in Between* (7 Stages Theatre, Atlanta, 2004) Iphigenia falls in love with Achilles, an androgynous rock star into alcohol and drugs. Iphigenia first meets Achilles through his video image in which 'he wears a close-fitting woman's tunic, fishnet stockings, boots, glitter lipstick, and black nails' (Svich 2004: 41). As the queer Achilles sings on the video, Iphigenia and the chorus of Fresa girls dance and move in orgiastic ecstasy, before Iphigenia and Achilles make love. Questioning her mythical past, this Iphigenia 'is keen to act against the role assigned to her by history', desiring 'a new life, free of the manipulations of her father and the prescribed social roles' (Rizk 2015: 224). Moreover, Achilles' queer performativity visualizes a moment of disconnection from the traditionally heroic representations of the hero, thereby celebrating an 'affective turn' (Warner 2012: 6) that was made possible only when artists adopted irony, unstableness and freakiness as tools for undoing past embodiments and heteronormative ethics.

The cultural reclaiming of the tragic texts was made possible after their installation in new media and digital environments, which enhanced their interpretational possibilities for the present. In these new and enhanced re-presentations of the ancient dramatis personae, 'we witness the character-in-the-language-text, we see the character-in-the-spatial/temporal-performance-text, and we sense the character-in-the-electronic-space' (Causey 2006: 38) which is the natural space of our twenty-first-century living experience.

Digital relocation of tragedy (alternate perspective)

Nothing of the abovementioned can be regarded as extremely *modern* after the video modernism of the seventies and the performances of The Wooster Group, which 'have furthered the aesthetics of video and performance through the digital processing of the videated image and the simultaneous generation of live and mediated images within performance' (Causey 2006: 35). The mediated presence of the actor (through either live cameras or filmed video projections) came to create a new theatrical language which redefined the traditional techniques of stage narratives, characterization, and space politics, inevitably affecting the directorial adventures of Greek tragedy. Still, the basic difference between the pioneering work of the Wooster Group and the *Regietheater* of the Director lies in the common fact that the work of a group implies a shared process and, perhaps, a commonly devised artistic product, while *Regietheater* assembles shared aesthetics, canons and anti-canons.

Accordingly, from Katie Mitchell to Ivo van Hove the European stages are 'haunted' by what I call a *phasmatic aesthetics of presence* for two reasons: First, the old ghosts of stage technology still occupy the stage (namely, archaic technologies and Piscator's legacy), and second, the mediated presence of the actor can be regarded as a ghostly duplicate of the 'real' presence in a visual dichotomy between digital ghost and matter. This *phasmatic aesthetics* which combines old and new technologies of presence, employs basic techniques that can be classified as follows.

Digital screens as *ekkyklemata* (dramatic characterization)

The staging of an ancient play emerges directly from the fusion of various elements from contemporary cultures, producing a new meaning that blends timelessness with contemporaneity. The simultaneous merging of digital images with live bodies creates a space of theatrical in-betweenness that calls the spectator back to a sensory familiarity overloaded with contemporary structures of viewing (TV, video games, social media). This televisual in-betweenness, is calling for video to 'act as a live participant in the performance, with almost equal status to an actor. For example, video footage of a person – recorded or live – may literally replace one of the actors', as Katie Mitchell (2008: 90) maintains for the uses of video in performance. Accordingly, in her *Oresteia* (1999) video projections were used primarily as commentaries on the action and the roles, which intensified the tone and emotion of the visual atmosphere, albeit their highly symbolic status: Mitchell had the ghost of Clytemnestra, covered in white plastic, physically presiding over the action of the first two plays and appearing via video in the *Eumenides* where it actually appears. In each case the ghost stood as a central figure of revenge and silenced femininity that haunt the stage. Still, much of the use of video was used 'to record and magnify the stage action' (Walton 2005: 205) and create an emotional, at times darkly melodramatic, mood. Accordingly, Cassandra's last speech 'was very deliberately chalked as a message on the floor and shown in video close-up on a screen above the palace façade' (2005: 205), intensifying the tragic irony of the scene. The *phasmatic* videated Cassandra was already absent and among the dead, mourning her life in Ted Hughes' 'supple, eloquent and ... often disturbing' new poetics of the tragic (Billington 1999; cf. Hughes 1999).

Except for conveying 'tone and emotion' (Rebellato 2010: 335), the video image is *extending, challenging* and *reconfiguring* the material body of the actor 'through technology' (Causey 2006: 16), carrying a *new subjectivity* for the role as a new digital *ethos* and a newly mediated character, although in many cases 'technology sheds light on reductionist renderings of the female subject in classical texts' (Sidiropoulou 2011: 118). In that sense, video projections become an integral part of the *mise-en-scène* and the meaning-making process of the performance, sometimes envisioning a new ethics of the tragic, a good example being Robert Icke's *Oresteia* (2015). Icke was using video cameras, sound recordings (as for a radio play) and screen projection, to bring faces and bodies in close-up as they were being filmed, in order to widen the *dramatis personae* and achieve digital characterization. Overall, wider contemporary concerns were reflected in the modern elements of the domestic setting and the modern costumes (the chorus was dressed as modern businessmen and women with briefcases and laptops), focusing on the play as a family business drama 'with a much more personal retelling of the myth' (Maurice 2017: 55). The extended digital characterization was mainly achieved by the manipulation of the camera angle, which, for example, aimed to project *an arrogant* Agamemnon (Angus Wright) who *was defending his profane choice* to go to war. With emblematic frontal close-ups, Agamemnon was pictured like a politician in a *televised news report, while his* 'mental anguish' as a leader (Billington 2015) was heightened by the digital presence of Clytemnestra, when he was standing silent in front of the large videated monologues of the Queen. Through the use of screen *ekkyklemata* that bring the new atrocious ethics out on stage, Icke presented the image of an 'increasingly uncertain' world, where the 'erosion of democracy' (Maurice 2017: 57) and the crisis of traditional family values become the focus.

Digital *periaktoi* (virtual scenery)

Video projections as scenographic devices are of common use in contemporary theatre. As Mitchell describes it, the video can therefore 'support the set design in communicating the world and ideas of the play', as, for example, 'using recorded footage of clouds in the sky moving across a white cyclorama' (Mitchell 2008: 90). For example, the *spatial fiction*[9] in Jan Fabre's *Prometheus Landscape II*, Jan Fabre/Troubleyn, 2011, transformed the 'reality' of the original Aeschylean surrounding into a dystopian twilight zone where heroism is deprived of its romantic enchantment and promise, and a 'self-world that knows no clear differentiation of subject and object' (Zavros 2017: 173). The large digital backdrop, in front of which Prometheus was X crossed in ropes, created a 'technological' landscape with satellite images of the sun or the moon the bright, more like a modern *place of the scull* where the old hero Prometheus, 'the sacrificial lamb of civilization...', was strung up ... like a lacerated Christ' (Manson 2011).

Sonic *ekkyklema* (diegetic commentary)

A sonic dramaturgy may use expressive sound images that can (or not) be equated with the concepts of the text, heightening thereby the atmosphere of the scene. This affective mechanism is not only broadening the emotion of the performance, but also brings about interpretations that do not necessarily exist into the dramatic character's world.[10] Even in the futurist fantasia of the 1920s, 'the sound images and the sound (phoneme), ... the more unusual and expressive they are, the better material they are for expressing *intense emotions*" (A. Kruchenykh *Phonetics of Theatre*, 1923, quoted and translated in Janecek 1996: 301). A proper example would be Katie Mitchell's *Iphigenia at Aulis* (National Theatre, London 2004) that employed digitally amplified sound in order to transform speech into extreme emotion and dramatic characterization, presenting an atmospherically 'hyperactive production' (Billington 2004) where the digital acoustics broadened the ethos of Iphigenia (Hattie Morahan):

> Iphigenia's microphone – quite despite her own best efforts – mutates the language of violence as gift, as glory, as national sacrifice, into precarious speech; in the powerful yet hollow reverb of her voice we hear the echo of her body in the process of its going missing. (Solga 2008: 155–6)

Narrative, pictographic or purely affective, all media rearrange the experience of the text into a new theatrical environment that looks and feels modern, but retells the stories, visually and aurally amplified. Finally, all audiovisual media can be recognized as performative metonyms for the new digital era, where (war, love, passion, family, and other) tragedies remain scandalous moral 'achievements' of the free human being now in a digital environment. Still, as Angeliki Poulou points out in this volume, the audiovisual media sometimes tell 'another parallel story as "context" or "subtext" to the main story presented on stage'.

Conclusions: Technologies of presence and digital conceptuality

Digital media are used to intensify the visual meaning of a performance and, when it comes to a classical text, offer broader interpretations or, even, reinvent a text. Historically, the majority of critics and scholars associate the meanings of the production with the use of cameras, videated close-ups and videographic scenography, all of which enframe a plural *mise-en-scène* as an integration of media which are '"jumping" between heteronomic spaces' of meaning (Lehmann 2006: 158). The symbiosis of the human actor and technology is thus put in the center of an identificatory process between contemporary audiences and distant classical texts, now visually adapted in distinctly twenty-first-century 'enhanced' versions.

Digital presences on contemporary stages, either aural or visual, concur with the essential theatrical mechanism of subject construction and enhancement, if we accept these procedures as an integral part of acting and directing (especially when it comes to a classical play that has lived through numerous of interpretations). In that sense, the recent distinction between 'the cinematic portrayal of psychology' (in Mitchell's 'live cinema' performances) and 'the use of media as a videographic backdrop, as in Ivo van Hove's *Antigone*' (Ledger 2018: 71–2) seems problematic, precisely because in any case the videated image intensifies the dramatic atmosphere and offers a more eloquent characterization of the *dramatis personae*, visually enhancing the narrative of the play in a new digital conceptuality. Moreover, this is a process of subject reconstruction following a Deleuzean *camera-consciousness*. Gilles Deleuze (1986: 76) claims that an oscillation takes place between the notion of objective and subjective image (real and mediatized), 'a correlation between a perception-image and a camera-consciousness which transforms it'. Although Deleuze talks about cinema, the transformative *consciousness* of media is equally valid in digital theatre as a mode of characterizing a role and a scenic environment.

More positively, the futurist utopian fantasy of the first half of the twentieth-century and the video enthusiasm of the 1970s are now transformed into a popular aesthetic style and an 'industrial' canon *per se* in the cultural market. Complying with the aesthetic centre of the mainstream, the potential political efficacy of Greek tragedy is often upgraded through a contemporarily artful performativity which reinvents the old theatrical typologies and tropes, and enriches them in broad terms. Besides, the tragic was born with an *ekkyklema* and still lives in the digital *ekkyklemata*. Equally virtually.

Notes

1. Vsevold Meyerhold's (2016 [1921]: 220) term for anti-naturalist, anti-illusionist theatre.
2. I have either seen live and/or in video all the recent productions discussed in this section.
3. Wagner's total theatre found a successful application at the festival of the Greek Theatre of Syracuse that was inaugurated in 1914. As early as 1922 Ettore Romagnoli chose the *Bacchae* as a tragedy which explicitly requires the inclusion of dance (along with music, song and prose). See Bordignon 2020: 31–2.
4. Cf. Townsend et al. 2014: xx.
5. Anti-art events combined readymades, found objects, art, détournement, paintings, appropriation, happenings, performance, body art, calling also for 'immediacy' (cf. Foster 1994).
6. The term was coined by Bernhard Diebold (1928: 28).

7 His *Orfeo ed Euridice* (La Monnaie/De Munt opera house, Brussels, 2014) is an example of the strategy of 'introducing reality into the theatre' (Semenowicz 2016: 195).
8 In January 2018 the 'On Stage 2018' guide was launched in the frame of the European Year of Cultural Heritage, see <https://europa.eu/cultural-heritage/news/stage-2018-guide-online_en> (accessed 5.6.19).
9 The term was introduced by Patrick Primavesi (2013: 167).
10 Cf. Ovadija 2013: 9–23.

References

Arndt, M. J. (1999), 'Theatre at the Centre of the Core (Technology as a Lever in Theatre Pedagogy)', in S. A. Schrum (ed.), *Theatre in Cyberspace*, 65–84, New York: Peter Lang.

Bathrick, D. (1989), 'Closing the Gaps: Erwin Piscator's Theater of the Spectacle', *Journal of Communication Inquiry*, 13.1: 70–9.

Berghaus, G. (2005), *Theatre, Performance and the Historical Avant-Garde*, New York: Palgrave Macmillan.

Billington, M. (1999), 'A Challenge for Our Time', *The Guardian*, 3 December, https://www.theguardian.com/stage/1999/dec/03/theatre.artsfeatures (accessed 5.10.19).

Billington, M. (2004), 'Iphigenia at Aulis', *The Guardian*, 23 June, https://www.theguardian.com/stage/2004/jun/23/theatre (accessed 10.10.19).

Billington, M. (2007), *State of the Nation: British Theatre since 1945*, London: Faber & Faber.

Billington, M. (2015), 'Oresteia Review: Icke Brings us Aeschylus for the Modern Age', *The Guardian*, 7 June, https://www.theguardian.com/stage/2015/jun/07/oresteia-review-icke-brings-us-aeschylus-for-the-modern-age (accessed 5.10.19).

Bleeker, M. (2008), *Visuality in the Theatre: The Locus of Looking*, Basingstoke and New York: Palgrave Macmillan.

Bordignon, G. (2020), 'Dalla filologia alla teatrabilità, e ritorno: il ruolo del coro danzante negli spettacoli classici al Teatro greco di Siracusa tra il 1914 e il 1948', *Danza e ricerca*, 12: 28–60.

Brecht, B. (1964 [1935]), 'The German Drama: Pre-Hitler', in J. Willett (ed.), *Brecht on Theatre: The Development of an Aesthetic*, trans. J. Willett, 77–81, London: Methuen.

Brecht, B. (1964 [1957]), 'Theatre for Pleasure or Theatre for Instruction', in J. Willett (ed.), *Brecht on Theatre: The Development of an Aesthetic*, trans. J. Willett, 69–77, London: Methuen.

Brown, H. (2016), *The Quest for the Gesamtkunstwerk and Richard Wagner*, Oxford: Oxford University Press.

Buscombe, E. (1981), 'Ideas of Authorship', in J. Caughie (ed.), *Theories of Authorship*, 22–34, London: Routledge and Kegan Paul.

Castellucci, R. (2004), 'The Universal: The Simplest Place Possible', *PAJ* 77: 16–25.

Causey, M. (2006), *Theatre and Performance in Digital Culture: From Simulation to Embeddedness*, London and New York: Routledge.

Clapp, S. (2015), 'Oresteia Review: A Terrifying Immediacy', *The Observer*, 7 June. https://www.theguardian.com/stage/2015/jun/07/oresteia-almeida-review-lia-williams-angus-wright (accessed 5.10.19).

Craig, E. Gordon (2009 [1911]), *On the Art of the Theatre*, ed. F. Chamberlain, Oxford and New York: Routledge.

Curtin, A. (2014), *Avant-Garde Theatre Sound: Staging Sonic Modernity*, Basingstoke: Palgrave Macmillan.

Daub, A. (2014), *Tristan's Shadow: Sexuality and the Total Work of Art after Wagner*, Chicago and London: Chicago University Press.

Deleuze, G. (1986), *Cinema I*, trans. H. Tomlinson and B. Habberjam, London: Athlone Press.

Diebold, B. (1928), 'Das Piscator—Drama', *Die Scene*, 18 (2): 27–9.

Dixon, S. (2007), *Digital Performance: A History of New Media in Theater, Dance, Performance Art, and Installation*, Cambridge, MA: MIT Press.

Fischer-Lichte, E. (2018), *Tragedy's Endurance: Performances of Greek Tragedies and Cultural Identity in Germany since 1800*, Oxford and New York: Oxford University Press.

Foster, H. (1994), 'What's Neo about the Neo-Avant-Garde?', *The Duchamp Effect*, 70: 5–32.

Friedman, K., et al. (2002), 'Volf Wostell', in K. Friedman, O. Smith, and L. Sawchyn (eds), *The Fluxus Performance Workbook*, 109–11, Aberystwyth: Performance Research e-Publications.

Goldberg, R. (1988), *Performance Art: From Futurism to the Present*, 2nd ed., New York: Thames and Hudson.

Grau, O. (2003), *Visual Art: From Illusion to Immersion*, trans. G. Custance, Cambridge, MA and London: MIT Press.

Green, A. (2014), 'Intermedia, Exile and Carolee Schneemann', in C. Townsend, A. Trott and R. Davies (eds), *Across the Great Divide: Modernism's Intermedialities, from Futurism to Fluxus*, 137–57, Newcastle upon Tyne: Cambridge Scholars Publishing.

Gropius, W. (1961), 'Introduction', in W. Gropius, A. S. Wensinger and O. Schlemmer (eds), *The Theatre of the Bauhaus*, trans. A. S. Wensinger, 7–14, Middletown: Wesleyan University Press.

Hostetter, A. and E. Hostetter (2011), 'Robert Edmond Jones: Theatre and Motion Pictures, Bridging Reality and Dreams', *Theatre Symposium*, 19: 26–40.

Huelsenbeck, R. (1974), *Memoirs of a Dada Drummer*, trans. J. Neugroschel, New York: Viking Press.

Innes, C. D. (1997), *Erwin Piscator's Political Theatre: The Development of Modern German Drama*, Cambridge: Cambridge University Press.
Janecek, G. (1996), *Zaum: The Transrational Poetry of Russian Futurism*, San Diego, CA: San Diego State University Press.
Jones, R. E. (1992), 'The Theatre of the Future', in D. Unruh (ed.), *Towards a New Theatre: The Lectures of Robert Edmond Jones*, 95–109, New York: Limelight Editions.
Ledger, A. J. (2018), '*The Thrill of Doing it Live*: Devising and Performing Katie Mitchell's International "Live Cinema" Productions', in K. Reilly (ed.), *Contemporary Approaches to Adaptation in Theatre*, 69–90, London: Palgrave Macmillan.
Lehmann, H.-T. (2006), *Postdramatic Theatre*, trans. Karen Jürs-Munby, London and New York: Routledge.
Ley, Graham (2007), 'A Material World: Costumes, Properties and Scenic Effects', in Marianne McDonald and J. Michael Walton (eds), *The Cambridge Companion to Greek and Roman Theatre*, 268–87, Cambridge: Cambridge University Press.
Manson, C. (2011), 'Jan Fabre's *Prometheus—Landscape II* (Montclair, NJ)', https://contemporaryperformance.com/2011/01/19/in-performance-jan-fabres-prometheus%E2%80%94landscape-ii-montclair-nj/, 19 January (accessed 30.7.19).
Marinetti, F. T. (2009 [1913]), 'The Variety Theatre', in L. Rainey, C. Poggi and L. Wittman (eds), *Futurism: An Anthology*, 159–64, New Haven, CT, and London: Yale University Press.
Marinetti, F. T., E. Settimelli and C. Bruno (2009[1915]), in L. Rainey, C. Poggi and L. Wittman (eds), *Futurism: An Anthology*, 204–9, New Haven, CT, and London: Yale University Press.
Marinetti, F. T., et al. (2009 [1916]), 'The Futurist Cinema', in L. Rainey, C. Poggi and L. Wittman (eds), *Futurism: An Anthology*, 229–33, New Haven, CT, and London: Yale University Press.
Maurice, L. (2017), 'The House of Atreus as a Reflection of Contemporary Evil: Performance Reception and *The Oresteia*', in E. Almagor and L. Maurice (eds), *The Reception of Ancient Virtues and Vices in Modern Popular Culture: Beauty, Bravery, Blood and Glory*, 37–59, Leiden and Boston: Brill.
McDonald, M. and M. J. Walton (2007), 'Introduction' in M. McDonald and M. J. Walton (eds), *The Cambridge Companion to Greek and Roman Theatre*, 1–10, Cambridge: Cambridge University Press.
McLuhan, M. (1964), *Understanding Media: The Extensions of Man*, Cambridge, MA: MIT Press.
McLuhan, M. (1967), *The Medium is the Massage: An Inventory of Effects*, London: Penguin Books.
Meyerhold, V. (2016 [1921]), 'Stanislavski's Solitude', in E. Braun (ed.), *Meyerhold on Theatre*, 4th ed., 218–22, London: Bloomsbury Methuen.
Mitchell, K. (2008), *The Director's Craft: A Handbook for the Theatre*, London and New York: Routledge.

Moholy-Nagy, L. (1961), 'Theater, Circus, Variety', in W. Gropius, A. S. Wensinger and O. Schlemmer (eds), *The Theatre of the Bauhaus*, trans. A. S. Wensinger, 49–70, Middletown: Wesleyan University Press.

Ovadija, M. (2013), *Dramaturgy of Sound in the Avant-Garde and Postdramatic Theatre*, Montreal: McGill-Queen's University Press.

Pavis, P. (2013), *Contemporary Mise en Scène: Staging Theatre Today*, London and New York: Routledge.

Piscator, E. (1980), *The Political Theatre*, London: Methuen.

Poll, M. (2018), *Robert Lepage's Scenographic Dramaturgy: The Aesthetic Signature at Work Adaptation in Theatre and Performance*, Cham: Palgrave Macmillan.

Pollux (1967), *Pollucis Onomusticon*, ed. Erich Bethe, Stuttgart: Teubner.

Pressman, J. (2014), *Digital Modernism: Making It New in New Media*, Oxford and New York: Oxford University Press.

Primavesi, P. (2013), 'Heterotopias of the Public Sphere: Theatre and Festival around 1800', in Erika Fischer-Lichte and Benjamin Wihstutz (eds), *Performance and the Politics of Space Theatre and Topology*, 166–81, New York and London: Routledge.

Rebellato, D. (2010), 'Katie Mitchell: Learning from Europe', in D. Rebellato and M. Delgado (eds), *Contemporary European Theatre Directors*, 317–38, London and Oxford: Routledge.

Rizk, L. (2015), 'Adaptation as Critique: Gender and Politics in the Plays of Effat Yehia and Amel Fadgy, Caridad Svich and Christine Evans', *Journal of Adaptation in Film & Performance*, 8 (3): 213–32.

Rodosthenous, G. (2018), 'Ivo van Hove's *Antigone*: A Contemporary Update', in S. Bennett and S. Massai (eds), *Ivo van Hove: From Shakespeare to David Bowie*, 74–8, London: Methuen.

Saltz, D. Z. (2001), 'Live Media: Interactive Technology and Theatre', *Theatre Topics*, 11 (2): 107–30.

Saltz, D. Z. (2015), 'Sharing the Stage with Media: A Taxonomy of Performer-Media Interactions', in S. Bay-Cheng, J. Parker-Starbuck and D. Z. Saltz (eds), *Performance and Media: Taxonomies for a Changing Field*, 93–125, Ann Arbor: University of Michigan Press.

Schneemann, C. (1996), 'Interview: Carolee Schneemann', in N. Kaye (ed.), *Art into Theatre: Performance Interviews and Documents*, 25–40, Oxford and New York: Routledge.

Semenowicz, D. (2016), *The Theatre of Romeo Castellucci and Socìetas Raffaello Sanzio: From Icon to Iconoclasm, From Word to Image, From Symbol to Allegory*, trans. P. Cichoń-Zielińska, New York: Palgrave Macmillan.

Sidiropoulou, A. (2011), *Authoring Performance: The Director in Contemporary Theatre*, New York: Palgrave Macmillan.

Solga, K. (2008), 'Body Doubles, Babel's Voices: Katie Mitchell's *Iphigenia at Aulis* and the Theatre of Sacrifice', *Contemporary Theatre Review*, 18 (2): 146–60.

Svich, C. (2004), 'Iphigenia Crash Land Falls on the Neon Shell That Was Once Her Heart (A Rave Fable)', *Theatre Forum*, 25: 27–51.

Townsend, C., et al. (2014), 'Introduction', in C. Townsend, A. Trott and R. Davies (eds), *Across the Great Divide: Modernism's Intermedialities from Futurism to Fluxus*, x-xxx, Newcastle upon Tyne: Cambridge Scholars Publishing.

Tripney, N. (2015), 'The Oresteia', *The Stage*, 6 June. <https://www.thestage.co.uk/reviews/2015/oresteia/> (accessed 10.10.19).

Wagner, R. (1892), 'Art and Revolution', in *Richard Wagner's Prose Works*, trans. W. Ashton Ellis and K. Paul, 1: 30–65, London: Trench, Trübner & Co.

Walton, J. M. (2005), 'Translation or Transubstantiation', in F. Macintosh, P. Michelakis, E. Hall and O. Taplin (eds), *Agamemnon in Performance 458 BC to AD 2004*, 189–206, Oxford and New York: Oxford University Press.

Warner, S. (2012), *Acts of Gaiety: LGBT Performance and the Politics of Pleasure*, Ann Arbor: The University of Michigan Press.

Zavros, D. (2017), 'Jan Fabre's *Prometheus Landscape II*: [De]territorialisation of the Tragic and Transgressive Acts of Arson', in G. Rodosthenous (ed.), *Contemporary Adaptations of Greek Tragedy: Auteurship and Directorial Visions*, 167–88, London: Methuen.

2

Digital media and Greek tragedy

A rhizomatic dramaturgy

Angeliki Poulou

Introduction

New media act as text-makers, developing a script, a dramaturgy, creating and re-creating current mythologies and ancient myths. In a way that digital performance functions as the myth, and artists as contemporary versions of the ancient tragic poet, transforming and visualizing fantasy worlds. Theatre directors, experimenting within their productions with the digital, modify the mythological 'megatext' in their artworks. In other words, digital technology, with its ability to construct worlds and atmospheres, fucntions as the myth. On some level, it may also satisfy the need for narration, acting as a rhapsode, resolving and rewriting the dissimilar dramatic elements. In addition to mimesis and illusion, the digital media act as performers on stage, in the words of Pierre Sarrazac (2012) as 'rhapsodes'. Technology acts as a performer.

The chapter aims to open a direct interdisciplinary dialogue between dramaturgy and the new media around key concepts of ancient Greek tragedy. Following an exploratory approach for understanding the creative potential of productions, I explore ancient drama in the digital era and ask the following research questions: How do the new media transform the narratives created on stage? How can we re-appropriate traditional concepts of drama? How does Greek tragedy represent the digital body, the sound mask and avatars? In what ways do contemporary artists deal with ancient drama conventions using the digital?

Digital writing

Digital writing concerning image, sound and interaction belongs to what is called scenic writing (écriture de plateau), indicating that the process of composition is realized first and foremost in scenic space. *Scenic writing* is a collage, an assortment of objects, words, music, sounds, texts, movements, devices and screens – miscellaneous features propounded as potentially exploitable sources in all theatrical creation. Just like the poets in the ancient Greek theatre, present-day directors do not merely deploy the means of expression provided by the genre of tragedy to achieve an intense dramatic effect, but having experimented, expounded on and perhaps exhausted their (already well known) function, they use them for a scenic game which by now regulates the experiences, the receptiveness, the openness of the audience.

Bricolage

The text of the performance results from a *scenic bricolage*. 'Bricolage' involves tinkering and transforming an aggregate of objects and assigning them new qualities and aims (Morin 1986: 179). It involves dissociating an object, an instrument, an idea or an institution from its system of reference and its very teleology, in order to induct it into a new system and assign it a fresh objective. *Bricolage* is further observed in the dramaturgy of sound and image which is deployed along with the wording of the text without always relating to it: at times it contributes, at times it works in counterpoint and it occasionally narrates another parallel, additional story, whether directly related or symbolic. As Genette notes (2018: 540), a new function overlaps and interweaves into the old structure, and discordance between these two coexisting elements lends an exciting tinge to the outcome.

In Castellucci's *Oresteia*, Aeschylus' text is communicated only through warped voices. The text is subsumed in the narrative, which is delivered through a processed and aurally altered voice. As the director says, 'We know perfectly well that tragedy is not poetry!' (Castellucci 2001: 57). His theatre works as a place where major dramaturgies are directly organized between 'sounding objects' (Mervant-Roux 2008: 39). Sound composition is almost always present, ever changing, forming a zone of permanent tension. Contrary to traditional theatre, where the text contextualizes the various sounds that are heard, here the beholder is alone with him/herself and is the one to tidy the discrepancies, to fill in the blanks between what is seen and what is heard, between different sound textures.

Dramaturgy can be seen as research on the coexistence of space, sound, body and technology in performative interactive practices, as a practice in the process of production, which is able to move a work 'onward' in interventionist ways that may frequently confuse, disorient or alienate. Digital dramaturgy may also be defined as 'new media dramaturgy', a term coined by Peter Eckesall (2017).

New media dramaturgy is a nexus between context, content, form, and audience ... In effect, New Media Dramaturgy is the name we use to designate both the composition of this kind of performance in and through new media art works, and its effects on an audience.... New media dramaturgy 'considers the way in which the materiality of technical elements matters'. (Eckersall, Grehan and Sheer 2017: 14).

Technology as myth

Theatre is transformed into a new medium every time that new media technologies become dominant, and is further adapted and disseminates the new cognitive strategies, which is what also happened in Ancient Greece (Hébert & Perelli-Contos 2001: 146), and is described by Eric A. Havelock (1981: 59). De Kerckhove points out that the Ancient Greek theatre was a product of the phonetic alphabet, which defined the sensory life of the Athenian community. This transition influenced the way that authors composed drama, since they could not have composed their tragedies, as we know them, without being literate (1980: 23-36). For Axelos (2005), a relentless urge leads human to an altered position, to exiting oneself through speaking and acting in a way that will later be called *mytho-logical* while simultaneously being almost *techno-logical*. In his view, the need to transcend a specific finite self leads human to myth and art/techne (technology).

Myth wields power similar to that of technology. For Axelos, 'the enigma of the cosmos is expressed and instantly activated in terms that will later be clarified and defined by words such as mythology and technology' (2005: 33). This is in accordance with considering new digital technologies as equivalent to myth by Hébert and Perelli-Contos (2001). In their view, digital theatre does not directly reflect reality but it can translate and reconstruct it into something else. Like myths, digital theatre can 'create virtualizations through the means and tools of the era into which it is inscribed' (2001: 132). They regard the theatre of image as 'equivalent' to myth, since they both have a rationale akin to the world of dreams, one that does not obey the rules of the linear model or rational thought, opting for the rules of metaphor and symbolism as a vehicle for shifting the outlook. Technology, as an opening towards a 'possibility', transcends the mimicry of nature and alters the question, 'what is this?' to the question, 'what could this become?' People build the horizon of their objects, create their world and enter the domain of possibility through technology.

Similarly, the directors of digital theatre, through the peculiar scenic writing they develop, beyond and above that of the text, emerge as the contemporary 'poets', who, just like the Athenian tragedians, alter the familiar myth, providing new versions while directing the creation of the performance. Creators are *auteurs*, in the sense that they do not merely aim at a successful representation of the text but they 'author' on stage.

Since the early 1990s, theatre and performance artists have been working on 'digital transformations' of myths and texts of ancient Greek tragedies, adapting them radically. Performances that became staged contemplations on contemporary technological culture, either utilizing its tools in sophisticated ways or raising crucial questions about it: *Bacchae* by ZT Hollandia, *Oresteia* by Romeo Castellucci, *Las Troyanas* by Fura dels Baus, *Antigone* by Luca De Fusco, *Philoktetes/MAN-O-WAR* by Crew, *EXPLORER/Prometheus Ontketend* by Urland and Crew, *Oedipus Reloaded* by Obermeier, *Death and the Powers* by Tod Machover, *Philoctetes* by John Jesurun, *Prometheia* by Medea Electronique, *La Medea* by Yara Travieso, etc.). While others explore the concept of sacrifice, war, postmodernity, insurgence, the law, the concept of the hero, of freedom etc.: *Ajax & The Persians* by Peter Sellars, *Alcestis* by Robert Wilson, *Oresteia* by Katie Mitchell, *Dionysos Stadt* by Christopher Rüping, *The Persians* by Ulrich Rasche, *(A)pollonia* by Kzryztof Warlikowski, *Atropa La Vengeance De La Paix* by Guy Cassiers, *Antigone* by Ivo van Hove, *Alexis, Una Tragedia Greca* by Motus, *Alpha* by Stathis Athanasiou.

Grand narratives and rhapsodicity

Ancient Greek tragedies created grand narratives about the cosmos, humans, chaos and meaning. Digital technology may in turn practice world-building, the construction of not only fragmented but also solid narratives. The performances that function as points of reference for the present article question postmodern fragmentation and subjectification in performing arts, thus contributing to the production of critical thinking, along with the return of the *Logos* and the grand narratives to the foreground. Steve Dixon claims that new technologies contribute to the transcendence of postmodernity. Regarding the postmodern as prone to fragmentation, subjectivity and the rejection of meta-narratives and meanings, while digital technologies in the theatre seek the exact opposite: coherence, meaning, unity, connection between the organic and the technological (Dixon 2007: 7).

The return to the narratives does not involve return to the text or to the traditional form in the theatre, but to world-building and the great schemas. It involves an opening to new narrative forms, such as stage writing (écriture de plateau), always in conversation with the neo-dramatic element.

Warlikowski's *(A)pollonia* is an onstage contemplation on the significance of sacrifice, from the archetypal myth of the sacrifice of Iphigenia, to Alcestis, all the way to the Holocaust. The director, who authored the adaptation/collage in close collaboration with the dramaturges and his permanent associates Piotr Gruszczyński and Jacek Poniedziałek, produces a new outlook on history and humans. He navigates history through micro-levels, he is interested in producing a new narrative about humans and the cosmos. The texts he used as a starting point are *Alcestis* by Euripides, *Oresteia* by Aeschylus and *Apollonia* by Hanna Krall, as well as the *Eumenides* by Jonathan Littell, *Elizabeth Costello* by J. M. Coetzee and *The Post Office* by Rabindranath Tagore. The director becomes a real author in this performance, which is not the interpretation of one work but a giant collage of texts, images, scenic traditions and techniques, historical issues, personages and myths.

The poetization of technology

Through arguing in favour of approaching technology as myth and as a world-builder and creator of grand narratives, we may perceive a first reply to the question of *poeticizing* technology. The digital media, on stage, in coexistence and/or confrontation with poetic discourse and physical bodies, can in turn be transformed, functioning dramatically. In digital theatre, technology is intensely present, as it is in everyday life. The difference is that here – on stage – technology may not have an 'instrumental' value, but it may be used mostly as a means towards experimentation, sensation and creation of emotions. Art may deprive them of their usual content, assigning them another or none, but the obvious one of play. What is more, it may be used for contemporary theatre to point out the extensive involvement of technology in everyday life, to portray the merging of the self and the machine, the 'intelligent' device, or it may also have a critical function by showing the audience the way they live. It turns spectators into observers of their very existence. It is up to them now to see if and to what extent they are satisfied with it. And the whole process is realized in the presence of the physical body, the action and discourse.

For Heidegger, poetry is connected to the 'revealing' of the world, through sensitivity and meditative thought, not through the violent visibility that present-day technology brings to bear. The revealing that holds away throughout modern technology does not unfold into a bringing-forth in the sense of poiesis. Poiesis as a mode of revealing requires a sensitivity to the movement of concealment and concealment made possible only in meditative thinking (Wendland, Merwin and Hadjiioannou 2018: 88).

Meditative thinking is an openness to the mystery of being and a willingness to dwell therein. Only through meditative thinking is enframing's totalizing tendency overcome and poiesis made possible. Poiesis, as a mode of revealing, does not occur in enframing. For Fischer-Lichte (2017), this is the challenge of the encounter between classical dramaturgy and the dramaturgy of the new media: presentness, physicality, the unveiling of things, their symbolization, the experience of the notional body as actual, the use of technical means so that the actor may be revealed as present and things as ecstatic.

The tragic

What gives the misfortunes of Greek tragedy this particular dimension, without which tragedy does not exist, is not that humans were willed a priori by the gods, but that they acquire meaning in connection with the great problems of human existence. A reading of ancient Greek tragedy and the tragic that takes account of the contemporary human concerns that relate to technoscience, expresses part of the present-day imaginary, the current standoffs, the present dilemmas.

This is the way that it explores contemporary quests concerning the human existence and condition: the transcendence of boundaries, human freedom, men and their devastation. The stage stands for this exactly: chaos in the world and the attempt to impose order on it, both on a dramatic level and on a performative one: conflicting forces, the various levels of the cosmos, conflicting views, gods and humans, this world and the netherworld, meditation and action. Chaos in the cosmos is depicted not only through dramatic discourse but also through digital technology: a barrage of images, sounds, a game of all dimensions (horizontal and vertical), a representation of the real, and the construction of potential environments, body doubles, direct contact and interaction, and telepresence. And all this flow of information, stimuli, sounds, images, temporarily coexists on stage; the boundary is the actor's body, and the eye of the viewer, which connects and orders these disparate elements.

A characteristic performance illustrating the above is Tod Machover's digital opera *Death and the Powers*(2014), created in collaboration with the MIT Lab. Based on Sophocles' *Oedipus at Colonus* and Shakespeare's *King Lear*, it attempts to take a new look, to produce a narrative about Human and the condition of existence, given the changes brought about by digital technology and technoscience (AI). Meditation does not follow the quotidian, micro-route through personal narrations, but exploits the 'opening' in space/time/myth/archetype offered by ancient Greek tragedy. The live global interactive simulcast of the final February 2014 performance of *Death and the Powers* in Dallas made innovative use of satellite broadcast and internet technologies to expand the boundaries of second-screen experience and interactivity during a live remote performance. In the opera, Simon Powers uploads his mind, memories and emotions into The System, represented onstage through reactive robotic, visual and sonic elements. Remote audiences, via simulcast, were treated as part of The System alongside Powers and the operabots. Audiences had an omniscient view of the action of the opera, as presented through the augmented, multi-camera video and surround sound. Multimedia content delivered to mobile devices, through the Powers Live app, privileged remote audiences with perspectives from within The System. Mobile devices also allowed audiences to influence. The System by affecting the illumination of the Winspear Opera House's Moody Foundation Chandelier.

Another performance that conceptualizes the tragic condition as idea and performative phenomenon (Lehman 2016; Poulou 2020) – addressing the intellect and the bodily perception of spectators – is the immersive opera *Oedipus: Sex with Mum Was Blinding* by ODC Ensemble (2019). The production was partly developed during the director's stay at the Center for Computer Research in Music and Acoustics at Stanford University, and features performers, musicians on stage, electroacoustic environments, live cinematic environment and neuroscience experiments. Artists and scientists collaborated in a new neuroscientific case study. The study asks: Are we free? Do we experience free will? Are there real alternatives, or is all that takes place the outcome of necessity? It is an exploration into determinism and self, where the answers describe either our majesty or captivity.

The 'rhapsode' figure returns to weave the great narratives on stage, made up of mythical, archetypical characters and events, but also of the present. Digital technology may satisfy up to a point the need for narration, for structure, by functioning as a 'rhapsode' (Sarrazac 2012), who unsews and resews the disparate dramatic elements. The polyphony and polyprism of ancient time returns through the multimedia of the scenic event, the hybridity and rhapsodicity on stage. A distinct voice is heard in parallel with the voices of the characters, adjusting the montage of the text: the 'rhapsode's' voice intervenes in the narrative. The 'rhapsode' invites the audience to form an opinion on the action on stage, offering a variety of perspectives.

Digital performativity

The scenic writing of contemporary directors/poets is supplemented by the performative (not merely mimetic) function of technological products. The term *performativity* denotes a non-essentialist approach to the concept of reality and questions the representation paradigm. Digital theatre deploys film, television and digital video on stage, in a *performative condition*: the means employed act and effect changes, functioning as sensory influences on the viewer. To put it differently, film, television and digital video are not just projected, they are also 'directed' and staged, since the theatre is the art of mise-en-scène, they are not mere accessories or accompaniments to the actors' action. They create, first and foremost, a 'sense of presence' (Féral and Perrot 2011: 11–40) through the virtual figures, the *dissembodied voices*, or 'acousmatic voices' (Chion 1994) and the digital avatars of actors on stage. Active vocality is reinforced by the new sound technologies. It signifies the transition from the logocentric hierarchy of the tradition of the text and linguistic content, to new areas, to soundscapes that invite the viewer/listener into new ways of recognition and signification. Therefore, the conventional unity of body and voice, guaranteed by the actor's physical presence on stage, is no longer a prerequisite.

Digital heroes are performative to the extent that they no longer represent but actually institute a new reality, to the extent that they impose a presence as actors or partners in the performance. The flow of information on stage is a factor in shaping the experience and involvement with the performance; it is performed in a continuum between live presence and live transmission, between the corporeal and the incorporeal dimension.

Jane Bennett talks about the 'vitality of matter' and the 'lively powers of material formation'. By 'vitality' she means 'the capacity of things – edibles, commodities, storms and metals – not only to impede or block the will and designs of humans but also to act as quasi agents or forces with trajectories, propensities, or tendencies of their own' (Bennett 2010: 13). The onstage video machinery participates in the narrative and impacts on viewer sensitivity. The setting, with its technological mechanisms, participates in the dramaturgy, which is no longer the exclusive prerogative of the actor. The sound amplifier or video recorder assists in focusing on a stage detail, thereby enlarging it. In the same way, a projector may segment and remorph the body anew (it may, for instance, change the frame within which the actor's gesture takes place). Lighting does, in fact, act on expressive materials, aiming to convey the aesthetic outcome to the viewer, who in turn remodels it. The actor's physical activity and stage lighting merge in a performative relationship, which aims at sensory efficiency.

Live video

Providing the audience with simultaneous visual access to the actors and their video avatars projected and transmitted in real time on the set, the performers play more and more with the performative potential of video during a performance on stage. They keep doubling the stage with the image, they prioritize the deconstruction of the image and the construction of reality, or at least the construction of reality through the image: long shots or close ups to foreground just a single detail of the face or the movement of the actor. Live video creates a sense of reality, it does not mimic, it transforms what is seen, while theatrical illusion or mimesis aims to make what is seen merely appear believable.

To take a case in point, when, in Warlikowski's (*A*)*pollonia* (2010), Clytemnestra prepares for Agamemnon's murder, he, intending to enter the mansion, removes his shoes. Clytemnestra speaks, yet on screen we can see Agamemnon's shoes and his feet walking towards the interior of the palace, where we know that the killing is to take place. Through live video Warlikowski 'repeats' the scene through the image, attempting to show what cannot be seen on the screen: what is outside the field, the deconstruction of the image and the construction of reality. The stage is at the same time 'a loop and a kaleidoscope' (Picon-Vallin 1998: 27). It is an almost cubist approach produced by combining detail and long shot, by the dematerialized close up and the actual figure, by a shot of the actor full face and sideways.

Absence/presence

Video obfuscates the concept of presence behind the one of representation, in that it allows the doubling of the actor (foregrounding the concept of the idol) and the substitution of the actor by his/her absence. So it turns the presence into an absence, emphasizing the absence of what is depicted. Live images therefore become the result of a construction and they are able to make the audience obliterate any human intervention in their construction.

So, when new media interact with ancient Greek tragedy, something very interesting arises as regards the issue of presence/absence, since in ancient Greek tragedy the characters and the events are seen as actually happening, even though they belong to an entirely different era. The incorporated presence of the actor in the theatre has always been a sign, or a mask, of an absence (Silk 1996 : 262).

Video means 'I see' in Latin. But what is it that one sees on video? It may be an *imago*. The *imago* is considered to be a richer word than its French derivative *image*, since it is used to denote a copy, a portrait, a statue, but also the shadow of one who is dead or a ghost. The reference to the *imago* takes account of the complexity of the *image*. In front of the video, 'the eye is reunited with the image, the video image is a ghost for the eye of the beholder. So, what one sees on the video is an *imago*' (Dufour 2008: 10). In digital theatre, the ghost enters the field of representation via technology, relaunching the debate about 'presence/absence' and the relationship between image and reality. The ghost, but also the video image, is a presence/absence. 'The latest technology, despite appearances, despite being scientific, increases tenfold the dominion of ghosts. The future belongs to ghosts' (Derrida & Stiegler 1996: 143).

In Kzryzstof Warlikowski's *(A)pollonia*, Orestes communicates with his mother's idol/avatar/image in real time through Skype. Then Hercules/Heracles and Athena join the Skype conference, where Orestes' trial is held. The trial held on Skype is a venue where the contemporary city debates and solves its issues. Digital communities are the Areopagus of the twenty-first century. On the one hand, there is the ease of communication afforded by technology, regardless of the spatial distance between the participants, or in this case even when the participants belong to different worlds and forms of existence; both the ghost and the gods appear on screen via Skype. On the other hand, their Skype communication proves to be ineffective, since understanding is absent. What arises here is the issue of communication quality. Here is a significant question: is this communication natural? Is it real? Is the presence on the dialogue window identical to the individual or transformed? Clytemnestra's ghost is the figure that appears on the Skype conference screen. Apart from the idol game, the video restores what has disappeared, creating ghosts with images. The video is an encounter with the shadow, a moulded shadow, convincing, lively and colourful.

Cyborgs

Instead of identifying with the action heroes, *immersive environments* invite the audience to join that world, not merely observe it from a distance, while the theatre had always been a *virtual reality*, where the actors notionally conspired with the audience to invent a joint belief.

In *EXPLORER/Prometheus Ontketend* by Urland and Crew (2015), the actors are not called upon to interpret a role or an emotion, but dressed in black in the dark, with sensors on their outfits, they have to perform movements with their bodies in order to create cyborgs on screen; they are asked to create their digital idol. Bridget and Deacon are virtual bodies, figures of a potential reality, reminiscent of avatars in *Second Life*. The two cyborgs are the primary agents of the action, the performers who are invited to embody the heroes and they are the agents of mimesis. Yet, they are both created in real time by the movements of the live performers who are equipped with a motion tracking system, and through a computer their movements are translated into a code that creates the digital bodies on screen (see also the discussion in Chapter 7).

The potential bodies are the new visual representations of the body, but they do not alter the physical composition of the flesh and bone bodies they refer to. The atopicity and fragmentation of the body in digital performance is an aesthetic practice that the deconstructive critics overstated, considering the potential body the central image of digital art, while in actual fact it works as an indicator, as yet another mark and representation of the perennial physical body.

Sound

The dimension of sound can interfere in the writing of a space in a successive, rhythmic function, performing the role of structure, of punctuation in spatial actions. It can also function as a setting and a frame (creation of environment) or be the subject/object. Finally, it can assist in the narrative (sound dramaturgy) of a spatial creation (sound mapping, becoming a narrative that supports identification (Faburel, Mervant-Roux, Torgue and Woloszyn 2014: 22).

Microphones, as well as projectors, also acquire dramaturgic function, as they are not regarded as mere technical elements of lighting or sound transmission. In fact, directors exploit them, loading them with figurative significations, seeking to eliminate distance from the audience and create an ambience of familiarity and intimacy, due to this artificial prefix. Sound amplification is also an occasion for a technological intervention that deploys the actor's voice in its own special way, allowing an intervention even in timbre, quality and intensity. Robert Lepage wonders: 'How can you be more and more intimate in ever larger venues? This is why, sometimes in an inept way, this technology is used' (Lepage 1997). Sound is a means of detonating images, thereby enlarging space. It also makes the 'off-field' visible; by the use of sound technology, in this case microphones, directors emphasize even more the innerness of the heroes, they prioritize their every move and word so that not a single one is lost to the eye or ear of the audience, everything is registered. Every voice will be heard, every murmur, every breath, every timbre, while in parallel they are frequently amplified or modified.

In Romeo Castellucci's *Oresteia*, the locus of the tragedy is also vividly portrayed through sound technology: voices sequestered from the body have been prerecorded and are reproduced warped in real time, the incessant noise of the first part of the performance is like a version of the citizens' chorus, which reprises the violence of the heroes. After all, Castellucci's favourite kind of theatre portrays the malfunction of existence in the context of artificial wreckage. Sound technology assists him greatly in achieving this effect. In his *Oresteia* sound functions as setting (it designs environments, conveys their aura) and as an element in dramaturgy (it expresses as yet another actor the action, tension, violence). It is the sound that along with the visual images of the actors' bodies makes the myth move before the eyes of the audience.

Sound technology in Castellucci's universe takes the form of an environment. Agamemnon's city, Argos, is noise, hence the intense sound plan, while in the *Choephori* there is absolute silence. Even the performers whisper. In the *Eumenides* some balance may be observed. The setting is reduced to a circle of light that reveals ghostly forms: figures of the past that haunt Orestes, feelings of guilt under the stare of the Furies. The new city has its new sound. The city in Castellucci's *Oresteia* is not vibrated by speech: the heroes do not speak, they do not express tragic conflicts through words but merely through cries (*Agamemnon*) or through silence and a few whispered words (*Choephori*), until some balance is achieved in the *Eumenides* and structured speech is heard on stage.

Rhizome: Intermedial and hypermedial

In the *Alexis, una tragedia greca* by Motus (2010), it is the rebellious city that invades the stage with the aid of technology. Motus presented their own version of Antigone. During the performance, photographs and videos are shown of Exarcheia in Athens, of social activism and self-managed venues, streets, images of slogans on the walls, posters, the place where a policeman killed Alexis Grigoropoulos, shots and archival material from demonstrations and clashes with the police. The material is projected on a large (14 metres wide, 10 metres high) PVC surface upstage. What is more, the audience watch video interviews with young people who speak about the killing of Grigoropoulos and the ensuing riots, about their lives and the crisis in Greece. During the Motus performance, the stage is bare, it looks like a studio with actors rehearsing. The action takes place both on video and on stage. The performance conjures up many dimensions, not 'layers', it is not a horizontal performance. Sound and image technologies contribute to this. There is no single angle, the audience may observe the scenic act from many viewpoints: through the story that is projected on the screens, through the 'open rehearsal' that the three performers have staged, through the myth and story/plot.

The digital theatre performances are characterized by *intermediality* (Chapple & Kattenbelt 2006: 20). *Intermedial theatre* (2006: 24; Bell 2000:

41–55) also deploys features of a *rhizome*. The *rhizome* comprises materials that on the surface appear not to belong with one another. These materials preserve their special characteristics and it is only through their connection with other elements that their purpose becomes clearer. For Deleuze and Guattari (1981: 31–2), the *rhizome* is characterized by an absence of hierarchy, plurality in counterpoint to a bipolar way of thinking, 'openings', lines of rupture and flight, interconnected surfaces. The *rhizome* is not made up of units but of dimensions, or to put it differently, it is transmuted by moving directions, ever changing its nature. Likewise, theatre functions as a *hypermedium* (Manovich 2001: 38), all the separate elements activated and organized in the mind and body of the viewer. *Hypermedial* theatre informs the viewer of the interaction between the various media, and therefore of the media themselves. There is no single viewpoint for the viewer, the focus of interest varies, action does not focus on any specific point: screens, projections of various sizes, sounds, lights, objects, the actors, the eye and the ear are confused, destabilized. The directors offer no single direction to the viewer, but invite him to watch a multidimensional spectacle, to choose, to move between these dimensions at will. They stage multiple plateaus, they create images, sounds, multidimensional atmospheres: the actor, the video screen, the computer, elaborate lighting, microphones.

Ancient Greek tragedy as a rhizome

Intermedial digital theatre, with its rhizomatic approach, appears to serve the rhizomatic mindset of ancient Greek tragedy. All the tragedians are in constant dialogue with literary tradition, mainly the epic, and they frequently recall this tradition to praise or criticize it. A prerequisite of successful theatrical viewing is for the viewers to experience a work on multiple levels concurrently. In the performances of ancient Greek tragedy in the digital theatre, there are hyperlinks between the ancient Greek tragedy and its adaptations, and with other texts. Perhaps overstating our case, we might see the current condition of ancient drama as rhizomatic: myth, the text of the poets, adaptations, the diverse versions of the myth, contemporary renditions: new links, concatenation, elements, names, fates, new readings, a never-ending process in short.

In addition, in ancient Greek tragedy, the basic issue is not moral (good and evil, right and wrong) but mainly an issue of identity, existence and coexistence, fate and measure. Also, the hero's 'self' is always facing adverse circumstances, so that the central question 'Who am I?' is ever present. Ancient Greeks, and Athenians in particular, used to define themselves in relation to others. An Athenian citizen saw himself as Greek because he was not a barbarian, as a man because he was not a woman, as a human because he was neither a god nor a beast, as free because he was not a slave.

Every element of the rhizome expands and connects with the rest. Equivalently, ancient Greek tragedy is 'an expression of the creative imagination of society that incorporates all the chaos through which it attempts to imagine (and establish) itself as other' (Gourgouris 2003: 157). In ancient tragedy, persons need to be defined through the other, they do not exist separately, what makes them persons is their relationship with others. It appears that tragedy implies that persons will never be complete without interaction with the others. The whole of *Oresteia*, for instance, is in dialogue with the traditions and practices of the city and attempts to revise them: the *Choephori* consist of a rupture with Agamemnon and a line of flight from him, leading to the *Eumenides*, where each murder presupposes the previous one and prepares the next, where even the end remains 'open', an open point and we know it is not final, the lines of rupture and flight are faintly visible.

Conclusions

This study addressed the changes that digital technology may effect on the traditional perception of ancient Greek tragedy, on the established approaches. What was discussed was the function of the new media as agents that developed a script, a dramaturgy, so that digital theatre is made equivalent to myth, and directors become a contemporary version of the ancient tragic poet.

The extensive use of technology does not weaken the conventional nature of ancient Greek drama; it does not deprive it of its poetic, otherworldly dimension. Given that realism, is not its exclusive function, but intervening in the real it may add dimensions and qualities. Furthermore, technology may serve *mimesis*, *representation* of an action, while functioning as a *performer*, acting, performing. The new media are able to further hone the *polyphony* of ancient Greek tragedy and its ability to create utopian/dystopian/reductive situations. Digital media assist ancient Greek tragedy in its *polyphony* by their *rhapsodicity*, they respond to its *intertextuality* by their *intermediality*. Now the concept of *mimesis* dovetails with *performativity*, while the contemporary version of aesthetic experience is changed from viewing to an immersive experience for the viewer or to a *hybrid* experience in an environment of augmented reality. Now the interaction with the audience, the deeper organic relationship between spectacle and viewer, is no longer served exclusively by the theatrical myth, or interaction, but with immersion. Its 'cathartic' function is amplified by the transformative power of the new media, through the atmospheres that they construct on stage and the multisensory involvement of the viewer.

The means of mimesis have changed greatly in the performances studied, while creators seek the 'metamorphosis' of the viewer though participation in a 'cyclical' theatrical experience. Digital technology of the image assists artists in the representation of the *ghost* or the divine, in its signifier *sensations of the real (effets du réel) and of presence*. Moreover, digital technology of sound, and the microphone in particular, also proves to be an equivalent of the mask, while it affects and immediately transforms the relationship between stage and auditorium.

The technologies of sound, image, interaction and immersion assist in this direction. As a result, new technologies are not merely employed for reasons of representation, just to bring the 'myth' on stage, but they frequently function independent of the text and the actors' performances, justifying the term 'audio' and 'visual' dramaturgy: they in turn act as performers or further relate another parallel story as 'context' or 'subtext' to the main story presented on stage. Ultimately, the performance resembles a *rhizome*, in the philosophy of Deleuze and Guattari: multi-layered, with continuous openings and lines of escape.

In analysing the 'pleasure' of digital environments, Janet Murray (2017) focuses on the concept of transformation. 'Kaleidoscopic narrative' capitalizes on the polymorphic ability of digital environments to be mutated. A parallel narrative of the same event and the freedom to support simultaneously alternative stories are characteristic of the creative use of digital media's polymorphic contribution in dramaturgy.

References

Axelos, K. (2005), 'Mondialisation Without the World', interview by Stuart Elden, *Radical Philosophy* 130: 25–8.

Bell, P. (2000), 'Dialogic Media Productions and Inter Media Exchange', *Journal of Dramatic Theory and Criticism*, 14 (2): 41–55.

Bennett, J. (2010), *Vibrant Matter: A Political Economy of Things*, Durham, NC: Duke University Press.

Castellucci, R. (2001), *Les pèlerins de la matière*, Besançon: Les olitaires Intempestifs.

Chapple, F., and C. Kattenbelt (2006), *Intermediality in Theatre and Performance*, Amsterdam and New York: Rodopi.
Chion, M. (1994), *Audio – Vision: Sound on Screen*, trans. C. Gorbman, New York: Columbia University Press.
De Kerckhove, D. (1980), 'A Theory of Greek Tragedy', *SubStance* 9 (29): 23–36.
Deleuze, G., and F. Guattari (1981), *Capitalisme et schizophrénie 2, Milles Plateaux*, Paris: Editions Le Minuit.
Derrida, J., and B. Stiegler (1996), *Échographies de la télévision*, Paris: Éditions Galilée.
Dixon, S. (2007), *Digital Performance: A History of New Media in Theater, Dance, Performance Art, and Installation*, Cambridge, MA: MIT Press.
Dufour, S. I. (2008), *L'image video d'Ovide à Bill Viola*, Paris: Archibooks.
Eckersall, P., H. Grehan and E. Scheer (2017), *New Media Dramaturgy Performance, Media and New-Materialism*, London: Palgrave Macmillan.
Faburel, G., M.-M. Mervant-Roux, H. Torgue and P. Woloszyn (2014), *Soundspaces : Espaces, expériences et politiques du sonore*, Rennes: Presses Universitaires de Rennes.
Féral, P., and E. Perrot (2011), *Pratiques performatives, Body – Remix*, Rennes: Presses de l'Université de Rennes.
Fischer-Lichte, E. (2017), *The Transformative Power of Perforance : A New Aesthetics*, London: Routledge.
Genette, G. (2018), *Palimpsests: Literature in the Second Degree*, trans. V. Patsogiannis, Athens: Cultural Foundation of the National Bank.
Gourgouris, S. (2003), *Does Literature Think? Literature as Theory for an Antimythical Era*, Stanford, CA: Stanford University Press.
Havelock, E. A. (1981), *The Literate Revolution in Greece and its Cultural Consequences*, Princeton: Princeton University Press.
Hébert, C., and L. Perelli-Contos (2001), *La Face cachée du théâtre de l'image*, Paris: L'Harmattan.
Lehman, H.-T. (2016), *Tragedy and Dramatic Theatre*, trans. E. Butler, London and New York: Routledge.
Lepage, R. (1997), *Les sept paroles de Robert Lepage, troisième mot, 'solo'*. Documentary on *Les sept branches de la rivière Ota*, Télé-Québec.
Manovich, L. (2001), *The Language of New Media*, Cambridge, MA: MIT Press.
Mervant-Roux, M. (2008), 'De la réalisation sonore historiquement intermédiale à l'activation par le son des scènes interdisciplinaires', in C. Naugrette (ed.), *Registres, revue d'études théâtrales, Théâtre et interdisciplinarité*, 13: 35–45, Paris : Presses de la Sorbonne nouvelle.
Morin, E. (1986), *La Méthode, La connaissance de la connaissance. Anthropologie de la connaissance*. Paris: Les Éditions du Seuil.
Murray, J. (2017), *Hamlet on the Holodeck, updated edition : The Future of Narrative in Cyberspace*, Massachussetts: MIT Press.
Picon-Vallin, B. (1998), *Les Ecrans sur la scène : Tentations et résistances de la scène face aux images*, Lausanne: L'Age d'Homme.

Poulou, A. (2020), *Ancient Greek Tragedy and Digital Theatre: Ruins, Metamorphoses, Dramaturgies*, Athens: Aigokeros.
Sarrazac, J. P. (2012), *Poétique du drame moderne*, Paris: Les Éditions du Seuil.
Silk, M.-S. (1996), *Tragedy and the Tragic*, Oxford: Clarendon Press.
Wendland, A.-J., C. Merwin and C. Hadjioannou (2018), *Heidegger on Technology*, New York: Routledge.

3

Digitizing the canon

Mediated lives and purloined realities in Jay Scheib's *The Medea,* Wooster Group's *To You, the Birdie!* and Persona Theatre Company's *Phaedra I—*

Avra Sidiropoulou

Introduction: Greek tragedy in the digital age

Since the mid-twentieth century, performances of Greek tragedy have been marked by the anxiety to preserve the enduring properties of the original text while researching and applying in performance updated stage idioms that could match its *antiqueness* to current perceptual codes. This anxiety is further imbued with the understanding that certain formal and religious aspects of the genre are difficult to represent, having no easy parallels to today. That said, staging the classics has been an appealing, if demanding, venture for many directors. Tragedy is an ideal platform for asking fundamental questions about humanity, society, politics and the self. It is also a genre that allows for experimentation and innovation, involving a variety of representational challenges that relate to bringing to (contemporary) life elements intrinsic to the ancient form, which are, however, foreign to spectators of the third millennium.

Quite understandably, modern productions of the classics have not been immune to the digital turn. The use of digital technology in performance has contributed significantly to the process of the ancient plays' reformulation and 'resurrection'. In this chapter, I will examine the use of multimedia in three contemporary productions/adaptations of Greek tragedy. Arguing that the hegemony of the mediated image has radically affected how directors read and how audiences reappraise the dramatic canon, I will look at Jay Scheib's *The Medea* (2005); Wooster Group's *To You, the Birdie!* (2002) and Persona Theatre Company's *Phaedra I—* (2019). These works rely heavily on video and sound technology to revise the structure and characterization of Euripides' *Medea*, Racine's *Phèdre*, and Euripides' *Hippolytus*, respectively. In all the above works, the complex negotiation of the source text with digital forms generates a cognitive turbulence that is both risky and inevitable – and perhaps also necessary – given the sensibilities of the modern spectator. Clearly, the Wooster Group's adaptation draws from the Greek myth of Hippolytus and Phaedra only *indirectly*; however, the strategies of digitization employed in the production are central to the focus of this chapter.

Today, we can safely assume that everything we experience in the theatre is profoundly mediated, through microphones, lighting or video screens. In fact, as Herbert Blau argues: 'There is nothing more illusory in performance than the illusion of the unmediated' (1987: 164). This acceptance goes hand-in-hand with the understanding that the expectations of a media-saturated audience have changed dramatically. Theatregoers tend to grow impatient at the absence of speed which characterizes traditional forms of dramatic theatre and are much more comfortable perceiving things through the frenetic rhythms of contemporaneity, which are constantly accelerated by technological progress and new forms of connectivity. Notably so the younger spectators who are addicted to the patterns of gaming, the expediency of apps and the counterfeit intimacy of social media. Add to that the fact that digital mediation builds a sense of recognizable space, pitting the outside world against dated literary and performative conventions and the artifice of the theatre. As theatre practice changes its priorities, revised interdisciplinary, hybrid modes of artistic research and expression are progressively emerging as important compositional tools.

Contemporary audiences become increasingly versed in alternative, 'porous' dramaturgies, 'artforms that are uncomfortable, discontinuous, destabilizing, frenetic, allowing for new information, theories and discoveries in science and technology to enter the domain of dramaticity' (Sidiropoulou 2018a: 117). The extensive use of multimedia in performance, besides 'updating' theatre's 'polyphonic system of information' (Barthes 2000: 263), no doubt mirrors an instinct for self-preservation and brings to the fore ontological questions about the multiple facets of performativity in a post-humanist era. After all, 'both human and non-human agents in contemporary performance can be said to possess a dramatic potency that is readable in terms of human experience' (Eckersal et al. 2017: 21). By virtue of its mediating properties, technology introduces heterotopic zones of endless possibilities.

In revisiting the Greeks, several artists[1] have used digital techniques as an integral aspect of narrative construction. The integration of media into the *mise-en-scène* adds meanings, nuances and allusions to the interpretation of the classical work. Indeed, it stirs up 'a contemporary sensibility . . . [that allows the text] to overcome the boundaries of history and culture and create a new sense that the dramatized world of the Greek tragedy is alive and current' (Campbell 2021: 235). For one thing, the media can unapologetically disrupt the sacred privacy of the archaic conventions, often revealing what in the original text was meant to be kept aside or merely alluded to (as for example, death on stage). Large choral parts can be displayed on screen in varying styles and to varying effect, and the chorus members can take up new exciting identities, to prevent the odd – principally dull – chord of old men declaiming on stage. Similarly, the use of masks is often replaced by projected animations and the Olympian gods – another alienating element germane to the tragic genre – are evoked by a mélange of distorted voices on play-back or a conjuring up of abstract digital 'presences'. Technology both domesticates and defamiliarizes the tragic form, manipulating perspective and making things appear bigger or insignificant, intimate or distant.

Digital expression helps a contemporary reading reframe the correspondence between the timeless and universal qualities of tragedy and the contemporary spectator's needs. Whatever feels foreign, incomprehensible or irrelevant in the source (the original text) can be revitalized by means of a visual strike of contemporary reference. Serving different functions and covering different needs, the presence of media in contemporary performance proposes new criteria for accepting the 'other' as 'own'.[2] Whether recorded or projected, the cultural co-ordinates of a global society we all can relate to intersect with the dramatic tradition of antiquity, creating geographies, time frames, and identities parallel to those experienced or embodied by the live performers. Philip Auslander's idea of 'televisual intimacy' posits that a contemporary audience whose existence is dominated by moving video images sees in those images a more convincing representation of the real than a live theatrical performance (1999: 12–16). The intimacy and shared space and time of live theatrical performance, ironically, becomes less 'real' because it is 'less familiar than the hegemonic media to which many of us are now accustomed' (Campbell 2021: 230).

Perhaps the most conspicuous and common use of multimedia in performance is its function as a visual/pictorial feature, which adds background and detail in places where the medium of theatre alone proves inadequate. The digital component brings film closer to the live arts, creating hybrid scenographies, which redefine and empower the narrational, sensory and emotional properties of stage images. In the late twentieth and the early twenty-first century, technology is becoming almost inseparable from theatrical design, occasioning jarring, ontologically pregnant collisions, whether through a simple projection of still images on the back wall of a black box theatre, a prerecorded action played back on a TV screen or more sophisticated *mediaturgies*[3] (Sidiropoulou 2018a: 158).

That being said, besides localizing the action in a literal sense, digital expression significantly generates psychic landscapes, yielding overt or subtle indication of mental states. Enabling the associative powers of projected imagery to take effect, the digital aspect redefines the perception of the real as something that seeps well into the mind. In so doing, it also generates impressions of the 'other', distending into the remotest past to allow for allegory to intrude into the realm of the private. The versatility of the medium allows different degrees of realism or abstraction, taking the spectator to existing or imagined and mythical places. In the productions discussed below, digital elements become a 'means of research and models not only for narrative purposes, but for reality itself: of each individual interpretation of reality' (Liakata 2018).

Three case studies

Jay Scheib's *The Medea*

American director Jay Scheib's *The Medea* (2005)[4] was performed at La Mama E.T.C. in New York City and in Adana, Turkey, as a multimedia adaptation based on different versions of the Medea myth by Euripides, Seneca, Müller and Cherubini. Conceptually, the production had Euripides' play narrated in reverse order. This was part of an attempt to trace the chain reaction that leads to a string of murders, such as the killings of Medea's two sons, of her brother and of King Creon and his daughter. According to the director-adapter, the action is narrated from the perspective of a detective story, in which 'we experience the presence of the end already in the beginning – but we read it anyway' (Scheib 2005).

The production featured video projections running constantly, creating a parallel narrative enriched with live and pre-recorded songs. The mixture of different media was meant to subvert and interrupt our received knowledge of the popular myth of the vengeful foreigner, who kills her children in response to her husband Jason's betrayal. Scheib's general intention to generate suspense was manifest also in the use of the camera angles, which manipulated the use of space, time and action. Applying digital technology, the adaptation deconstructs the idea of a perfect Aristotelian plot, yielding strong visual images and evoking recognizable references and daily rhythms. As the production's dramaturg Peter Campbell explains, Scheib's *The Medea* 'is not imprisoned in the past' of the myth of Medea or its past iterations, although it is aware of them and exploits them' (2010: 177).

Scenographically, *The Medea* features a versatile performance space, with an array of plastic chairs, a large mirror and a built-in white room with no ceiling, where many of the projected scenes are live-fed from an onstage camera operator. The room, where Medea often seeks refuge, is lined with a panoramic, kitschy picture of a tropical island. The inside can only be seen when the doors are open, but some of the action happening there is documented through the video cameras that have been placed inside. This enclosed area is Scheib's idea of 'a poor, sort of impoverished *skene*,' the equivalent to a building behind the playing area that in ancient Greek theatre was originally a hut for the changing of masks and costumes but eventually became the background before which the drama was enacted.[5] For the Greeks it was behind the closed doors of the *skene* that unspeakable violence took place.

Leah Gelpe's video design places cameras inside the room/*skene*, so that 'some parts of the play are made as if on a miniature sound stage, with scenes being projected live, run backwards, and frozen in time' (Scheib 2005). Gelpe characterized the role of the camera as 'devolution not evolution,' a catch-phrase which 'became the organizing principle for the entire play – it is potentially a fitting description of our times' (Scheib 2005).

The performance starts backwards. Jason, who recites Müller's text into camera, lies on the floor under a piece of rubble, facing upstage. The first glimpse that the audience gets of him is through a close up of his bloody face projected on a screen. The convention of mediated identities is established from the onset of the performance. The projection of what goes on in the room is constant, running parallel to the live action. Sometimes it is used to support what is happening mainstage; at other times it becomes the focal point of action, as in the killings of Medea's sons, which are partially seen and partially screened. As Campbell points out, 'by incorporating and obscuring both live and mediated images, the production obfsucates the scenography as it presents disconnected and fragmented images of the action of the actors. Furthermore, as these scenes are sometimes played backwards or paused, the use of video echoes the narrative reversal and enhances the dramatic subversion' (2010: 180). In effect, the cameras reveal what is taking place behind the scenes, sometimes against the archaic convention of never representing violence onstage.

This consistent engagement with the media creates a heterotopy and heterochrony of myth. Digital story-telling sets out to cover the entire expanse of Medea's history through to the present, deepening and expanding the perception of time and creating spaces inhabited by memories relived and facts re-accessed. The digital narrative helps resist structural linearity, dethroning common representational conventions and facilitating a different understanding of how our sense of reality can be shaped or modified in performance. In her divisions and multiplicities, Medea is caught in an uncomfortable zone between past and present, the public and the private, the self and the 'other', mundane reality in all its little details and mythical allusion. The use of media underlines the intertextual nature of the adaptation and echoes a story which condenses past, present and future into an abstract 'now', as the spectators try to process untold details of a popular myth.

In the process of updating Euripides' play to generate a confused, hurt, vengeful woman in a pop-saturated world, technology is instrumental. It recontextualizes setting, story and character, bringing the notions of suffering and recognition down to a more human – if deliberately prosaic — level. It also adds touches of contemporary hypernaturalism and parody, as in the scene where the screen displays the two sons and the nurse happily eating apples, against Medea's and Jason's nearly seven-minute-long rough love-making. As the action begins to unfold (or rather, *de-fold* to follow Scheib's concept of 'devolution'), *The Medea*'s intermedial nature becomes even more pronounced. The title character starts speaking directly to the camera, while her sons and the nurse watch some of the action on the two monitors positioned at the front of the stage. Most of the characters use microphones. At the end of the play, they all dance on camera to the music composed and performed by Margareth Kammerer.[6] A lit candle is extinguished in a close-up on the screen, signalling the end of the performance.

While serving as a mechanism of ironizing the myth, the video sequences clearly generate affective impact in the most emotionally fraught moments of the play, whether by juxtaposing live and mediated storytelling or by repeating a scene in a different form or scale. This, for example, happens in the opening sequence of the production, where the freshly murdered Jason is projected onto the monitor at the front of the stage, while the confused nurse wanders among the chairs aimlessly. This also happens in the video portrayal of the killings of Medea's sons. The murder scene is repeated on screen, which structurally blurs the boundary between reality and memory, past and present.[7] The simultaneous, often competing use of different media, including video projections and live and pre-recorded music, is part of Scheib's investigation of 'found reality' (notes), a 'crossing a variety of disciplines as a means of forcing the theatre into unusual shapes, and actors into reality . . . an approach to Reality on the stage that . . . might rival our Reality on the Street' (Scheib 2005).

In many adaptations of Greek tragedy, video footage is used as a background for clarifying elaborate or ambiguous parts of the spoken text and providing additional details of narrative exposition. In its most literal use, media adds missing information via projecting explanatory images and newsfeed on screen. This may explain why digital technology has become an important aesthetic and structural tool in performances of documentary theatre. At the same time, digital storytelling can generate layered commentaries and introduce new and subtle interpretative perspectives on the text. That being said, in Scheib's production, the projections, rather than clarifying the text, emphasize the eclectic nature of the adaptation – as various sources are used together with Euripides' original – and the stylistic variety that characterizes the different modes of acting, from heightened poetry to low-brow vernacular and soap-opera melodrama. More than anything, the projected images overthrow any expectations of linearity, simultaneously undermining the tragic tone normally expected from any reading of *Medea*. These images satirize the insignificant rituals of our everyday experience, the anti-heroic routines of otherwise 'grand' and tragic characters. There is something bizarre as well as moving to hear Medea unfold her lofty revenge plans, while we continue to enjoy Kammerer's guitar playing and singing from inside the room. This is a statement that life will go on, and Medea's history will survive, even in a mediated form.

Wooster Group's *To You, the Birdie!*

The Wooster Group's controversial work *To You, the Birdie!* (2002),[8] based on Paul Schmidt's translation of Jean Racine's *Phèdre*, reconfigured the French tragedy by thoroughly digitizing visual and auditory storytelling. Revisiting the classical story of unrequited love, the production transformed Phèdre's passion for Hippolytus into a jarring, highly ironic multimedia exploration of contemporary cultural assumptions about image and body representation. Director Liz LeCompte used a game metaphor, borrowing the title of the play from badminton, which gave the production its leitmotif. In fact, the game of fortune in Jean Racine's tragedy was represented by a relentless match of badminton, which had Hippolytus compete against the referee Venus. The use of multimedia undermined classical conventions and modes of characterization and representation, producing a highly parodic effect. Sometimes video projections and sound manipulation introduced parallel sets of action that contrasted ironically with what was happening on stage. At other times, they added detail and depth to those actions performed live, functioning as a kind of subtext to what is happening in the foreground.

In LeCompte's metaphor, the palace of Troezen, where Phèdre and her stepson Hippolytus meet during Theseus' absence on a military expedition, is transformed into a badminton court, where tempestuous emotions, recriminations and lamentations are played out in mostly understated, deadpan style, matched by the perfect symmetry of the space. Serving this concept, the set design – delineating clear and geometrically defined playing areas – is abstract enough to allow for the digital images to take centre stage. There is a platform with a set of steps on both sides, and the back of the set suggests a swimming pool, with benches behind it. The flat screens move up and down, and there is also a glass panel behind one of the monitors. The visual environment framed by the proliferation of TV screens is meant to convey the play's ever-shifting actual and imagined spaces and reflect on Phèdre's physical, mental and psychological state.

Here too, digital mediation redefines classical conventions. Especially in relation to the presence of divinity, it reconceptualizes the notion of 'divine' which is at the heart of tragedy, but which contemporary audiences often have trouble accepting. The co-existence of the physical and the digital presence of Venus – who is not listed among Racine's characters yet plays a pivotal role in Euripides' *Hippolytus*, as she instigates Phaedra's passion for her stepson – creates the necessary conceptual backdrop that helps acknowledge the absurdity of gods meddling in human affairs. The contrast of Venus' mediated presence on video overseeing the match with Phèdre's live wheelchair presence supports LeCompte's reading of the play from the get-go: this is no clean version of the myth, but a startling encounter of fact and fiction, bringing a relatively ordinary love story to the digital realm of the gods.

What makes the use of the media particularly original is its revealing hidden aspects of the characters' personalities, especially in regard to their little vanities and vices. Such is the case with the portrayal of King Theseus, when he returns from his war expedition, as a massive animated statue whose muscular strength and pseudo-heroic body-builder's poses are further enhanced in the video. Willem Dafoe's Theseus lies down and a close-up of his torso is projected onto the plasma screen, digitally transformed into a piece of art. Other technological quirks are less meaningful, even if they produce comic effect. Despite suffering from incontinence and being constantly attached to a potty-throne, Phèdre spends a great deal of time trying on different pairs of shoes, as the projections of her Prada collection (mis)matching her live legs and feet comically illustrate. At the back of the stage, Hippolytus and his tutor Theramenes engage in man-to-man locker-room confessions, exacerbated by graphic images projected on the television screens. While the two men fiddle with their genitals underneath their skirts, the screen displays a distorted sequence of crossing and uncrossing of knees, which yields a hilarious imbalance, without necessarily leading to any character epiphanies.

Yet, the originality of LeCompte's concept lies in making technology a determining factor of identity construction. Blurring the boundaries between the real and the imagined, the mediated image takes over not just as a visual counterpart of the live narrative but also as an essential, ontological agent.

Recalibrating representations of selfhood, the performance is layered with alienating voice-overs, while Phèdre's and Theseus' figures on the video screen are sometimes split into two. The interpenetration of video and live action complicates the fraught understanding of *liveness* (to refer to Auslander 1999) and *aliveness*, the paradox of processing two different levels of reality simultaneously. The audience oscillates between empathy and estrangement, which produces a kind of 'nostalgia for the pure body,' uncontaminated by the 'noise' of mediation (Sidiropoulou 2018b.), especially in those moments when Phèdre's as well as Hippolytus,' Theseus' and Theramenes' virtual selves dominate the physical ones. Both visual and auditory framing challenge and reconfigure the performers' – especially Phèdre's – subjectivity. The characters become both actors in and observers of their stories.

Inevitably, the division/multiplication of the self ultimately results in a destabilization of the spectator's perception. Exposing Phèdre's fragmentation, the digital presences update existing mechanisms of characterization. There is little opportunity or even desire for unified psychology, and whatever empathy exists is the result of all our conflicting emotions in search of closure. The fact that the 'self' can now be split, multiplied and manipulated at the director's will no longer concerns the 'death of character' (an idea introduced by Elinor Fuchs in her seminal study of 1996), but 'rather of a character's rebirth or re-incarnation as a hybrid, existing in a state of liminality between corporeality and imagination' (Sidiropoulou 2018b). The irony of seeking completion through division is, after all, a recurrent trope in mediatized performance.

Matthew Causey rightly views the televisual screen as 'that privileged object that emerges from the separation of the self' but also as 'the technology of the self-mutilation revealing the appearance of the double as the approach of the real' (Causey 2006: 21). As he argues, 'the question of the drama is not one of representation, of the thing and its reflection, but rather of the splitting of subjectivity' (2006: 21). Forced to become her own viewer, as she mimics her version on screen, Kate Valk (the actress playing Phèdre) establishes a dialogue of herself as a performer and the character's 'body as a spectacle of tragedy and femininity, incapable of any greater physical action than being looked upon' (Monks 2005: 210). This dichotomy is aided by sound and voice manipulation. Notably, Phèdre's soliloquies are whispered into a microphone by Scott Shepherd, the actor playing Theremenes. Shepherd's monotone delivery deflates the tragic element and sabotages the queen's imperial identity. In fact, Shepherd, who is mostly placed upstage, recites the text of all the main characters (Phèdre's, Hippolytus and Theseus) except for Phèdre's Nurse Oenone's, while the actors act out the words. The existing voice-overs and pre-recorded dialogic parts that are communicated in the actors' voices convey a sense of distance and displacement. The body is decomposed, caught in the duality of living entity and machinery component.

In the body of work that the Wooster Group have developed over their long career in experimental theatre, video is no longer a mere addition of a new medium in performance, but one of its integral elements (see also Sampatakakis' Chapter 1). Indeed, the 'expansion of the use of video in performance increases the fragmentation of perception. Now, it is no longer the image that is fragmented into live and mediated components, but the space itself, and with it, the performance' (Jakovljevic 2010: 94). The intrusion of the hyper-real aggravates the audience's disorientation, by celebrating the mediated presence as an equally, if not more, valid identity in today's 'post-existential' culture. Ironically, the use of media holds the mirror up to the entrapment and loss of authenticity which results from our experiences becoming overly mediated. In this sense, the Wooster Group's involvement with multimedia forms also interrogates the impact of the digital agency on human relationships and social interaction.

Persona Theatre Company's *Phaedra I*—

Phaedra I— (written and directed by Avra Sidiropoulou), premiered at the Tristan Bates Theatre in London in 2019.[9] The production revisits Euripides' classical story of Phaedra's passion for Hippolytus, based on a new, elliptical and palimpsestic text, which is partly inspired by the myth handed down to us by Euripides and later taken on by Seneca and Racine. In keeping with the Euripidean premise,[10] the action is set in motion with the spell that goddess Aphrodite casts on Phaedra, which both liberates and traps her into seeking sensual pleasure in her stepson, Hippolytus. We are made witness to sequences of charged interactions between Phaedra and the chorus of Athenian women, who are castigating but also acting envious of her existence, at the threshold of transgression, well outside the rules dictated by her societal role.

The prevailing use of video projections and mapping establishes a dynamic visual landscape – the performer's costume is her whole world. Phaedra sits on a platform centre stage for the entirety of the performance. She is mostly static, allowing for her costume to also function as a projection screen.[11] In its purest form, the visual element absorbs scenographic semiosis entirely. Throughout the play, the video stills and projections offer indications of location, at least as far as an actual, identifiable setting is concerned. In the opening sequence, where Phaedra interacts with the chorus of women, the long white dress bears the projected image of an ancient Greek pillar, which takes us straight to the mythic past of Athens, to which constant references are being made in the dialogue. When Phaedra's private, corporeal self grows into a public space, her memories cease to be personal; they evoke shared experiences. Images of urban life as well as of natural catastrophes from the recent history of Greece reinforce the devastating clash between the country's past and present with a touch of irony. Significantly, the fire spreading images at the opening of the play carried through to the final visual of scattered debris in a field.[12]

As the stage is covered by Phaedra's super-sized dress, the live character is completely surrounded/submerged and then swallowed by this fabric construction: the dress becomes the extension and the prison of Phaedra's physical self. Her body is transformed into an entire self-contained universe where she dwells in complete mental isolation. The body-landscape is initially white and still, desert-like and uninscribed by past experience, a *tabula rasa*. The moment the action begins, however, light, colour and movement are cast on it through the video, just as the Aphrodite's spell is cast on Phaedra's body. Phaedra's existential angst is reciprocated by Aphrodite's mediated presence. The play opens and closes with the dominant presence of the goddess, who exists as a constant vocal reference but who is also portrayed as a visual of fire spreading wide, setting up the scene for the drama to unfold.

In general, the video projections create narratives that develop with the text and the actress' performance. This compositional method helps build a parallel story line, which far from being descriptive, directly linked to the myth, or merely substituting for missing text, provided 'additional emotional and cognitive content' (Liakata 2018). In the apparently domestic scene where Phaedra shares her sentiments of boredom and disenchantment with Theseus, the audience is shown a video of an elegantly positioned cluster of male and female naked bodies, writhing in white sheets, in a languid sequence of obviously joyful play. In this case, the image visualizes the subtext underneath Phaedra's *post-coitum* musings. The integration of dialogue with visually absent Theseus' pre-recorded voice also serves to that effect. Sometimes, the images add a surrealistic, humorous feel, as in the nightclub scene, where Phaedra is first introduced to Hippolytus. A projection of the bottom half of a woman's body in short skirt and fishnet stockings, seated on a bar stool, captures both setting and mood. Phaedra crosses and uncrosses her legs, while the performer continues to sit still underneath her huge costume. As a male torso enters the projection, the video generates a sensual feel, well matched to the soundscape of mixed tipsy voices commenting on Phaedra's lust for her young stepson. In fact, the video follows Phaedra's fantasy: a steamy dance with the object of her desire, depicted as two male hands moving slowly and intimately up and down parts of a glittery female dress.

Repeatedly, projections reveal stereotypes of femininity and the prejudices of the Chorus about Phaedra: the video of Phaedra's sexy dangling stilettos luring Hippolytus into small talk alternate with pink rose petals that fall over Phaedra as she sings a country ballad entitled 'Younger Bones' and dances in a moment of teenage elation. Such images are meant to reflect the chorus' own projections on Phaedra's 'picture-perfect' life and her role in reinforcing the patriarchal narrative of marriage as an institution from which women can benefit socially and economically. Serving to underline the protagonist's conflicting emotions, the sequence 'Contempt' follows Phaedra's transformation from a love-torn, dejected woman into an enlightened character, who philosophizes on the nature of rejection and on being human and vulnerable. The video image depicts a barren, cracked piece of earth, which trembles throughout, suggestive of an earthquake. Phaedra's speech, blending high poetry and confrontational direct address, is nearly synchronized with the quavering landscape. Standing still, the performer laments Hippolytus' rejection of her love, which she attributes to her invisibility. The combination of image, intermittent sound and staccato sentences underlines the disjointed, disconnected sensation of the scene.

The most prominent function of digital media in this production, however, concerns the introduction and validation of the play's missing characters. The text presents an added layer of complication, because the title character incorporates all characters in the original myth. In terms of sound, this happens in most of the scenes by means of pre-recorded voices that stand for Aphrodite, the chorus of women, the mixed crowd in the nightclub, and Theseus. On stage, the performer interacts with herself as performer and the projected snapshots of her life, but more importantly, with her other selves. In this sense, she is caught in an internal conflict to reconcile her various personas, shaped through relentless interrogation with her electronic counterparts. The complexity of her performing all the parts is further aggravated when these different roles stand in dialogue with their mirrored self. Each scene conveys this narrative convention in different ways, so that we soon begin to accept and enjoy it. Only Hippolytus remains voiceless, a choice that underlines the carnal, irrational aspect of Phaedra's desire for him. Even more startlingly, the digital element bestows the absent actors a digital body and a face. In most cases, this is a fragmentary identity, torn into pieces that are scattered all over Phaedra's costume and adding to the overall impressionistic effect of the show. Once again, Hippolytus stands out from the rest of the characters. He is given a full body, his overriding carnality drawing attention to Phaedra's sexual fantasies of her stepson. Significantly, in the most climactic scene of the play, in which Phaedra confesses her love to Hippolytus, also speaking his lines, the male character is digitally personified in the video images of three different men's semi-naked bodies crawling up and down Phaedra's body. The body multiplication is there to suggest that Phaedra is enamoured not with one specific person, but with the idea of falling in love and being sexually fulfilled.

At the end of the play, as Phaedra exits the stage naked, leaving behind everything she possessed, the video is still left playing against the cadaver of her dress, which lies on the floor crumbled. The projection of a field of colourful debris on her discarded 'dress-skin' keeps playing in slow motion until it shrinks to a snapshot of a funnel devouring every remaining bit of garbage, as the play fades to dark. The symbolic significance of this extended image poses questions about Phaedra's future: one wonders whether Phaedra is a free woman, who has been liberated from the burdens of her past and ready to embark on new adventures; or whether the final visual suggest some kind of regret, and a 'deconstruction and reconstruction of her personal moral code/value system' (Sidiropoulou 2019b). While the play is open-ended, the final scene suggests that Phaedra finally breaks away from whatever held her captive. The ending therefore implies a sense of personal salvation; Phaedra emerges out of the rubble cleansed, a survivor. The rubble, however, is more than just a statement on Phaedra; we are surrounded by the debris of a culture of instant and cheap gratification in which people – women and men alike – suffocate alone, in their search for a modicum of meaning.

Conclusions

Given how generously performance keeps metamorphosing, the authorial iconization of the stage, along with fresh notions of dramaturgy as an operation of theatre-making, call for revised ways of training the spectator to appreciate mediatization as a powerful arbiter of narrative structure and sensual engagement. The discussion of the three productions above set out to illustrate only some aspects of media's significant role as a compositional (instead of a merely scenographic) tool in contemporary theatre. The encounter of the future – represented by the inexhaustible possibilities of the media aesthetic – with the remotest past of the Greek plays is testimony to the fact that the guilt-free intercourse of *logos* with digital forms is fraught with tensions, anxieties, mutual recriminations and fiery emotions – the makings of an exciting, meaningful, if sometimes troubled relationship.

It is no surprise that radical updating strategies such as projected images, intercepted voices, virtual and even augmented reality have infiltrated many stage adaptations of tragedy as a way of reenergizing and making an old text relevant today. Yet, while multimedia forms have helped explore and explode representational boundaries and sharpen directorial interpretation, it is worth noting that over-reliance on the digital has complicated the audience's relationship to the classics further, leaving open axiomatic questions about the symbiosis of source text and creative process, of adaptation and reception. Active in this debate are the polemics of theatrical revisionism who cling onto the 'fidelity discourse' that permeates theatre criticism. This attitude tends to renounce any radical readings of the 'sacrosanct' source text as irreverent, claiming that the ethics of direction are intrinsically linked to paying respect to the playwright's 'intentions;' a term, which is in fact as dangerous, as it is ultimately redundant.'[13] In my exploration of the functions of technology in the productions and adaptations of classical plays I have focused on, I have tried to argue that the digitization of the Greek tragic plays can in fact help bridge the gap between the archaic and the postmodern, between ancient metaphysics and our century's awareness of the post-tragic.

Notes

1 Some of the most representative being Romeo Castellucci, Ivo van Hove and Katie Mitchell; from the younger generation see the work of Robert Icke in the United Kingdom.

2 One also recalls Hans-Thies Lehmann's conceptualization of the 'real' and the 'extra-aesthetic' in postdramatic theatre:

> The aesthetic cannot be understood through a determination of content (beauty, truth, sentiments, anthropomorphizing mirroring, etc.) but solely – as the theatre of the real shows – by 'treading the borderline', by permanently switching, not between form and content, but between 'real' contiguity (connection with reality) and 'staged' construct. (2006: 103)

3 Unpacking the development of new media dramaturgies, Eckersall et al. refer to a recent shift in approaches to experience design in the use of theatre and performance technology, which

> might be characterised as one in which the human sense of what occurs, the overt anthropo-scenography of our traditions, is gradually diminished in favour of an object-oriented scenography informed by what the technology itself seems to want to say. In this study we see technologies that are overtly visible, externally mechanical, operating on and against bodies, centrally regulated and controlled alongside dispersed, multiple, interactive, liquid media. (2017: 11)

4 *The Medea: Play with mixed music & mixed media, after Euripides Seneca Mueller Cherubini* was performed by Dima Dubson, Oleg Dubson, Dan

Illian,* Margareth Kammerer, Jennifer Lim*and Zishan Ugurlu* with original music performed by Margareth Kammerer, video design and direction by Leah Gelpe, scenic design by Michael Byrnes, costumes designed by Oana Botez-Ban, lit by Lucrecia Briceno and dramaturgy by Peter Campbell; assistant director Shira Milikowsky; production manager Mercedes Murphy; adapted and directed by Jay Scheib.

5   See https://www.britannica.com/art/skene (accessed 28 March 2022).
6   Kammerer wanders through various scenes but her troubadour presence is not always acknowledged by the other players, though it is often projected in the video screen. According to the programme notes, the musical score 'combines selections from Cherubini's 18th century "Médée" (Medea), well-known Italian love songs, and original songs based on texts from Heiner Müller into a score for solo voice and classical guitar'.
7   According to the reversed order that the production proposes, if Medea's sons died in this scene, their presence in the previous scene (which occurs later) cannot be accounted for.
8   For full production credits see https://thewoostergroup.org/to-you-the-birdie (accessed 28 March 2022).
9   The play was performed by the British-Australian actress Elena Pellone. The set, costume and video design was by Mikaela Liakata, the lighting by Anna Sbokou, and the original music by Vanias Apergis. The production was dramaturged by Eleni Gini and Miranda Manasiadis and assistant-directed by Julia Kogou and Maria Hadjistylli. The project was realized with the kind support of the J. F. Costopoulos Foundation.
10 At the opening of Euripides' tragedy *Hippolytus* (428 BC), Aphrodite, goddess of love, in her prologue, lays out for the audience her revenge plot on the title hero for refusing to honour her.
11 For more on the possibilities of projections, see Eckersall et al. 2017: 25–53.
12 Those sequences had a special emotional significance for the Greeks among the London audience members, as the play was performed just a few months after the catastrophic wildfires in the Attica region of Mati in July 2018, which led to the death of 102 citizens, and left the entire country in a state of national mourning.
13 The current debate in adaptation scholarship differs from this reactionary attitude. In fact, it views chronologically earlier works not as superior or more influential than their successor, but as 'points of reference that are available for interpretation, recontextualisation and remodelling'. In fact, 'radical adaptations can reinforce just as much as they can subvert their predecessors, and the focus is on the existence of a relational rather than a hierarchical tie-in between the two' (Komporally, 2017, p. 4). For a discussion on the ethics of directing see Sidiropoulou (2021). For the mechanisms of recontextualization in contemporary productions of Greek tragedy see Sidiropoulou (2015).

References

Auslander, P. (1999), *Liveness*, London: Routledge.
Barthes, R. (2000), *Critical Essays*, Evanston, IL: Northwestern University Press.
Blau, H. (1987), *The Eye of Prey: Subversions of the Postmodern*. Bloomington, IN: Indiana University Press.
Campbell, P. (2010), 'Jay Scheib's *The Medea* as Postdramatic Performance' in H. Bertel and A. Simon (eds), *Unbinding Medea*. London: Legenda.
Campbell, P. (2021), 'Postdramatic Greek Tragedy' in V. Liapis and A. Sidiropoulou (eds), *Adapting Greek Tragedy: Contemporary Contexts for Ancient Texts*, Cambridge: Cambridge University Press.
Causey, M. (2006), *Theatre and Performance in Digital Culture*. London and New York: Routledge.
Eckersall, P., H. Grehan and E. Sheer (2017), *New Media Dramaturgies*, London: Palgrave Macmillan.
Fuchs, E. (1996), *The Death of Character: Perspectives on Theatre after Modernism*, Bloomington, IN: Indiana University Press.
Jakovljevic, B. (2010), 'Wooster Baroque', *TDR* 54 (3): 87–122.
Komporally, J. (2017), *Radical Revival as Adaptation*, London: Palgrave Macmillan.
Lehmann, H. T. (2006), *Postdramatic Theatre* trans. K. Jürs-Munby, London and New York: Routledge.
Liakata, M. (2018), panel discussion in 'Tragedy 2.0. Greek Tragedy and the Digital Era' International Conference, Cacoyannis Foundation, Athens.
Monks, A. (2005), in S. Mitter and M. Shevtsova (eds), *Fifty Key Theatre Directors*, London and New York: Routledge.
Scheib, J. (2005), *The Medea*, programme notes.
Sidiropolou, A. (2015), 'Adaptation, Re-contextualisation and Metaphor. Auteur Directors and the Staging of Greek Tragedy', *Adaptation* 8: 31–49.
Sidiropoulou, A. (2018a), *Directions for Directing: Theatre and Method*, London: Routledge.
Sidiropoulou, A. (2018b), 'Identity, Technology, Nostalgia: The Theatre of Ivo van Hove, Robert Lepage and The Wooster Group', *Archée: Arts Médiatriques & Cyberculture*, http://archee.qc.ca/wordpress/identity-technology-nostalgia-the-theater-of-ivo-van-hove-robert-lepage-and-the-wooster-group/ (accessed 25 June 2020).
Sidiropoulou, A. (2019a), *Phaedra I—*, unpublished production script.
Sidiropoulou, A. (2019b), 'Greek Ancient Drama in the UK', *Greece in the UK* 15: 20–4.
Sidiropoulou, A. (2021), 'Adaptation as a Love Affair: The Ethics of Directing the Greeks' in V. Liapis and A. Sidiropoulou (eds), *Adapting Greek Tragedy. New Contexts for Ancient Texts*, Cambridge: Cambridge University Press.

Part Two

The chorus and the digital: Rediscovering the politics

4

'Inventing' the ancient tragic chorus

Communality and the digital in the 1999 *Oresteias* by Katie Mitchell (NT, London) and Georges Lavaudant (Odéon, Paris)

Estelle Baudou[1]

Introduction

Any director who wants to stage a Greek tragedy faces historical and aesthetic difficulties regarding the ancient chorus. Archaeologically, we don't know much about the performance of the tragic chorus, leaving a director to decide how the group moves and speaks with no other help than the text itself. Besides, choral practice is unfamiliar for contemporary Western theatre (Billings, Budelmann and Macintosh 2013: 3). Whilst choral forms have been developed both in theatre texts and on stage since the 1980s and thus become a way to renew Western theatre (Baur 1999), the tragic chorus and its ancient united form still appear as a mysterious aesthetical model and potentially an idealized community. Indeed, the ancient chorus is marked out by its collectiveness – politicized for Simon Goldhill (2007: 55–6) and more cultural for Helene P. Foley (2007: 356). Directors consequently have to find a way to perform this community out of its original time and space (Vernant and Vidal-Naquet 2001). In other words, staging the tragic chorus is much more a socio-political problem than an aesthetical or historical one (Baudou 2021: 22-24) and the main question, while performing the Ancient tragic chorus in contemporary times, is to find a way to express its communality not only physically and orally, but also politically and culturally. Nevertheless, none of those archaeological, aesthetical and historical difficulties is insurmountable: they have rather provided a source of fascination, incentivizing artists to find new solutions (Banu 2001).

'Inventing' the tragic chorus and its communality with the digital

According to Anne-Violaine Houcke (2012), the concept of 'invention' is particularly useful for understanding classical reception in contemporary arts. The verb 'invent' is derived from the Latin 'invenire', literally *to find* something or even *to meet with* it. This sense of 'invention' supposes a physical or an intellectual movement towards something pre-existing the moment of discovery itself (2012: 43–4). The tragic chorus existed in the past, yes, but contemporary directors still have to 'invent' it with each production. This process of 'invention' is therefore a revealing one, demanding imaginative engagement. Anne-Violaine Houcke illustrates how Pier Paolo Pasolini and Federico Fellini used cinema to 'invent' ancient myths and ancient ruins, the camera acting as the eye revealing reality. At the same time, she states, they managed to extract antiquity from its clichés and engaged it in a fictional reorganization – therefore 'inventing' it (2012: 45).

During tragedy's academic and artistic reception history, a long list of clichés has developed, notably surrounding the chorus. From a philological and literary perspective (Gagné and Govers Hopman 2016), the ancient tragic chorus is generally seen as a poetic, philosophical and collective comment of the on-going action. Indeed, it is dramaturgically true to say that the *stasima* deliver the chorus' point of view on the situation and clarify its historical and dramaturgical contexts, adding both a memorial and epic function to its initial role as commentator. However, the word 'comment' is problematic, implying that the chorus plays a secondary role to that of the protagonist. It has been generally admitted that the chorus has been progressively moved off-centre during the performance history of ancient tragedy. However, it is now well known that this traditional approach has been mostly dictated by readings of Aristotle's *Poetics* (Wilson 2000: 5) and thus by a strictly literary approach. That is why the assumption of a static and external observer has to be questioned. Therefore, it is crucial to keep in mind that the chorus, despite its commenting function, is not a minor figure in Ancient tragedy: the main characteristic of the Ancient chorus is to '[mediate] not only spatially, but temporally and formally between audience and actors' according to Helene P. Foley (2007: 355). So, if the chorus' major function is to form the link between action and spectator, it consequently becomes central to the performance. This central position combined with a status representative of the religious and political institutions of Athens (Wilson 2000) confirms its communal dimension. A further risk of cliché must be highlighted here: that of idealizing the ancient chorus as a ritual and/or political community and picturing it as a perfectly unified group.

Many stage directors have managed to avoid this idealization of the tragic chorus by developing new expressions of its communality: Richard Schechner offered a ritual experience of Greek tragedy relying on the chorus (*Dionysus in 69*, 1968), Peter Stein invented the model of the citizen chorus (*Die Orestie*, 1980) and Ariane Mnouchkine created a danced chorus united by emotion (*Les Atrides*, 1990–92). All these celebrated performances found a way to extricate the ancient chorus from its clichés of solemnity and neutrality, drawing focus towards one of its communal aspects (rituality, citizenship, emotion). As argued by Sebastian Kirsch in this volume, the chorus, as a non-protagonist figure, can particularly contribute to our understanding of the relation between Greek tragedy and the digital. This invites the question: when looking at contemporary performances of Greek tragedies, how does the digital, as a multiform technology (video and sound) but also as a creative process involved in theatre making, participate in the 'invention' of the ancient chorus and its communality? This chapter will answer that question, analysing two performances produced in 1999: *The Oresteia* by Katie Mitchell (NT, London) and *L'Orestie* by Georges Lavaudant (Odéon, Paris).

1999 Oresteias: Inventing the chorus and the digital

The digital is the modern and liberal technique *par excellence*: with the generalization of the internet and social media, it is known for isolating individuals while constantly connecting them, entailing a paradoxical experience of sociability. Consequently, the digital has been used in contemporary performances to illustrate the fragmentation of the world and of the self (Perrot 2013). In her PhD thesis, Angeliki Poulou (2017) shows how this is particularly true when performances of Greek tragedy engage with the digital. However, this chapter will demonstrate that the digital *can* contribute to the 'invention' of the ancient chorus without condemning its communality to fragmentation. To do so, one must consider the early democratization of digital techniques in the 1990s, before the global development of the internet and also before the widespread use of these technologies within theatre making in the twenty-first century. I will analyse two performances of Aeschylus' *Oresteia* that utilized similar resources; firstly because they were both produced the same year and secondly because they were both staged in state theatres: the first by Katie Mitchell at the National Theatre (London) and the second one by Georges Lavaudant at the Odéon (Paris). It is worth mentioning here that the archives of both theatres hold documents relating to the performances (videos, photographs, hand-outs, press cuttings and rehearsal notes) and this chapter draws on this material.

These performances are of particular relevance because they illustrate a shift regarding the use of the digital in the performance of Ancient tragedy and specifically in the 'invention' of the chorus. Indeed, Poulou (2017: 140) notices that digital productions of the twenty-first century based on Greek tragedies generally adapt ancient texts, mixing them with other materials without adhering to a single translation. On the contrary, Katie Mitchell and Georges Lavaudant both worked with contemporary translations of Aeschylus' trilogy, respectively by Ted Hughes (Aeschylus 1999) and Daniel Loayza (Aeschylus 2001). As a consequence, they directly faced the problem of the Ancient chorus because they had to deal with the text of the *stasima*; and they both used the digital to 'invent' the chorus. Produced in 1999, just before the large spread of the digital in theatre performances, these two *Oresteias* illustrate the shift from intermediality to multimediality. Indeed, according to Poulou (2017: 166), there is intermediality as soon as the performance engages with the performability of the digital, thus modifying the theatrical experience. Both productions initially appear to work with multimediality because they mainly use digital sounds and images as tools amongst others. In fact, both directors use the digital to draw the audience's attention towards one of the traditional functions of the tragic chorus by enlarging it. Aeschylus' trilogy tells a cycle of revenge and these two performances are specifically questioning the notion of heritage, notably in creating choruses embodying collective memory – political memory in *The Oresteia* and cultural memory in *L'Orestie*. The communality of those choruses is therefore rooted in a collective memory and I will analyse how the digital takes part in its 'invention'. Nor is the digital limited to repeating or relaying the ancient chorus: both performances tend towards intermediality, enabling them to perform the memorial process itself. So I will demonstrate how the digital creates the opportunity to 'invent' a communality that suits the audience's time and space.

The Oresteia by Katie Mitchell

In 1999, Katie Mitchell was a rising star of British drama. After being assistant director at the RSC, she was funded by the Winston Churchill Memorial Trust to travel across Eastern Europe in 1989 and to meet various theatre directors. She then gained critical acclaim directing *The Phoenician Women* in 1995 at the RSC, for which she won the Evening Standard Award. This performance reflects her stay at the Polish theatre company Gardzienice but also her experience of the collapse of the USSR in the Balkans, and both elements are still visible in her 1999 *Oresteia*. In the manner of Gardzienice, the actors are considered as an ensemble responsible for telling the story to the audience and they are all taking part in the chorus. Moreover, the dancing and the singing are influenced by Balkan folklore and the NT's archive reveals that the team considered Agamemnon as Milosevic at least in some phases of rehearsal. However, if the Balkan War is a major reference in the first part of the performance, *The Home Guard* (*Agamemnon*), the second part, *The Daughters of Darkness* (*Choephori* and *Eumenides*), focuses then on the familial situation.

In this performance, Katie Mitchell introduces the digital as part of her aesthetic (Rebellato 2010). The set (by Vicky Mortimer) is an almost empty rectangular area with spectators on both sides and two big screens at each end. Live and pre-recorded videos (designed by Chris Pleydell) are projected there, mediatizing the power of the characters as well as performing the persistence of the past in the present. Recorded sounds are used both to create an atmosphere and to perform off-stage actions. Digital effects are almost omnipresent here, yet they never reach the intensity of *Waves* (2006) or *Some traces of her...* (2008), in which Katie Mitchell interweaves theatre with cinema. Nevertheless, the digital, from multimediality to intermediality, takes part here in 'inventing' the ancient chorus (see also Sampatatakakis' discussion of *phasmatic aesthetics of presence* in Chapter 1 above).

From collective memory to collective responsibility

Dramaturgically speaking, the three choruses of *The Oresteia* act in the present to make the past acknowledged. Besides, in this production, the communality of the chorus is directly rooted in its collective memory. First, the chorus of elders in the *Agamemnon*, who are veterans wearing poppies in their buttonholes, are keeping the memory of the war alive. Secondly, in the *Choephori*, the Theban captives carry a memory of the destruction of Troy and of their own abduction, made visible in their mourning outfits and songs. This memory entails a desire of revenge that is performed through their enthusiasm towards Orestes' plan to kill his mother and then in their plotting behaviour inside Clytemnestra's house. Finally, the Furies, dressed as bureaucratic workers from the 1940s, attend Orestes' trial to defend Clytemnestra's ghost. Katie Mitchell does not consider the chorus' members as external commentators or narrators and insists on the consequences of their memories within the on-going action. With the incorporation of digital techniques, they are regularly immersed in the situation and thus start sharing responsibility around it.

The elders of the *Agamemnon* first appear in the *parodos* to recount the Trojan War. At this point, audio and video recordings accompany their epic and memorial functions. First, on a Dictaphone, they play an extract of Calchas' and Agamemnon's discourses both justifying the sacrifice of Iphigenia. Thus, the audio recording not only takes over on the chorus' memorial function but also dissociates the veterans from their leaders' decisions, as if they could keep the story objective. Later, when they tell the story of the Trojan War itself, the screens display a 'war montage' made of images from wars of the twentieth century (NT archive: RNT/SM/1/446i, section D: 14). But those videos are not objective proofs: at that point, the elders are much more involved emotionally and their status switches from archivists to witnesses. However, the digital does not simply illustrate the epic function of the chorus: by allowing an oscillation between desired objectivity and inevitable subjectivity in the story telling, the digital also reveals the ambiguity of collective memory.

Later in the play, when Clytemnestra kills Agamemnon, a loud alarm signals the murder to the elders who immediately panic; the digital allows the chorus to start commenting upon the off-stage event but also immerses it in the situation. In her PhD thesis, Poulou defines the immersion provided by the digital as a hybrid experience dissolving the common limits of reality and mixing the body with its environment (2017: 153–5). Here, because of the alarm, the elders seem suddenly physically connected to the murder of Agamemnon, shaking and shouting. Consequently, the chorus members and their collective memory are no longer innocent: from witnesses they may become accomplices. The immersive power of the digital engages the responsibility of the chorus towards the situation, at the same time enlarging its political function. Similarly, in the *Choephori*, the Theban captives are immersed in the suffocating atmosphere of Clytemnestra's house by a few digital effects (an intercom and heavy electronic sounds): their oppression is obvious and the chorus is suddenly responsible for rebelling against those in power. Furthermore, this collective responsibility is at the same time performed in the making of live videos.

Mediating function and power

In *The Oresteia*, the actors create some of the images displayed on the screens in real time, and live video is particularly used to illustrate the power of the characters. In fact, the chorus is successively involved in this mediatisation on both sides of the camera. Just after the murder of Clytemnestra, one of the Theban captives holds the camera to broadcast Orestes' victory and later, in the *Eumenides*, the chorus' authority is emphasized by live close-ups of their severe faces. In both cases, the digital is not only a multimedial tool illustrating the chorus' point of view but also an intermedial tool performing its responsibility towards the situation. This production can be understood to denounce the abuses of mediatization: the manipulation of images and the performance of power, which are both familiar to the spectators. In 1999, live broadcasting of political discourses and major events played a huge part in the spectacle of power, particularly within the Balkan conflict (Colleran 2012). The mediatisation of power in *The Oresteia* questions thus the collective responsibility of the chorus and also that of the audience. Indeed, this intermediality 'invents' the chorus' mediating function in two different ways: by confronting it with contemporary issues of media coverage and by immersing the audience in the actuality of mediatization.

The analogy between the play and contemporary events is transcended by the immersion of the spectators within the performance. In Katie Mitchell's *Oresteia*, mediation is both bodily (Struan Leslie) and orally performed by the chorus, through a storytelling virtuosity in the manner of Gardzienice: it narrates and shares its collective memory with the audience in a very engaging way. Thus the chorus, which stands in the centre of the bi-frontal set up, manages to involve the spectators. Then, however, sounds and images surround the audience and achieve its immersion within the performance, enlarging the chorus' mediating function. Since the digital simultaneously reveals the ambiguity of collective memory and the issues of mediatization, this immersion has a political dimension. The spectator is therefore directly confronted with the issues that the chorus is struggling to comprehend: how do we deal with the past and our memories of it? What is our responsibility towards the consequences of this past in our present? So, thanks to the intermediality of the performance, the audience may be able to experiment the chorus' communality.

Persistence of the past within the present

I have demonstrated that the chorus' communality is deeply rooted in a collective memory that can turn into a collective responsibility at any time. Consequently, the chorus is directly involved in the cycle of revenge, in which each action is the consequence of a previous event. This persistence of the past in the present is also embodied by ghosts: Iphigenia's ghost is joined by Agamemnon and Clytemnestra once they have been murdered and their presence justifies on-going actions. Videos establish a further link between past and present: pre-recorded footage preserves traces of past events (the Trojan war and the sacrifice of Iphigenia) and live video allows the characters to communicate with the ghosts (Orestes and Electra with Agamemnon and, later, the Furies with Clytemnestra). The digital is thus once again enlarging the chorus' memorial function. However, pre-recorded and live videos refashion the experience of time within theatre performance; the digital also performs the memorial process itself.

In their analysis of intermediality in Katie Mitchell's ... *some trace of her*, Markos Hadjioannou and George Rodosthenous show how the encounter between cinema and theatre crystallizes the persistence of the past within the present. First, they explain that 'the cinema screen brings to light an image of a past reality that is being projected, but this reality does not belong to the viewers' present reality. The screen confirms that the world exists, but it does so by placing a filter between the two worlds' (Hadjioannou and Rodosthenous 2011: 49). So, pre-recorded images are traces of the past world in present times. In *The Oresteia*, they are a multimedial tool revealing the ambiguity of the memory of the chorus and the characters but also of the audience. With videos created in real time on stage, 'the experience of time [...] is refashioned in the intermedial in-between of theatrical presence and cinematic pastness. The world being created on-screen is thus directly implicated in the *liveness* of the theatrical performance' (2011: 49–50). So, intermediality abolishes the distance between past and present realities by making them coexistent. In *The Oresteia*, this contributes to a justification of the sequence of revenge by connecting the ghosts with living people, but it also confirms the immersion of the chorus and the audience within the situation, engaging their responsibility. The chorus faces the emergency of dealing with the past, which haunts their present reality. Therefore, the digital relays the memorial function of the chorus by maintaining traces of the past world in the present reality (pre-recorded video), but also performs the memorial process itself by creating an intermedial in-between across time periods (live video).

The combination of those two levels of video reveals the complex stratification of memory and is thus a metaphor of the reception of Greek tragedy in performance. Indeed, while staging an ancient play, contemporary directors regularly deal with multiple traces of the past and their transformations across times, then find a way to perform these historic imprints in the present, for example by declaring the timelessness of Greek tragedy or by deciding to modernize it. In fact, the intermedial encounter of cinema and theatre proves the coexistence of the past with the present and states that Greek tragedy can be immediate.

This production clearly performs the persistence of the past within the present. However, and despite the use of the digital, it doesn't report the fragmentation of the chorus' point of view and the loneliness of the modern individual. Instead, because the chorus is the matrix for the performance, the digital reveals the hybridity of collective memory and builds communality. The digital becomes a tool used to 'invent' the tragic chorus: videos and sounds draw attention to the chorus' memorial function and enlarge it. But, as demonstrated, multimediality regularly turns into intermediality. The digital then becomes performative and immerses both the chorus and then the audience in the performance, thus 'inventing' their communality. Katie Mitchell's *Oresteia*, by performing the hybridity of collective memory, responds to the increasing individualism of the end of the twentieth century but also to the emergency to assess both international and local situations at the turn of the millennium.

The Oresteia by Georges Lavaudant

Performed for the first time in the autumn of 1999, *The Oresteia* by Georges Lavaudant is also preoccupied with collective memory, but in this case the issue is much more cultural than political. In fact, the memory of the Second World War occupies the political and the judicial stages in France since the end of the 1980s with the trials for crime against humanity, the publication of memorial laws and various commemorations. There is no need, then, to acknowledge in the French theatres, as Katie Mitchell does, the persistence of the historical past within the present reality. Instead, Georges Lavaudant develops a cultural response to the political imperative of memory.

In 1999, *L'Orestie* is Georges Lavaudant's first performance as director of the Odéon in Paris. By staging this monument, he obviously shows his legitimacy but also his originality. Indeed, the reception of Greek tragedy in France has been shaped by *L'École de Paris* and its political reading of ancient drama. In this context, the poetic and aesthetic approach of Georges Lavaudant appears distinct, even if he is not the only one to do so (see for example: *L'Orestie* by Serge Tranvouez in 1997 or *L'Orestie* by Olivier Py in 2008). In *L'Orestie*, he 'invents' the ancient chorus by multiplying the quotations and the clichés, and this Mannerist aesthetic is a provocative way to play with a respectable culture within a respectable institution.

The chorus' communality is here rooted in a cultural communality and the digital is one of the tools used to 'invent' it. At the same time, digital sounds and images enlarge the chorus' ritual function by performing a communion between past and present realities. Thus, as we will see, the performance tends towards intermediality.

The digital as a Mannerist tool

The set of *L'Orestie* (Georges Lavaudant and Isabelle Neuveux) is very sober: an almost empty beige box with a sandy floor framed by large hangings. The choruses fit perfectly within this general austerity: comprised of two to three members wearing dark colours, they are very static and solemn. Consequently, Georges Lavaudant seems to maintain and even revivify an old cliché about the chorus. Indeed, many critics describe the performance as a ceremony whose officiators are the chorus members. However, this austerity is not the principle of the performance but rather a basis on which then accumulate other clichés, and references in a kind of Mannerism. Thus, as noted in contemporary reviews, each chorus refers to another work of art: the elders of the *Agamemnon* are dressed like the citizen chorus of *Die Orestie* by Peter Stein (Solis 1999 and Leonardini 1999), the Theban captives evoke Mediterranean mourners in Pier Paolo Pasolini's cinema or Luigi Pirandello's theatre (Leonardini 1999), and the Furies resemble the old women in Francisco de Goya's painting (Solis 1999 and Leonardini 1999). Moreover, the acting of the chorus starts with the distant narration of the elders, then goes to the lamentation of the *Choephori*, and finally ends with the discussion of the Furies. This progression, which follows the dramaturgy of the trilogy, shows a wide knowledge of the reception of the Ancient chorus by utilizing different performing traditions about it: distant comment, ritualized behaviour, and common conversation. Thus, the chorus embodies a cultural memory aware of the issues of art history and particularly of classical reception.

The performance deconstructs the clichés of Greek tragedy as static and solemn, by situating them into the long history of reception. The digital, which is only used at the very end of the play, tells the most recent stage of this history. When the Furies come around Athena to pray and celebrate peace, videos are projected for the first time of the performance on the back wall: while Athena speaks the play's final lines, the audience can watch images of ancient ruins. Pre-recorded videos, as the last Mannerist tool of the performance, 'invent' thus the chorus' cultural memory by enlarging it to a digital memory – and the digital demonstrates, as in Katie Mitchell's *Oresteia*, the hybridity of this memory. Moreover, because it occurs as the performance concludes, the sense of chaos created by the digital also brings back the audience from ancient Greece to their contemporary world, relaying the ritual and mediating functions of the chorus.

Rituality of the digital

In this closing scene, the audience is suddenly overwhelmed by a chaotic aesthetic contrasting with the austerity of the rest of the performance. Indeed, the digital images and sounds surround the spectators and immerse them in a communion between past and present that has been described by several critics (notably Pascaud 1999: 70). During the final prayer, while images of ancient ruins start being projected, recorded whispers in ancient Greek are played. Gradually, the sounds become louder and engine noises from cars, boats or helicopters come over the whispers, turning the ancient prayer into a hybrid, technological and thus modern celebration.

However, in this instance, the digital is not exactly modernizing Greek tragedy but rather creating the possibility to perform the link between past and present realities. According to Jean-Pierre Leonardini: 'At last, in front of a panorama of Ancient Greek ruins shown on a screen, with a great deal of horns and urban rumblings, the shadows of the silhouettes seem to shuttle between yesterday and today' (Leonardini 1999). Because of the set-up, the actor's shadows are actually projected onto the screen. So, living people are not only superimposed onto but also brutally integrated within images of Ancient ruins. In other words, the liveness of theatre is transferred into the past of the recording. However, those characters, because they are part of a Greek tragedy, are relics of a much more ancient time than the images themselves. Consequently they reveal, by their liveness, the ruination suffered by those buildings and make their presence across epochs acknowledged. This concluding scene explores the interrelation of past and present worlds: the use of the digital is not limited to overprint ancient and contemporary realities and tends to an intermediality that performs the 'to and fro' movement of the reception of Ancient drama. As in Katie Mitchell's *Oresteia*, intermediality 'invents' the chorus' mediating function by creating an immediate experience of Greek tragedy.

Nevertheless, the communion of past and present realities enabled by this 'to and fro' movement does not rely on an idealization of ancient Greece. Indeed, as demonstrated, the digital reveals the hybridity of memory and thus deconstructs the idealisation of this culture. In fact, the digital transforms the ancient chorus' ritual into a digital and chaotic celebration and converts its memory into digital knowledge. This may be read as a provocation of the well-educated audience of the Odéon. Even so, Georges Lavaudant's irony is not an attack and intends to build complicity with the spectators of an institution he had recently joined as director. The use of the digital doesn't denounce the fragmentation of post-modernity here, but rather 'invents' a communality that suits the audience's time and place. Indeed, this intermedial final passage invites the spectators to collectively celebrate the joyful chaos of their cultural history within the liveness of performance.

Within the Mannerist aesthetics of *L'Orestie*, the digital is first of all a multimedial tool, adding a digital declension to the cultural memory embodied by the chorus. Thus, the performance 'invents' the chorus' memorial function by making it partly digital – the digital in turn managing to embed the chorus's communality into post-modernity. Furthermore, the digital 'invents' the chorus' ritual function because it turns the performance's final prayer into a modern celebration, similar to the 'bacchic digital ritual' discussed by Chloé Larmet and Ana Wegner in Chapter 5 below. The encounter of cinema and theatre in this instance represents the interrelation of past and present realities, highlighting the reception process of Greek tragedy and thus 'inventing' the chorus' mediating function. Therefore, this final section 'invents', with the digital, a communality based on a hybrid culture. By doing this, Georges Lavaudant not only builds complicity with his new audience but also responds to the fragmentation of a more and more globalized world.

Conclusions

The Oresteia by Katie Mitchell and *L'Orestie* by Georges Lavaudant 'invent' the ancient chorus with the digital and thus begin to free it from the clichés accumulated in its performance and reception history. Indeed, in Katie Mitchell's production, the digital manages to immerse the chorus in the situation and consequently to highlight its responsibility. Therefore, the trope of a static chorus merely commenting upon the action is avoided. Moreover, the chorus' involvement in the mediatisation of power highlights the ambiguity of its collective memory. So, this performance disabuses the audience of the notion that the chorus is an ideal community. If Katie Mitchell conscientiously avoids all the clichés about the chorus, however, then Georges Lavaudant instead accumulates them through his Mannerist aesthetics – an accumulation which, ultimately, results in a deconstruction. Indeed, the chaotic final celebration performed with digital sounds and images destroys the idea of an austere and solemn chorus. So, the digital participates in exonerating Greek tragedy from its clichés and, while doing so, draws particular attention to the political function of the chorus in *The Oresteia* and on its ritual function in *L'Orestie*.

These productions use the digital to enlarge the chorus's pre-existing functions. In both cases, the communality of the chorus is rooted in collective memory (historical in *The Oresteia* and cultural in *L'Orestie*) and the digital relays first of all the chorus' memorial function. Collective memory was a prevalent political issue in 1990s Europe due to the ongoing Balkan War and, in 1999, to the imminence of the third millennium and to increasing globalization. This context explains the choice to perform Aeschylus' trilogy, which illustrates the persistence of the past within the present and the difficulty implicit in putting an end to violence and building communality. In both productions, the digital participates in the dramaturgy by revealing the ambiguity and the hybridity of memory.

Furthermore, as demonstrated, the presence of digital video within theatrical performance refashions an audience's experience of time. Such encounters between the pastness of cinema and the liveness of theatre illustrate the process of reception and state the immediacy of Greek tragedy. Within this immediacy, intermediality 'invents' the mediating function of the chorus by creating a communality rooted in hybridity, suiting the audience's own time and space. In Katie Mitchell's performance this communality is political and questions the spectator's responsibility, whereas Georges Lavaudant makes it cultural and invites complicity with his new audience by calling for a joyful and chaotic collective memory. In doing so, both are responding to their own preoccupations and to their national context. The use of the digital in those productions is thus the result of personal, local, and global moments. Taking into account the history of technologies, this moment represents a shift between multimediality and intermediality in theatre performance in general and the reception of Greek tragedy in particular. As evidenced, intermedial performances using ancient drama as a material only increased with the move into the twenty-first century.

To conclude, it is worth noting that the eruption of intermediality accompanying both performances coincides with a shift in their directors' careers. Indeed, in 1999, Georges Lavaudant was nominated as director of the Odéon – his last posting in a French state theatre. Katie Mitchell, on the other hand, went on to engage deeply with intermediality, directing many intermedial performances where the cooperative ensemble, made of actors and technicians making videos in real time, replaces the ancient chorus as the matrix for the performance (see Cornford 2020). The aim is no longer to 'invent' communality but rather to perform the fragmentation of the postmodern world and individual. In Katie Mitchell's later direction of other Greek plays, also seeking to build communality, she does not use the digital: in *Iphigenia at Aulis* (2004) and *Women of Troy* (2007), collective trauma replaces collective memory and the communality of the chorus is performed through social behaviours and particularly through dance (see Solga 2008; Radosavljević 2020; Sampatakakis in Chapter 1 above). *The Oresteia* can therefore be seen as representing the end of her 'Gardzienice' phase, before her move towards a Stanislavskian approach to performance.

On the other hand, Georges Lavaudant's use of the digital was very circumstantial at the time. In his second version of *L'Orestie*, performed in 2019 at the festival 'Les Nuits de Fourvière' (Lyon), a screen displayed prerecorded images at the back of the set throughout the show and influence its atmosphere from the very beginning (in contrast to digital imagery as a final surprise in the 1999 performance). Moreover, Georges Lavaudant has moved away from using actors' shadows in projection; now their silhouettes stand out against the retro-lighted screen and seem isolated in their suffering. Obviously, the time is not to celebrate communion any more and this performance is in fact darker than the previous one. For both Katie Mitchell and Georges Lavaudant, their 1999 *Oresteia*s represent a final interpretation of the ancient chorus' communality with the digital before lapsing into the fragmentation and the loneliness of the third millennium's opening decades.

Note

1 While writing the second version of this chapter I was funded by the European Commission: my project has received funding from the European Union's Horizon 2020 research and innovation programme under the Marie Sklodowska-Curie grant agreement No 839770. I also want to thank here Claire Barnes for her helpful proofreading.

References

Aeschylus (1999), *The Oresteia*, trans. T. Hughes, London: Faber and Faber.
Aeschylus (2001), *L'Orestie*, trans. D. Loayza, Paris: Flammarion.
Banu, G., ed. (2001), *Études théâtrales* 21.
Baudou, E. (2021), *Créer le chœur tragique. Une Archéologie du commun (Allemagne, France, Royaume-Uni; 1973–2010)*, Paris: Classiques Garnier.
Baur, D. (1999), *Der Chor im Theater des 20. Jahrhunderts*, Tübingen: M. Niemeyer.
Billings, J., F. Budelmann and F. Macintosh, eds (2013), *Choruses, Ancient and Modern*, Oxford: Oxford University Press.
Colleran, J. (2012), *Theatre and War: Theatrical Responses since 1991*, New York: Palgrave Macmillan.
Cornford, T. (2020), 'Katie Mitchell and the Technologies of the Realist Theatre', *Contemporary Theatre Review* 30 (2), 168–92.
Foley, H. P. (2007), 'Envisioning the Tragic Chorus on the Modern Stage', in J. Elsner, H. P. Foley, S. Goldhill and C. Kraus (eds), *Visualizing the Tragic: Drama, Myth, and Ritual in Greek Art and Literature*, 353–78, Oxford: Oxford University Press.
Gagné, R., and M. Govers Hopman, eds ([2013], 2016), *Choral Mediations in Greek Tragedy*, Cambridge: Cambridge University Press.
Goldhill, S. (2007), *How to Stage Greek Tragedy Today*, Chicago: University of Chicago Press.
Hadjioannou, M., and G. Rodosthenous (2011), 'In Between Stage and Screen: The Intermedial in Katie Mitchell's "...some trace of her"', *International Journal of Performance Arts and Digital Media*, 7 (1): 43–59.
Houcke, A.-V. (2012), 'L'invention de l'antique dans le cinéma italien moderne: la Poétique des ruines chez Federico Fellini et Pier Paolo Pasolini', PhD diss., Université Paris-Nanterre.
Leonardini, J. P. (1999), *L'Humanité*, 27 December.
Pascaud, F. (1999), 'Le Talon d'Eschyle', *Télérama*, 15 December: 70.

Perrot, E. (2013), 'Les Usages de la vidéo en direct au théâtre chez Ivo van Hove et chez Guy Cassiers', PhD diss., Université du Québec, Montréal, Université Sorbonne Nouvelle, Paris.

Poulou, A. (2017), 'La Mise en scène de la tragédie grecque dans l'ère numérique', PhD diss., Université Sorbonne Nouvelle, Paris, Université Nationale et Capodistrienne d'Athènes. Longer version in Greek: 'Η σκηνοθεσία της αρχαίας ελληνικής τραγωδίας στην ψηφιακή εποχή'.

Radosavljević, D. (2020), 'Curating the Invisible: An Archive-Embedded Interview with Struan Leslie', *Contemporary Theatre Review*, 30 (2): 236–44.

Rebellato, D. (2010), 'Katie Mitchell, Learning from Europe', in M. M. Delgado and D. Rebellato (eds), *Contemporary European Theatre Directors*, 322–35, London: Routledge.

Solga, K. (2008), 'Body Doubles, Babel's Voices: Katie Mitchell's *Iphigenia at Aulis* and the Theatre of Sacrifice', *Contemporary Theatre Review* 18 (2): 146–60.

Solis, R. (1999), *Libération*, 21 December.

Vernant, J. P., and P. Vidal-Naquet ([1972] 2001), *Mythe et tragédie en Grèce ancienne I*, Paris: La Découverte.

Wilson, P. (2000), *The Athenian Institution of the Khoregia: the Chorus, the City and the Stage*, Cambridge: Cambridge University Press.

5

Augmented vocal chorus

Sounds of digital chorus in Euripides' *Bacchae*

Chloé Larmet and Ana Wegner

Introduction

Since the major contribution of Erika Fischer-Lichte (2014) on the staging of *Bacchae*, the reasons for the renewed interest for Euripides' last tragedy in the twentieth century after an absence of many centuries are well known. According to her analysis, it has (mainly) to do in the 1960s with firstly the social context of the time allowing an 'analogy between the events of the tragedy' (2014: 5) and the situation of the world in the sixties (social protests, society transformations and political violence) and secondly, the influence of anthropological understandings of the ritual as a mean to a new social order (Turner 1982). George Sampatakakis points out the same arguments even if the two scholars disagree on globalization as far as *The Bacchae* are concerned. That said, Sampatakakis' thesis is of great interest for us as he asserts that 'the Bacchae is a play for the theatre of the 20th and 21st centuries, that is to say for the theatre of the mise-en-scène beyond psychological characterization and closer to the modern ritualization of theatre' (Sampatakakis 2017: 190).

A 'modern ritualization' is precisely what this chapter would like to discuss in a contemporary creative context to understand the influence of digital technology (especially in terms of sound) on the *Bacchae*'s chorus. As shown by the studies of Claude Calame, the choral parts have various mediation functions which coincide with three choral voices: the performative voice, the affective voice and the hermeneutic voice (Calame 2017: 94–102).

The ancient chorus is therefore polyphonic and, with *The Bacchae*, such definition is even more accurate for different reasons. The first is the interweaving of the dramatic and performative functions of the chorus in *The Bacchae*, as has been shown by Anton Bierl (2013). Moreover, Euripides built a dramaturgy with a choral duality since there are actually two choruses in *The Bacchae*: the one composed by Dionysus' worshippers arrived from Lydia and entering into Thebes to impose the Dionysiac cult, and a second one formed by the Theban women exiled to Mount Citheron for having denied the divine birth of Dionysus. 'This "second" Theban chorus is only imagined offstage and never shown in the orchestra to the audience' (2013: 214). But nothing in Euripides' text prevents us from hearing this second chorus, which can be called acousmatic (Chion 1984). Each gesture, each word of Euripides' text, especially in the choral parts, would have its sonorous foreign replica, as if an acousmatic presence was haunting the tragedy. Such acousmatic logic of *Bacchae's* chorus may complete Sebastien Kirsch's hypothesis (developed in Chapter 6 below) of why digitalization in contemporary stages mainly concerns the non-protagonist figures of Greek theatre. Between polyphony and acousmatic voices, Euripides' *Bacchae* offer a variety of sounds to be explored by artists and scholars. And if some things can't be heard by human ears, maybe the digital tools can help us discovering the sounds of Euripides' *Bacchae*.

This chapter presents an analysis of scenic adaptations of *The Bacchae* which pave the way for such a fascinating journey on the digital chorus' sound: an 'eletrocandomblaica' opera in *The Bacchae* of José Celso Martinez Corrêa's *Bacchae* (São Paulo, 2016); an acousmatic and polyvocal chorus in Georgia Spiropoulos' *Bacchae* (Paris, 2010); a synthetic and polyphonic chorus in the workshop *A Vocal Approach of Ancient Greek Tragedy: acting with texts, sounds and synthetic voices* (Athens, 2018). To conclude and to echo Estelle Baudou on the invention of the Ancient tragic chorus (Chapter 4 above), we will consider the digital chorus as an innovative and fruitful tool for both artists and scholars to apprehend the complexity of the chorus in Greek tragedy.

Bacantes (*The Bacchae*) of José Celso Martinez Corrêa: An electrocanbomblaica opera (São Paulo, 2016)

José Celso Martiz Corrêa (also called Zé Celso) is one of the most creative, involved, and innovative artists of the Brazilian theatre history. In 1958 he co-created the Teat(r)o Oficina company and since then Euripides' *Bacchae* played a significant role in the troupe, as it did for the constellation of Latin American's artists who were adapting, invoking, and re-working ancient Greek texts in modern theatre at that time (Andújar and Nikoloutsos 2021). Their first adaptation dates back to 1986 and was a matrix for a second version (1996) analysed by Erika Fischer-Lichte (2014) through the prism of carnival, festival and ritual, notions that allowed her to understand the specific relationship built by the show between the actors and the audience.

The most recent version (2016) shares with the 1996 creation many original musical compositions, the sets, some of the costumes, a part of the cast and the general dramaturgical structure. But Zé Celso insists on *The Bacchae* (2016) being a new *mise-en-scène*. The show uses the arrival of Dionysus in Thebes to disturb the social order as an opportunity for the troupe to question the political tempest still devasting Brazil (the 2013 protests and Dilma Rousseff's impeachment in 2016). About six hours long, the show uses a Portuguese translation of Euripides' text which emphasizes musicality, plays on words and daily expressions (translation by C. Hirsch, D. Assunção, M. Drummond and Zé Celso). Once on stage, the actors are free to adapt the text according to the pleasure of the *mise-en-bouche*. The text has to be pronounced, repeated, sung, eaten and digested before being fixed once for all, in compliance with the artistic approach of Oswald de Andrade ([1928]1991), an essential reference for the Teat(r)o Oficina since the 1960s.

A mixed choir for 40 voices and more

The Bacchae of 2016 is focused on the chorus with one principle in terms of composition: heterogeneity; and one methodology: blurring the frontiers – between the actor and his character, between the chorus, the corypheus and the protagonist, between bare and amplified voice, masculine and feminine, actors and spectators, and so on. Zé Celso duplicated Euripides' dual feminine chorus by adding a masculine choir, featuring sometimes a group of satyrs and sometimes Pentheus' soldiers ('Pentheus' choir'). The *mise-en-scène* stages a progressive absorption by the Menades' chorus of estranged voices: the masculine chorus merges with the feminine one and destroys any gender distinctions, the actors featuring Dionysus (M. Drumont), Tiresias (Zé Celso), Pentheus (F. Steffen) or even Cadmos (R. Bittencourt) join the chorus from time to time and form a sounding mass of 35 actors and six musicians.

Such a layered chorality is enriched by the use of wireless headset microphones for some actors, while the ones featuring the corypheus (S. Prado/C. Iglesias), Agave (J. Medeiros) and Semele (C. Motta) wear even smaller microphones attached on their face and almost invisible. Such discrete dispositive allows the text to be heard clearly without giving the impression that the voices are separated from the chorus. The actors are dancing, singing, kissing, laughing or climbing the bleachers and the intimacy they have with those digital objects turn them into an extension of their own bare skin. Thanks to the strong physicality of the *mise-en-scène*, Zé Celso creates a choir both digital and physical. The enriched chorality also relies on the multiplicity of the soundscapes evoked in Euripides' tragedy and the choice of Zé Celso to juxtapose musical references. The end of the fourth stasimon illustrates perfectly such sonorous heterogeneity. When Pentheus, dressed as a Menade, leaves for the Citheron, Dionysos warns his Bacchae with a few words, the latter are said with a regular speaking voice and the sound of a drum is heard, playing songs from Afro-Brazilian religious rituals. When the chorus starts singing the fourth stasimon, the drum's momentum breaks into melodic singing and speaking voices, as in a musical show. Several instruments join the dance (an electric guitar, one bass and a drum set) and the rest of the strophe is performed like a rock music concert with the line 'Up now, you hounds of madness, go up now into the mountains' (1210) shouted as in a *heavy-metal* show. Then the voice of Agave, microphoned, emerges from the chorus along with only two unamplified voices for the contrast and some jazz music, creating a breach with the precedent *crescendo* voices. The various speakers dispatched into the room amplify and multiply Agave's voice, as if one voice were to become a whole choir. The whole fourth stasimon alternates between melodies borrowed to the carnival, blues or even bossa nova and each time the musical style changes the actors deploy another vocality. Going from singing to speaking voice, from choral to solo, from bare to digitally amplified voice, this ten minutes long scene seems to linger in time and is significant of Zé Celso's *modus operandi*.

Another important aspect of the show's dramaturgy is the inclusion of music from popular Brazilian culture with lyrics that resonate with specific scenes of the piece. When the audience hears such well-known songs they often start singing along with the actors. The spectators are constantly encouraged to cheer, speak, sing and shout and the voices of the audience add themselves to the actors' in order to form a greater choir. Some vocal puns used by the actors can even be repeated by the audience, as for the bleating sound made by actors in reference to Dionysus that some spectators play with during the show. Thanks to a heterogeneous choir based on a complex sound dramaturgy, Zé Celso's *Bacchae* create 'a choric performance, not merely representing but bringing forth a festive community that extended to the spectators and actively incorporated them' (Fischer-Lichte 2014: 89).

A digital ritual

Such a communion with the audience is a well-known specificity of the Teat(r)o Oficina work and has also to do with the place they perform in. Built in 1993, the Teat(r)o Oficina's scenic space has become one of the most important performance spots in the city São Paulo. Lina Bo Bardi and Edson Elito designed it to match the artistic ambitions of Zé Celso. They were inspired by the *terreiros* (places of worship for many Afro-Brazilian religious rituals), the *sambodrome* (the avenue in which the carnival parades) and the football stadiums (the ultimate place of gathering in the Brazilian culture). Entering this one-of-a-kind space, the audience immediately gets rid of the usual behaviour habits of a traditional theatre performance.

The set is made of a 25m-long corridor with metallic bleachers on each side. One cascade, one tree in the middle of the set, windows and doors: the list of things to take into account for dealing with the acoustic is long and such an extraordinary space influences among other things the techniques with which the actors can use the microphones. For those digital tools doesn't merely have a supporting role (allowing the voice to be heard), they are also a part of Zé Celso's artistic project to join tradition and modernity together. The Brazilian director and actor forged the phrase 'ópera eletrocandomblaica' to describe *The Bacchae* of 2016. 'Opera' implies a dramaturgical structure based on the overlapping speaking and singing voices while the neologism 'electrocandomblaica' refers to the *candomblé*, an Afro-Brazilian religion seasoned with Catholic and Indigenous American traditional elements, and to the electronic usage of microphones, video cameras and projections, and electronic instruments such as samplers and synthesizers.

The ambition of Zé Celso's *Bacchae* isn't merely to transpose Dionysus' arrival in Thebes into the political context of Brazil and even more specifically into the Bexiga neighbourhood of São Paulo city where the Teat(r)o Oficina stands. In fact, the performance intends to connect the Dionysiac cult with the rituals of the *candomblé*. What the troupe extracted from those traditional rituals is the possibility for the participants to enter a trance thanks to dance, singings and drums. Such state of ecstasy is to be activated through a poetic and musical approach but also thanks to the crossing of imaginations. When looking closer to the renewed dramaturgy of Zé Celso's *Bacchae,* one can observe many associations between the gods and cosmogony of the Afro-Brazilian religions and the religious context of the antique Greece as described in Euripides' tragedy. The eclectic musical repertoire displayed in the *mise-en-scène* is also part of this search of an ecstatic condition. The troupe draws its inspiration from football games, carnival parades and pop music concerts in order to create a cathartic environment. Microphoned voices merge with the audience cries and laughters and to that regard the digital tools reveal themselves to be an essential link between the intimacy of a body and the mass gathered in a same heterogeneous and vibrant sound.

Zé Celso's *Bacchae* stage a digital yet physical choir in which frontiers between gender, hierarchy, and social status are blurred and displace the usual coordinates of a theatre performance. The Teat(r)o Oficina uses the centrifuge force of an abundant chorus in search for a common ecstatic condition, which is the exact opposite reflection of our next digital chorus: the lonesome and vocal *Bacchae* of Georgia Spiropoulos.

Acousmatic chorus: *The Bacchae* of Georgia Spiropoulos (Paris, 2010)

Georgia Spiropoulos' *Bacchae* (Paris, 2010) is described as a vocal and scenic action for one interpret, electronic, and lights. The description speaks for itself: one voice, put on a digital augmented stage, acts. In other words, Spiropoulos' ambition is to explore the tragic and dramatic capacities of voice using Euripides' *Bacchae* as an experimental material. With the collaboration of the vocalist virtuoso Médéric Collignon, the Greek composer created a piece at the crossroad of music, theatre and digital arts in which Euripides' tragedy becomes an exciting 'archaeology of sounds' (Sterne 2012). The combination of digital technologies, sound archives, and an antique theatrical material such as Euripides' allows us to hear the multiple echoes, past and future that resonate in *Bacchae*.

Virtual and vocal masks

The musician and composer Georgia Spiropoulos reduced the tragedy of *Bacchae* to its skeleton and created a vocal and scenic action of 24 minutes long. To do so, she chose to focus herself on four characters (Dionysus, Pentheus, The Messenger, and Agave) plus the choir, and used the alternation between Episodes and Stasima as a rhythmic structure. On stage, the set is simple: the black box is left as such, five standing microphones are dispatched along with their respective speakers and defines four areas, each of them matching one character (Dionysus has two microphones). A few neon lights mark the upstage out and draw oblique lines as a tormented horizon. The solo interpreter, Médéric Collignon, is dressed in black with his bare arms, wears no significant make-up, and goes from one microphone to another according to the character involved in the episode. During the stasima, the lights and electronics become the only interpreters and Collignon's outline disappears in the sudden blackness of the stage. As we can see, Georgia Spiropoulos opted for a radical simplicity in terms of *mise-en-scène*. The only images on stage are those of Collignon's body and the shadows created by the neon lights on the walls. Everything is made to give sound the maximum space and to free the spectator's imagination of any pre-existing illustration.

Georgia Spiropoulos' intention is to give voice to the first role in order to explore the multiplicity that lies in any vocal phenomenon. Using the

IRCAM software Max/MSP, she designed vocal identities for each character by creating a combination of 'natural' and virtual masks. Such a choice perpetuates the Greek tradition of acoustic masks through digital tools in a way analysed for instance by Vovolis (2009). In Spiropoulos' words, 'vocal masks are seen as a metaphor of Euripides' *dramatic personae* in which masks of the same actor are used as virtual scores which register the vocal trace of the performer and give further vocal agility, extensibility, mutation, multiplication and augmented vocality' (Spiropoulos 2010: 1). Those masks are actually the result of three types of sound mask, each of them having a specific effect on the voice: the natural mask, be it vocal or instrumental, uses vocal techniques and phonation types to impact the timbre; the virtual mask changes the timbre, the amplitude, and the colour of the voice through electronic treatment, the microphone, and the electromagnetic waves; the double mask combines simultaneously virtual and natural mask to create a hybrid voice.

Each character can be identified by its vocal mask and sound, here, allows the interpreter to transform himself almost endlessly. What is interesting in this kind of transformation is its plasticity and performative quality due to sound. A vocal mask is not something that is fixed once for all for sound isn't strictly speaking an object but a phenomenon with an 'objectile' quality (Bonnet 2012). The interest of Spiropoulos' work lies exactly here: by using vocal masks to stage *The Bacchae*, the composer points out the inevitable flexibility of identity and fulfils by doing so the Dionysiac ritual (Swift 2013).

One moment illustrates such dissemination of identity through sound: the third episode. Georgia Spiropoulos chose to divide it into two distinct moments. The first one, called 'Citheron' stages The Messenger with a breathy and aspirated voice (natural mask) sustained by a virtual mask made of pulse sound and granular synthesis. Euripides' verses (677–774) portray the Bacchae in the Citheron, first as a 'miracle' of life, then as a violent strength of destruction. In Spiropoulos' version, only a few words can be heard distinctively and the whole passage creates a tensed and oppressive atmosphere in contrast with the calm melody associated with the Menades that closes the Citheron section. Then the confrontation between Dionysus and Pentheus begins in a moment called 'Prophecy'. Médéric Collignon stands behind the 'Dionysus microphone', his eyes closed and his shoulder relaxed. A high-pitched electronic sound, like a foreign siren seems to come out of his lips and slowly transforms itself into the whispered words of Dionysus: 'You don't listen' he says. In the background we can hear the sound of instruments playing a melodic *ritornello*: it's the presence of the chorus behind Dionysos voice. The six speakers broadcasting the Chorus' voice are put into the audience area and create a dispositive in which sound surrounds the spectators' bodies, as if they were to be touched by the acousmatic choir. Bit by bit, the melodic chorus spreads notes of music into the God's whispered voice which becomes like a vibrating lament, a long and profound cry. Médéric Collignon then accelerates the rhythm and goes back and forth from Dionysus' voice to Pentheus', changing microphone each time he does so. The spectator feels he can almost hear in the same musical sentence the vocal masks of the two enemies.

If Dionysus' and Pentheus' vocal masks seem to be in a clear and almost caricatural contrast with each other, the alternation between one voice and another slowly tempers such difference. Dionysus' voice borrows a growling quality for a moment and Pentheus' timbre comes closer to Dionysus within an inch of falsetto voice. The contours of each one's identity has been blurred, the bacchic ritual can begin and everything is ready for the future disguise of Pentheus. It is no hazard if the third stasimon, following this Dionysus-Pentheus duo, differs from the other Spiropoulos' stasima by being partly improvised rather than taped (the same goes for the Exodos). To the virtual mask made of clipping, spectral stretch and filtering Médéric Collignon adds tapping sounds, whistles and a variety of growling voice effects then amplified in live by the electronic devices. Natural and virtual masks merge into each other to create a hybrid and mysterious chorus. During these few seconds of the third stasimon, the virtual choir designed by the Greek composer resonates with all its layers of sound, as if the acousmatic chorus was suddenly strong enough to appear in a vibrating shadow.

Polyphonic presences: An acousmatic and hybrid chorus

Movements between natural and virtual masks are at the core of Spiropoulos' work and reveal a specific approach of the chorus. At first, the roles are well distinguished: the scores of the choir are electroacoustic taped and the episodes are performed in live, with the voice of Collignon augmented by the different virtual masks. The third stasimon is a turning point since for the first time there is an interaction between the interpret and the offstage choir, as if the spectator were to be put into contact with the acousmatic chorus through the body of Médéric Collignon. The collaboration with the multi-vocalist allowed the two artists to explore various avant-garde vocal techniques such as those performed by Sainkho Namtchylak and Demetrio Stratos and to confront them with digital sounds. It is striking to hear in *The Bacchae* how natural and virtual masks are intermingled, each of them amplifying and responding to the other. A powerful dialogue takes place between the human and the machine, between artificiality and nature, which creates a hybridity that echoes perfectly with the character of Dionysus and that the spectator can actually see on stage. Collignon's body seems to be infected by the digital sounds and transforms itself, as if he was possessed by an invisible presence. At the same time, the microphones and speakers visible on stage appears too tangible to contain such mysterious sounds and their concrete and common presence only strengthen the extent of their vocal and acousmatic body. Eventually, the Choir exists outside the frontiers of both the human and digital, through this exploration of hybrid vocality.

To that extent, Spiropoulos' *Bacchae* is part of a more global research dedicated to oral traditions and their relationship to death rituals. With *Klama* (Paris, 2006) for instance, she explored the balance between the choir and live electronics and the consequences for the very act of composition by means of technological tools such as Open Music, Max/MSP and Audio Sculpt (Spiropoulos 2007). The Greek composer has a long-lasting obsession for voice and her adaptation of *The Bacchae* is enriched by such research which appear in the form of sound archives that haunt the whole piece before exploding in the Exodos. In the latter, one can hear fragments of Demetrio Stratos' voice and of recordings of death rituals of New Guinea and Solomon Islands for instance. Such acousmatic presences rise as Agave is holding her son's head, surrounded by the Choir. The 'second' chorus mentioned by Bierl (2013) can finally be heard and, in Spiropoulos' imagination, it has the features of those foreign oral traditions.

On stage, the interpreter has disappeared and the spectator can feel the vibrations of those lamenting sounds, as if the Choir were to put a sensitive spell on everyone in the room. Along with those traditional sounds, the musical references to Xenakis haunt these digital *Bacchae* and an expert ear will recognize in Spiropoulos' work his compositions using idiomatic vocal writing such as *Oresteia, N'Shima* or *Akanthos* and *Nuits* (Spiropoulos 2013). Building acousmatic and polyphonic *Bacchae*, Spiropoulos achieves her goal: allowing each spectator to feel the vibrations of the antique tragedy, along with an infinity of past and future vocal identities.

Touch of synthetic voices: 'A vocal approach to ancient Greek tragedy' workshop experience (Athens, 2018)

To end our journey with the sounds of the digital chorus in Euripides' *Bacchae*, we want to present some results of a workshop called 'A Vocal Approach of Ancient Greek Tragedy: acting with texts, sounds and synthetic voices'. It took place within the European event 'Tragedy 2.0 – Athens 2018 – Ancient Drama & the Digital Era', organized at the Michael Cacoyannis Foundation of Athens in October 2018. We were a team of four people: Chloé

Larmet and Ana Wegner, the two authors of this chapter, one 'coryphaeus', Roberto Moura (a specialist in polyphonic singing and the Feldenkrais Method), and one digital master, Christophe d'Alessandro (musician and researcher at the CNRS, who designed with his team at the Sorbonne University (LAM) the synthetic singer 'Cantor Digitalis'). Using vocal techniques and the counter-intuitive Feldenkrais method, we arranged the participants of the workshop (a group of fifteen people, most of them actors or singers) into three layers of voices: polyphony songs, untransformed by any kind of external technology; amplified voices with standing microphones; synthetic voices using *Cantor Digitalis*, a singing synthesizer controlled by chironomy, meaning using stylus and fingers on a graphic tablet (D'Alessandro et al. 2019). Playing with different types of voices, actors were invited to expand their listening, hoping to catch this profound inaudibility of Dionysus, in between the changing vocal qualities of the *Bacchae*, and thus the irrational and mysterious part of each voice.

The senses of voice: Following a hidden rhythm

Instead of looking for answers through theoretical explanations or analysis, we decided to tackle the mystery head on and to work on the unheard sounds of ancient Greek. We asked one of the actors (who had performed in various productions in ancient Greek) to read the first *stasimon* slowly and distinctly, as if he were a coryphaeus. The rest of the participants gathered in front of him, as a chorus, and repeated each sound, each syllable and each word. The specificity of this exercise was that not only did the group have to follow and imitate the words and the tone of voice but they also had to mirror the movements of the coryphaeus' body. He changed the orientation of his movements according to the rhythm of the text: each punctuation mark was for him a sign to modify the trajectory of his body, to accelerate or slow down his walking, to throw himself on the ground etc. Every comma or punctuation mark in the text became for him a choreographic sign, as if the text was a partition to be felt inside his body, with the changes in his movements. Inspired by the work of Cicely Berry, such an approach allows us to move towards a text thanks to physical rhythm while the question of the words' signification at first is suspended. The results of these experiments were a success, judging by the reaction of the chorus.

At first, repeating the sounds in ancient Greek provoked some laughs and difficulties. Twisting one's tongue and mouth to be able to create unfamiliar sounds can be a real challenge, especially if one stays focused on the potential, but unknown, signification of those words. In other words, repeating sounds that have no meaning is easy, like singing a melody, but when those sounds constitute language, things change: instinctively, one looks for an unknown intentionality. In this exercise, the fact that the chorus had to follow the movements of the coryphaeus while repeating the text in ancient Greek acted as a creative diversion. Bit by bit, the chorus' focus shifted from the meaning of those words they didn't know to the inscription, in their body, of the text's physical rhythm. As they did so, their pronunciation gradually improved: they *felt* the meaning of the text through rhythm instead of looking for it abstractly. This essential role of the rhythm is at the core of Cicely Berry's work:

> [...] the essence of the meaning is locked in the rhythm – whether smooth or broken. It is in the length of the phrases and how they knock against each other [...] Meaning is rhythm, and rhythm is meaning. (Berry 2012: 17)

Hearing the text with one's legs to feel its rhythm and unlock its meaning – such is the challenge to which we rose with the ancient Greek. But we did not stop there for the alterity was yet to be expanded. After a few improvisations with the structure moving the coryphaeus/mirror chorus, we decided to integrate the synthetic voices into the pattern. The instructions were basically the same: one coryphaeus leads a chorus following the rhythm of the text, in modern Greek this time. Every time the coryphaeus meets a variation of the rhythm, be it a punctuation sign or a breathing pause, he changes the orientation of his movements. But a radical difference occurred: in order to play synthetic voices with the Cantor Digitalis, you must be sitting still in front of a computer and a graphic tablet. When the Cantor Digitalis acted as a coryphaeus, the person had to guide the movements of the chorus only with the help of sound. And the reverse situation – a moving coryphaeus and a chorus made of four people playing the Cantor Digitalis – implied the same challenge: expressing clear choreographic indications with the sole vocal (and synthetized) sounds.

We observed in those two situations a similar contamination of each voice's qualities. The human chorus, following the instructions of the machines, produced uncommon sounds, mirroring the prosodic and melodic variations of the Cantor's sentences. What appeared then was something otherwise inaudible: the living and breathing person behind the machine. To put it differently, this vocal role-play of a machine-coryphaeus shed some light on the marionette quality that defines the relationship between the Cantor player and the vocal synthesizer. When the situation was reversed and the Cantors had to follow the instructions of a human coryphaeus, the contamination also took place. The synthetic voices had to keep their inexistent ears open to the breathing of the human voices, to its fragility and hesitations, its limits in terms of length and tonal range. In both cases, something happened: the synthetic and bare voices merged together to create a living polyphony.

As ancient Greek language or inert machines, the confrontation with vocal alterity triggered the creativity of the participants and displaced their focus on the rhythm of the text. This diversion allowed them to come closer to this mysterious vibration of *Bacchae,* a vibration they could now feel in their own bodies.

(Dis)placing the voice: A sensitive challenge

Feeling the voice: such is the paradoxical challenge to which actors and singers need to rise, whether digital tools are involved or not. And here lies maybe the singularity of the workshop 'A Vocal Approach of Ancient Greek Tragedy: acting with texts, sounds and synthetic voices'. Since the voice synthesizers we used, the Cantor Digitalis, require a tactile approach, the question of sensitivity was present from the beginning. The aim of the workshop was then to prove that the sensitive activation of voice, which is external and easily observable in Cantor Digitalis, echoes the same sensitive logic of the very 'natural' or 'unmediated' vocal gesture. To put it in other words: the relationship between an actor and his/her voice, be it synthetic, microphoned or unmediated (by any technical object), is made of a paradoxical sensitivity. In fact, the vocal training of the actor has always to do with going back and forth between sensitive perceptions and the mental explorations of the virtual image of the body.

The physical and virtual perceptions of one's voice during the act of enunciation is the only method for an actor to master: not only the vocal gesture itself, but also the virtual vocal bodies that result from it. This virtual dimension was essential to renew the approach of the voice in the art of the actor in the second part of the twentieth century in Europe and overseas. Antonin Artaud (1938) already wished for a voice that breaks ties with both the physiological limits of the body and the ideal of a beautiful and well-placed voice. To that matter, the French director and actor Jean-Louis Barrault considers that:

> Like the singer, the actor needs to place his voice. But he also needs to be able to 'displace' it. [...] He must have the capacity to move from one vocal placement to another, without any fatigue. (Barrault 1972: 58–9, our translation)

'Displacing the voice': the expression highlights the aim of vocal training which cannot be reduced to the physical structure of the vocal organ – vocal cords, diaphragm, larynx etc. To that extent our pedagogical approach met perfectly the dramaturgical stakes of Euripides' *Bacchae*, in terms of displacement: displacing the norms and values of the city comes in the piece with a vocal revolution and an expansion of the chorus' usual partition in ancient Greek drama.

The challenge which we tackled during the workshop was to put the physiological into movement *through* the voice in order to discover new places of sensibility in the actor's body. To illustrate this process, one can picture voice as a sensitive trigger that awakens each spot of the body whenever it touches it. The mere expression '*placer sa voix*' is a good example of this tension between physicality and imagination we mentioned earlier. *A priori,* the expression 'placing one's voice' implies that voice is like an object that the actor can manipulate, putting it in one place or another inside (or even outside of) his body according to the needs. But such manipulation is more complex than it seems, for the voice does not let itself be objectified so easily for many reasons (Bonnet 2012). The first has to do with the physiology of the vocal gesture: the voice only exists when different organs are activated at the same time, which means that a voice is always a voice *in movement*. Another reason of this non-object quality of voice is linked to a complex articulation between interiority and exteriority: voice resonates at the same time from the inside of the body and from the outside of it – a phenomenon called the 'sensible chiasm' according to the French phenomenologist Merleau-Ponty (Merleau-Ponty 1964). How is it possible, then, to place, manipulate and even displace something that cannot be reduced to an object?

One traditional exercise in vocal training consists of giving the voice an actual body by means of a tool as trivial as a tennis ball. The process is quite simple: the participants are sitting on the floor in a circle. Successively, they roll a tennis ball on the floor towards another person while voicing a vowel. The aim of the exercise is to start the vowel's sound at the exact instant when the hand launches the ball and to end it when the ball touches the hand of the other person. The tennis ball becomes the visible body of the voice and at the same time it is focus. Hearing the voice becomes, in this exercise, a question of visual and tactile perception. But this exercise is also useful for questioning the ability of each actor to separate him/herself from his/her voice when in relationship to another speaking on singing entity (be it a person or a vocal synthesizer) on stage. By such separation, the exercise is a step towards creating a chorus in which each individuality persists but puts itself at the service of a collective identity.

Voices, digital or not, become like pieces of a puzzle: independent, separate and yet forming an entity when put together in a certain shape. Our approach to choral voices was inspired by an exercise created by Peter Brook in the seventies to train the actors and presented in Gerald Feil's movie *The Empty Space* (1976). He asked a group of actors to make sounds all together and to point at the same time in the direction which the sound of their voice was supposed to follow. His instruction underlines the fact that this simple exercise can be interpreted in two different ways: either the actors are in a conscious attempt to produce a sound reflecting a personal expression; or they manage to consider sound as something that does not belong to anyone and that can be oriented by everyone in a same direction. To create a sound that 'does not belong to anyone', the first step is, according to Brook, to give the sound a specific physical orientation – a step that our exercise with the tennis balls reproduced. To consider the orientation of the sound in space is a way to displace the hearing and speaking (or singing) habits of the actors. The focus shifts from an individual relationship (the sounds of the voice betray the emotions of the self) to a collective and active tension: to direct, collectively, the sound in a specific direction into space. The voice is no longer considered as a mere shelf for intimate emotions but creates meaning by itself, thus allowing a new range of vocal possibilities to explore *alongside* the digital tools instead of *in conflict with* them. We extended the principle of the tennis ball exercise to the voice synthesizers and the microphones and it was an immediate success. All separated voices suddenly merged with one another and began to create freely as a hybrid and polyphonic chorus, made of hidden rhythms and vibrations.

Conclusions

Based on the analysis of contemporary artistic works, this chapter followed the sound of three digital chorus inspired by Euripides' *Bacchae*. A journey that began in Brazil with Zé Corrêa's 'electrocandomblaica' and its festive community made of heterogeneous voices in a one-of-a-kind theatrical space, reaching for an ecstatic and ritual horizon. Secondly, we listened to the apparent solely voice of Médéric Collignon in Georgia Spiropoulos' *Bacchae* to discover an acousmatic chorus in which virtual and vocal masks appear and transform themselves endlessly. The last section of our chapter presented some results of a workshop where actors had to play with different layers of voices, digital or not, in order to touch the profound inaudibility of Euripides' *Bacchae* and to explore a paradoxical sensitivity for voice, since the voice defines who we are in a way that nothing else can. Each minute of each day, those vibrating sounds are the sensor of our intimacy, our emotions, our ideas, our relationship to the world and to ourselves in such a way that many of us are convinced voice is the most familiar thing to be. And yet, the three digital choirs analyzed in this chapter lead to the same conclusion: when confronted at digital technology, voice reveals an essential alterity and gains a playful and mysterious quality. 'Augmented' *Bacchae* then become an opportunity to question the limits of vocality and, at the same time, of everyone's profound identity: a digital bacchic ritual to long for.

References

Andújar, R., and K. P. Nikoloutsos (2021), *Greeks and Romans on the Latin American Stage,* New York: Bloomsbury Publishing.

Artaud, A. (1938), *Le Théâtre et son double (suivi de) Le Théâtre de Séraphin,* Paris: Gallimard.

Barrault, J.-L. (1972), *Mise en scène de* 'Phèdre' *de Racine,* Paris: Éditions du Seuil.

Berry, C. (2012), *From Word to Play: A Handbook for Directors*, London: Oberon Books.

Bierl, A. (2013), 'Maenadism as self-referential chorality in Euripides' Bacchae', in R. Gagné and M. Govers Hopman (eds), *Choral Mediations in Greek tragedy,* 211–26, Cambridge: Cambridge University Press.

Bonnet, F. (2012), *Les mots et les sons: un archipel sonore*, Paris: Éd. de l'Éclat.

Calame, C. (2017), *La Tragédie chorale. Poésie grecque et rituel musical,* Paris: Les Belles Lettres.

Chion, M. (1984), *La voix au cinéma*, Paris: Cahiers du Cinéma.

De Andrade, O. ([1928]1991), 'Cannibalist Manifesto', *Latin American Literary Review* 19 (38): 38–47.

D'Alessandro, C., S. Delalez, B. Doval, L. Feugère and O. Perrotin (2019), 'Les Instruments chanteurs', *Acoustique et Techniques* 89: 36–43.

Euripides (2009), *Bacchae and Other Plays,* New York: Oxford University Press.

Fischer-Lichte, E. (2014), *Dionysus Resurrected: Performances of Euripides' The Bacchae in a Globalizing World,* Chichester: Wiley-Blackwell.

Fónagy, I. (1991), *La Vive voix: essais de psycho-phonétique*, Paris: Payot.

Merleau-Ponty, M. (1964), *Le Visible et l'invisible,* Paris: Gallimard.

Sampatakakis, G. (2014), Book review: 'Erika Fischer-Lichte, *Dionysus Resurrected: Performances of Euripides' The Bacchae in a Globalizing World*', *Logeion* 4: 387–97.

Sampatakakis, G. (2017), 'Dionysus the Destroyer of Traditions: "The Bacchae" on Stage' in G. Rodosthenous (ed.), *Contemporary Adaptations of Greek Tragedy: Authorship and Directorial Visions*, 189–211, London: Methuen Bloomsbury.

Spiropoulos, G. (2007), '"Klama": the Voice from Oral Tradition in Death Rituals to a Work for Choir & Live Electronics', Proceedings SMC'07, 4th Sound and Music Computing Conference, Lefkada.

Spiropoulos G. and Georgaki (2010), A. 'Virtual masks in the masks in "The Bacchae" by Georgia Spiropoulos (IRCAM, 2010): Exploring Tragic Vocality in Max/MSP Environment', SMC 2013 Conference, Stockholm.
Spiropoulos, G. (2014), 'Real-Time Composition of Sound Environments', ICMC/SMC 2014 Conference, Athens.
Sterne, J. (2012), *The Sound Studies Reader*, New York: Routledge.
Swift, L. (2013) 'Conflicting identities in the Euripidean chorus', in R. Gagné and M. Govers Hopman (eds), *Choral Mediations in Greek tragedy*, 130–54, Cambridge: Cambridge University Press.
Turner, V. (1982), *From Ritual to Theatre. The Human Seriousness of Play*, New York: PAJ Publications.
Vovolis, T. (2009), *Prosopon: The Acoustical Mask in Greek Tragedy and in Contemporary Theatre*, Stockholm: Dramatiska institutet.

Artistic works

Akanthos (1977), [Music] Comp. Iannis Xenakis, Paris: Salabert Ed.
Bacantes (2016), [Theatre Production] Dir. José Celso Martinez Corrêa, São Paulo: Teatro Oficina. Video available online: https://www.youtube.com/watch?v=LInR5MozrsE&list=PLTN97D_XfEQGoDPCvDPof_4WwxYACII9d&index=2&t=1020s&fbclid=IwAR0ZY1bxG2T6-6GSqoXHWEIpjTiJTtWdn5K3novZ-ozEHCOxsDl-tpwL3Sg&app=desktop (accessed 3 July 2020).
Bacantes (1996), [Show] Dir. José Celso Martinez Corrêa, São Paulo: Teatro Oficina.
Bacantes (1986), [Show] Dir. José Celso Martinez Corrêa, São Paulo: Teatro Oficina.
The Empty Space (1976), [Film] Dir. Gerald Feil, New York: Seven Valleys Entertainment.
Klama (2005–06), [Music] Comp. Georgia Spiropoulos, Paris: IRCAM.
Oresteia (1965), [Music] Comp. Iannis Xenakis, London: Boosey & Hawkes.
N'Shima (1975), [Music] Comp. Iannis Xenakis, Paris: Salabert.
Nuits (1967), [Music] Comp. Iannis Xenakis, Paris: Salabert.
The Bacchae (2010), [Show] Dir. Georgia Spiropoulos, Paris: IRCAM. Video available online: https://www.youtube.com/watch?v=O2tuXZmpDuw&fbclid=IwAR1rXZ--r2gq3LsxiN7xSCngnrjFEMHSQlP9XdytAHaoWTUUFrQedQZMqVo&app=desktop (accessed 3 July 2020).

6

Tragedy and the digital environment

Ancient desiring machines, choruses and Oedipus

Sebastian Kirsch

Introduction

Tragedy and the digital: The connection suggested by the title of this chapter is anything but obvious. What should the traces of a theatrical form whose heyday ended almost 2500 years ago have to do with the digital upheavals that in recent decades have turned the modern globe into an almost totally interconnected planet? Why (and how) to build a bridge between tragedy in the fifth century BC and post-2000 digitalization? In other words: how are we to read the conjunction 'and' here?

This chapter will approach this question by considering the changes indicated by the keyword 'digital' as a mutation in the deep structures of Western societies, which concerns the history of institutions as well as that of the subject. From this perspective, digitalization must be depicted as a decisive challenge of framings that belong to a long-term history and can even be seen as residuals of an ancient 'Copernican turn'. This is also where tragedy will come into play, since the invention of the tragic protagonist can in fact be understood as a reaction to this very turn. Accordingly, the author will argue that, considering digitalization, it is the non-protagonist figures of Greek theatre (i.e. the chorus, but also the messengers) that are of particular interest today.

To develop this systematically, the first two parts of this chapter will deal separately with 'tragedy' and 'the digital'. The third part will then explore the 'and' between them, using Sophocles' *Oedipus* as a case study. As for the issue of tragedy, I will generally take up recent discussions that have shed new light especially on the importance of the chorus for the whole of ancient theatre (Annuß 2014, 2017; Bodenburg, Grabbe and Haitzinger 2016; Enzelsberger, Meister and Schmitt 2012; Haß 2014, 2021; Kirsch 2020). As far as digitalization is concerned, my remarks will rely on two concepts that were introduced into the theoretical discussion just on the eve of the 'digital revolution' and have been further developed especially in recent media theory. The first concept (on which greater focus will be placed) is 'environmentality' (or 'environmental governmentality'), a notion originally developed by Michel Foucault (Foucault 2008: 260–1). But I will also draw on the distinction between 'social subjection' and 'machinic enslavement' as proposed in Deleuze's and Guattari (1987). However, the first thing to clarify here is the notion of ancient Greek theatre itself, on which this chapter relies.

Tragedy: Chorus and environmental knowledge

In the first place, I would like to emphasize that ancient Greek theatre should be seen as montage: this theatre was put together from two very different stages, i.e. the orchestra and the skene, and accordingly brought together chorus and protagonist as two completely heterogeneous types of being-on-stage. The protagonist developed just on the threshold of the classical fifth century. Speculations even concentrate on a name and a date: it is Thespis who is said to have exposed the first actor around 534 BC and thus 'invented' the tragic form as such. In contrast, the chorus is much older and has multiple origins vastly scattered in space and time. As far as we know, it was very important in the pre-classical rural Dionysia, which suggests that it was linked to agriculture and fertility cults. And beyond this, the traces of the chorus lead and disappear into diverse directions and cultures, e.g. Minoic, Egyptian, Persian or Semitic. Therefore, its appearance in the surviving ancient Greek plays resembles a process of emergence: the chorus is adopted in the younger theatre frame like an erratic boulder that no poet has come up with but nevertheless seems to be so constitutive of the whole structure that one cannot neglect it.

What may sound trivial at first contains many complicated aspects that require great attention. Here, I will highlight three of them some more. Firstly, it is absolutely crucial to keep in mind that the Greek stage form, being the aforementioned montage, contained not only two, but three different parts: the skene as the protagonists' stage, the orchestra as a dance floor for the chorus, and the theatron where the audience was placed. I am emphasizing this since I consider it most important that this triad totally eludes the modern idea of theatre as a complicated duality of actors and audience. The most obvious consequence of this is that modern times frequently did not know what to do with the somehow superfluous chorus: whether to count it among the actors or to make it part or even a representative of the audience. But it is equally essential to understand the epistemological background of this difference, which ultimately results from two mutually incompatible ideas about what it means to see, and thus concerns two very different concepts of visibility. The French historian Gérard Simon has shown in more detail that the entire ancient world conceptualized seeing as a physiological process between bodies being in each other's presence (Simon 1988). In this understanding the optical is based in a deeply somatic relationship. Therefore, a body and its image cannot be separated here: seeing and touching someone/something belong together.

A striking consequence of this is that the idea of light refraction cannot emerge within the ancient frame, and it was only this idea, which enabled modern attempts to visualize and represent something or somebody in terms of a picture or a mirroring image. One can actually see that the dualistic framework of modern theatre (for example, the picture frame stage) which confronts the actors and the audience *vis à vis* is equivalent to the younger concept of the optical. And on the other hand, ancient theatre indeed cannot be apprehended in terms of the picture stage. Instead one should approximate the relation between the three stages in terms of contagion and bodily affection.

Thus, the chorus did not fit into the dualistic frame of the picture stage and its optical/mirroring framework. This brings me to a second point: since in modern times the chorus and everything related to it had become more or less an enigma the simplest solution seemed to connect it to terms like 'public sphere', 'the people', 'community' or 'collective' – a commonplace which even today is referred to quite often. But why is this in fact a huge misunderstanding?

To start with, one has to take in account here that the association between 'chorus' and 'public' is usually grounded in another dualistic framework. This time it is not the opposition between actors and audience but that between the public and the private, an idea which, in fact, informed huge parts of political thought from at least the eighteenth century. However, what makes it complicated to see the mistake here is that the modern public/private distinction was for its own part derived from a distinction famously introduced in the fifth century BC. It is the distinction between polis itself, understood as the (male) sphere of political actions, and then oikos as the closed space within, i.e. the household being ruled by women. So, considering these ancient origins it may at first sight seem somewhat plausible to locate the tragic chorus within this framework. The falseness of this conclusion, however, begins to become apparent when one recalls the very fact that the chorus is much older than the strong division between polis and oikos: The latter was only the result of a momentous epistemological turn on which the whole development of the classical polis was based. Generally speaking, this turn was a shift from thinking in more tertiary structures to a more binary thinking. Therefore, if one takes a closer look on the rise of the polis/oikos distinction, one will find that also in this case a third term got suppressed or even lost: it is the term kosmos which had been of tremendous importance in pre-classical times. And indeed, it is noticeable that the tragic chorus, especially in its stasima, often appears to be a bearer of a memory that includes a wide range of cosmic topologies. For example, the fifth stasimon in Sophocles' *Antigone* (the Hymnos kletikos), in which the chorus begs Dionysos to come, naming a multitude of sacred locations and cultic sites associated with the god; or the chorus built by Aeschylus' *Suppliant Women*, i.e. the fifty Danaids tracing back to the mythological figure of Io: Io was transformed into a cow by Zeus and chased by a monstrous horsefly sent by Hera; and this chorus is able to list all the mythological landscapes and countries that its ancestress crossed during her earth-spanning escape.

In order to get a better idea of the chorus' 'cosmic connection' one should keep in mind that in ancient Greek the term kosmos did not denote a strong divine and transcendent order as we find it in Christian traditions, but is better understood as a name for the interconnectedness of everything alive. In this sense, kosmos is a word for a non-human sphere that precedes and exceeds entities like polis and oikos, but at the same time enables their establishment in the first place. However, I would like to expand on that by relating the arrangement kosmos/polis/oikos to another ancient tertiary structure that later narrowed into binary: the case of the 'middle', which was in ancient Greek a third voice next do active and passive, and which for its own part became more and more invisible in later linguistic developments, while at the same time the active/passive opposition grew increasingly strong. It is evident that the dualism between polis and oikos resembles that between active and passive. But how does then the excluded kosmos relate to the middle?

Usually the middle is defined as denoting that a subject is both the agent of an action and simultaneously concerned with the action itself (e.g. 'I am washing myself'). However, this is a bit simplistic. The stoics for example characterized the middle as a marker for an agency that cannot be said to be passive although it seems not to act intentionally (Diogenes Laertius VII, 1: 64) – just as 'cosmic' forces do, such as an ocean, a tree, a desert or a mountain. And furthermore, the middle is often used to express events with strong affective values. Take for example the verb form klaiomai, which means 'I am crying for me'. But if we follow linguist Emilé Benveniste who emphasized that the subject denoted by the middle is primarily a carrier of a process taking place it would be more appropriate to translate this as 'There is crying happening to me' (Benveniste 1971). Thus klaiomai expresses a woe so forceful that it exceeds the single cryer and relates to all the other virtual tears that have once been cried and will be cried in the future. Why not call this a cosmic crying . . . ?

If one sums this up it is striking that the attributes of the middle also apply to the tragic chorus: its agency, often hesitant and dithering, clearly differs from the strong intentional actions of the protagonists, but can on the other hand by no means be reduced to 'passivity'. And of course the example of the 'cosmic crying' which is too strong for just one mouth is reminiscent of numerous scenes of lamentation the tragic chorus appears in, from the wailing girls in Aeschylus' *Seven against Thebes* to the mourning mothers in Euripides' *Suppliants*. We can therefore conclude that the chorus is in fact related to all the cosmic forces which lie beyond the public/oikos couple as well as they undermine the active/passive contrast. Therefore it seems fair to say that the chorus, when it appeared in the urban theatre, did work as a memory of these forces, transporting and injecting them into the developing dualistic frame of the classical polis and at the same time forbidding its closure.

All of this leads to my final point. If we consider the chorus that part of Greek theatre which was in many ways connected to the older triadic epistemology, we can simultaneously recognize that the protagonists often take the side of the younger, dualistic thinking. To be clear, this is more of a helpful rule of thumb than an absolute law. But it helps to explain, for example, why tragic protagonists are not seldom endowed with a strong will to invoke their 'ego' (which is the very first word the oldest protagonist we have utters when entering the stage: Xerxes in Aeschylus' *Persians*), to found or, like Oedipus or Creon (in *Antigone*), to (re-)erect cities and houses on their own. And on the other hand, we often find that this kind of energy remains strange to the chorus, who, due to its 'cosmic' remembrance, is often the bearer of a knowledge not centred on a personal ego. In ancient tragedy this knowledge sticks to a widespread mythological horizon populated by countless hybrids of humans, animals, gods and even landscapes. But beyond this mythological 'canopy' we can characterize it as an environmental knowledge: a knowledge of multiple beginnings that does not allow for the idea of one grounding since each and every beginning is always already permeated by immeasurable environmental forces. Therefore what tragedy calls hubris is ultimately an attempt to suspend this environmental condition.

One should also keep in mind that tragedy does not stage a simple opposition between the chorus' 'cosmic' or 'environmental' heritages and then the protagonists' hubris. It is still more complex, because at the same time the chorus can be seen as the very instance of Greek theatre which enables the protagonists' appearances in the first place. Since the chorus is for its own part a multi-headed 'environment', one of its most important functions is to 'donate' the necessary space for the protagonists, providing them with the reasons and the possibility to step on the skene at all. (Just think of the chorus waiting in front of the palace before the tragedy of Oedipus commences.) Put in more general terms, one could say that the tragic chorus is ultimately two-sided: On the one hand, it stands in a close relationship to the protagonists, even if they are carrying out their battles on their own stage, and in this context it is usually also involved in the scene itself. But on the other hand, being related to cosmos, the chorus also touches on the absolute and antecedent outside of the polis' orders – and this is usually where he switches from its scenic entanglements to the stasima. Therefore, all in all the montage of protagonist and chorus generates (again) a complex threefold figure, consisting of the skene as the protagonists' location, then the 'interior' side of the chorus, relating to the protagonists' logics without merging with it, and finally its 'exterior', opening the whole constellation to kosmos.

The digital: Environmentality (Foucault) and enslavement (Deleuze/Guattari)

As I already mentioned, my aim is to discuss the effects of digitalization here by drawing especially on two terms: primarily 'environmentality' which goes back to Foucault, but also Deleuze's and Guattari's distinction between 'social subjection' and 'machinic enslavement'. What are these notions about?

Foucault coined the term 'environmentality' (*environmentalité*) just in a short, but extremely interesting manuscript which belongs to his 1979 lectures on governmentality (Foucault 2008: 260-1). In order to understand the thrust of this term, one must briefly recall that Foucault's governmentality analyses did not only complement his older remarks on sovereignty and disciplinary power (Foucault 1977). Rather he relativized them considerably against the background of the development of neoliberalism since 1945. Therefore it is no wonder that his notes on environmentality open with the diagnosis of a recent 'massive withdrawal with regard to the normative-disciplinary system' (2008: 260).

In *Discipline and Punish* Foucault had argued that the traditional legal power of the Ancien Régime, which was committed to the principles of spectacularly punitive sovereignty, was successively overlaid by new, more finely woven techniques of surveillance during the eighteenth century. His main example, which has become perhaps even too familiar since then, was Jeremy Bentham's plan for a panoptic prison: a circular building with numerous individual cells that could potentially always be observed by an invisible guard in a central tower. At that time Foucault had emphasized that disciplinary power, being a power of permanent visibility, produces and simultaneously subjugates individuals who try to become identical with their own pictorial appearance: 'under the surface of images, one invests bodies in depth.' (1977: 217) But moreover, back then he had also declared: 'Our society is one not of spectacle, but of surveillance' (1977: 217) – and it is especially this diagnosis he later would definitely take back in the light of governmentality.

A first step to this self-correction was Foucault's insight that the eighteenth century did not just witness the rise of surveillance but also of another type of power he initially had no proper name for (and which later was to be named governmentality). In his 1977 lecture Society must be defended he stated:

> From the eighteenth century onward (or at least the end of the eighteenth century onward) we have, then, two technologies of power which were established at different times and which were superimposed. One technique is disciplinary; it centers on the body, produces individualizing effects, and manipulates the body as a source of forces that have to be rendered both useful and docile. And we also have a second technology which is centered not upon the body but upon life: a technology which brings together the mass effects characteristic of a population, which tries to control the series of random events that can occur in a living mass, a technology which tries to predict the probability of those events (by modifying it, if necessary), or at least to compensate for their effects. (Foucault 2003: 249)

These remarks are enlightening since they give a first indication of how the history of protagonist and chorus 'beyond' their ancient appearances can be written further. It is fair to say that the inheritances of the protagonist should later shape the disciplinary subject whereas the more or less 'hidden' role of the chorus, which did not fit into the panoptic organisation, became the neuralgic point for the 'new' technology 'centered upon life'. This becomes even clearer in another passage of the same lecture that reads like this:

> What we are dealing with in this new technology of power is not exactly society (or at least not the social body, as defined by the jurists), nor is it the individual-as-body. It is a new body, a multiple body, a body with so many heads that, while they might not be infinite in number, cannot necessarily be counted. (2003: 245)

One can easily see here that this new, non-panoptical and non-disciplinary technology of power is concerned with the question of a 'third' sphere that is neither public ('society') nor private ('individual'), i.e. the very question that once was related to chorus and kosmos. Accordingly, governmentality aims to occupy and to regulate all those aspects of life, or rather of the living, that go beyond the level of contoured entities. That means its focus lies on the very mutual processes of becoming between individual bodies and their surroundings I associated especially with the chorus' being an 'environment' on his own part and 'donating space'.

The next important point is an observation Foucault made in his first lecture on governmentality. In *Discipline and Punishment* he had painted the differences between sovereignty and panoptic surveillance in bright colours. But now he declares:

> The idea of the panopticon is a modern idea in one sense, but we can also say that it is completely archaic, since the panoptic mechanism basically involves putting someone in the center – an eye, a gaze, a principle of surveillance – who will be able to make its sovereignty function over all the individuals [placed] within this machine of power. To that extent we can say that the panopticon is the oldest dream of the oldest sovereign: None of my subjects can escape and none of their actions is unknown to me. The central point of the panopticon still functions, as it were, as a perfect sovereign. (Foucault 2009: 66)

In other words, while surveillance inverts sovereignty by reversing the primarily punitive approach into a productively improving one, the structural frame of both powers does not really change. This is also why Foucault uses the expression 'normative-disciplinary system' later. From the perspective of this chapter we can therefore say that the whole difference between sovereignty and surveillance was ultimately just an internal difference within the protagonist horizon. It was only governmentality that would begin to exceed this protagonist field, historically starting already in the late eighteenth century.

It was not until the mid-twentieth century that technologies developed which fitted the governmental approach perfectly. First and foremost it is cybernetics which, being the science of feedback and (self-)control processes, was better suited than any other technology before to making the field of mutual becoming its main manoeuvring area. And it is precisely in this context that Foucault situates what he calls 'environmentality'. Therefore, among the main aspects of 'environmental technology' are: 'the definition of a framework around the individual which is loose enough for him to be able to play', 'the possibility for the individual of regulation of the effects of the definition of his own framework', and, above all, 'not a standardizing, identificatory, hierarchical individualization, but an environmentalism open to unknowns and transversal phenomena' (2008: 261).

If one reads these notes today, one can easily see how the story continued, since by now all these aspects are well-known parts of a neoliberalism shaped by digital networks. So it is no wonder that Foucault's term 'environmentality' has been taken up frequently in recent times for the analysis of 'algorithmic governmentality', 'ubiquitous computing' and generally a digital control power that has effectively shifted from panoptic surveillance to the 'capturing' of series and clusters of pre-individual movements, gestures, traces and affects (Rouvroy 2013). The crux is here that in the ages of Big Data, environmentalization takes the form of a massive appropriation (but also management) of everything that lies beyond classical conditions of subjectivation: Transformed into 'algorithmic governmentality', environmental power works simultaneously 'below' and 'above' traditional mechanisms of institutional inscription, coming-to-language, mirroring in the image of the other, sexualization etc. Moreover, it even 'bypasses consciousness and reflexivity, and operates on the mode of alerts and reflexes' (2013: 153). And it does not allow for the process of subjectivation to happen, because it does not confront 'subjects' as moral agents [...]. The only 'subject' algorithmic governmentality needs is a unique, supra-individual, constantly reconfigured 'statistical body' made of the infra-individual digital traces of impersonal, disparate, heterogeneous, dividualized facets of daily life and interactions (2013: 157).

This would be a Foucauldian perspective on today's digital world. Before I return to tragedy I want to complete this now with Deleuze and Guattari's term 'machinic enslavement' which, being opposed to 'social subjection', basically aims at the same point but allows for one or two further remarks. The decisive passages can be found in the chapter '7000 B.C. Apparatus of Capture' in *A Thousand Plateaus*. Here, Deleuze and Guattari define 'social subjection' as a mechanism which constitutes a human being as a 'molar' entity, i.e. 'a subject linked to a now exterior object, which can be an animal, a tool, or even a machine' (1987: 457). By contrast, 'machinic enslavement' points to an instrumentalization and exploitation of the 'molecular' dynamics in which molar relations between subjects and objects emerge and take shape in the first place. Unlike subjection, it is about the modulation, control and economization of pre-cognitive and pre-discursive components, of unconscious micro-percepts and circulating affects that cannot be linked neither to an individual nor to a privileged human entity. Therefore, there is enslavement 'when human beings themselves are constituent pieces of a machine that they compose among themselves and with other things (animals, tools), under the control and direction of a higher unity' (1987: 456, 457).

Again, it is not difficult to apply these two layers to the protagonist/chorus distinction, with subjection relating to the field of the protagonist and enslavement to that of the chorus. But what is of special interest here is that the distinction also delineates two different ways of thinking about technique and about work instruments: If 'subjection' brings about a 'subject linked to an exterior object' it also enables the classical construction of an actively working being (man) and a passive material object which is worked on, i.e. the so called 'hylemorphism' as we find its first elaborated formulation in Aristotle, a hundred years after tragedy. And on the other hand the buzz-word 'machinic' points to the idea of a self-differentiating matter which does not allow for the hylemorphistic opposition between active shaper and passive matter, but emphasizes their mutual becoming. If this logic then can be enslaved it is about colonizing exactly those processes that also environmental governmentality tries to capture.

And: Oedipus and beyond

Oedipus is a particularly good example to discuss the different realms of subjection and enslavement, respectively sovereignty and environmental governmentality in tragedy because the protagonist of this piece has traditionally been considered the model of the modern subject in general (see also Poulou in Chapter 2 above). What became invisible this way, however, was that those logics which cannot be reduced to the field of subjection are in fact extremely important in Sophocles. In this last part I therefore want to show where to find these non-protagonist (shall we say: non-Oedipal?) logics in *Oedipus* and argue that they indeed, in a quite astonishing way do echo the topics that are at stake with digital control power.

First, a remark on Oedipus himself. One of the biggest clichés about his tragedy concerns the oracle he was given in Delphi, particularly that segment which predicted he was to 'mingle with the mother' (hos metri men chreiie me meichthenai, v. 791). It is a commonplace that Oedipus read this as a horrible prophecy, saying that he would have to sleep with the woman who gave birth to him. What is much less well known, however, is that this oracle has in fact two other meanings which Oedipus totally neglected: the expression 'to mingle with the mother' as we find it here could also mean 'to become king in the polis one was born in', and then also simply 'to return to mother earth', that is to die (Vernant and Vidal-Naquet 1990: 110–11). Now, against the background of what has been said here, one can see that these three meanings perfectly match the triangle of oikos (sleeping with your mother), polis (becoming king in your hometown) and kosmos (return to mother earth). Thus the fact that Oedipus was unable to connect 'mother' to another level than oikos obviously bears witness of his positioning within the younger epistemological frame. And indeed his tragedy could also be read as a tragedy of the ultimate impossibility of this reduction.

In other words, in Oedipus himself we find environmental knowledge only ex negativo. But do we also have some 'positive' formulations in this piece? After all I have developed, the first thing one would do to find an answer is certainly to take a look at the chorus. But then the surprise will be all the greater that just in this tragedy the chorus seems to take the protagonist's side very strongly: At least in his inner scenic involvement we find it again and again submitting itself to the 'tyrant' Oedipus. The chorus calls the protagonist the first of all men (andron de proton, v. 33) and expects him even explicitly to re-erect the city (anorthoson polin, v. 46). It is therefore all the more striking that in this tragedy we can find the clearest traces of environmental knowledge not in the chorus but in the messengers, particularly in the blind seer Teiresias and in the shepherd who is questioned at the end of the play. In what sense?

Let me refer, once more, to Foucault here who for his own part gave a lecture on Sophocles' *Oedipus*, in the context of his interest in legal practices and procedures of truth (Foucault 2014: 22–74). His main discovery was there that Oedipus' investigation into the 'Laius murder case' follows the ancient practice of the sumbolon and the 'law of two halves'. However, I only want to focus on one aspect of this lecture which is indeed highly illuminating here: It is Foucault's claim that this tragedy whose entire plot coincides with Oedipus' investigation is in fact primarily about a battle between different forms of knowledge.

The field on which this battle takes place is defined by three levels, through which, Foucault says, Oedipus' quest for the origins of the plague leads. According to the 'law of halves', each of these tableaus explains two aspects of the complete case and, on each tableau, a different type of knowledge is at work. The first one deals with the gods and their media. Apollo is questioned in Delphi and his answer conveyed to Kreon, and Teiresias the seer must explain and clarify the god's words. Two issues are explained thus: through Apollo we find out that a murder has taken place; through Teiresias the murderer is identified. But this means that the criminal case has actually already been solved here – the detective story is over, the seer has already proclaimed Oedipus himself to be the murderer. However, divine knowledge is not enough; there is no visible proof for what has been said. Oedipus does not believe the seer, so his quest continues.

On the second level, the particulars of the crime of Laius' murder and the circumstances of Oedipus' birth are explained. This middle level is that of

Oedipus and Jocasta themselves, that is, the level of wife and husband, of mother and son, of the (royal) couple and therefore that of the protagonists. But after everything on this level has been said and done, there is still something missing: Without the authenticating eye-witness testimony of the servant who observed Laius' murder, the case cannot be solved. Upon closer inspection, the second, protagonistic level is actually the one that is not just dominated by the greatest uncertainty, but also by the greatest blindness.

We still need the disclosure of the servant. With this we arrive on the third, the deepest level: that of the shepherds, the servants and slaves. Only with these do the last two pieces come together that put back the shards of the sumbolon: The servant gives an account of the attack on Laius, the shepherd of the abandoned infant Oedipus being handed over to his surrogate parents. It turns out that, exactly like on the first level of the gods (and radically unlike the middle protagonist level), we already know everything on this level too: Laius' servant even had himself transferred to the surrounding countryside (chora) so that he would not be confronted with his knowledge on a day-to-day basis.

Upon closer inspection, it becomes apparent that the knowledge of the gods and the knowledge of the slaves, the first and the third levels that is, share the same essential characteristics, which is even more surprising considering the fact that they have, of course, completely different dispositions. This means that – unlike the protagonists, who talk incessantly – all of the figures of these two levels have to be made, if not forced, to speak in the first place: Apollo has to be interviewed and translated, Teiresias only discloses his knowledge under threat of punishment, and the slaves, in turn, have to be found, the servant even having himself transferred out of the polis, out of the palace. At the same time, these two forms of knowledge are grounded in plural phenomena that seem so insignificant, unspectacular and meaningless that they are simply overlooked by the protagonist level. Elsewhere, where they do draw attention to themselves, they are not even recognized as their own genre of knowledge any more. Apollo's prophecy refers to the stellar constellations and Teiresias' divination is based on his ability to read the flight paths of flocks of birds. Oedipus dismisses both as insignificant: He thinks that Kreon's translation of the oracle is a personal scheme and he also suspects that the seer is telling a profane lie, whereas he himself is taking up the exclusive reading of human or, more precisely, significant signs and traces. On the level of the protagonists, the slaves' knowledge must also be considered non- and un-important: knowledge which we might characterize as practical, impersonal knowledge that is constituted in a way that is eminently technical, a network-like 'know-how'. It is everyday knowledge, which appears as trivial from a royal (i.e. protagonistic) perspective.

So, we can say that these two forms of knowledge – the knowledge of the seer and the knowledge of the slaves – refer to one another like the two sides of a Moebius strip, which surrounds the level both of the protagonists Oedipus and Jocasta and of the chorus as an exterior environmental sphere. But above all these two forms of knowledge are each associated with techniques that are no longer recognized by the protagonists as such. Foucault describes the reason why Oedipus denies the tekhné of the seer's knowledge in the following words:

> On the one hand, if Teiresias speaks the truth, this is not exactly a tekhné (for Oedipus) for the excellent reason that Teiresias has a natural bond with the truth. He is born with the truth, the truth is born in him, the truth grows like a plant within his body, or as another body in his body. [...] Teiresias says: 'I nourish the truth in me,' and Oedipus says: 'You know the truth, suneidōs, you know it immediately.' So, there is no technique, since there is this connaturalness [...] of Teiresias and the truth. (2014: 54)

The key point is here that the prophetic reading of the flight of birds is literally a technique that cannot be understood in terms of prosthesis or supplement, but rather solely in terms of primordial environmentality and machinic assemblage. The seer lives and reads, so to speak, in the midst of the flock of birds, with whose movements he is in somatic-affective contact and with which he communicates beyond the paradigm of the visual mirror (Teiresias is blind!). But, upon closer inspection, it is precisely that relational notion of technique that – if we take away the reference to Apollo – is returning with all it is worth today: with computing working beyond the visual frames which defined the former analogue media and with human beings finding themselves more and more embedded and disseminated in technological environments that affect them from all sides.

But something similar can also be claimed for the technique of the slaves and, in particular, the shepherd. Like the seer with his flocks of birds, the shepherd lives together with herds of sheep and goats; and like the seer, the shepherd has also trained in a specific technique (guarding his herd), which the royal protagonists are not even able to know of in the first place. And again, this technique is not in the relation between subject and object (which would make it hylemorphistic), but in mutual becoming. But we can describe it also as a governmental technique in the strict Foucauldian sense. It is a governmentality of everyday life, which includes ultimately all the non-spectacular, non-personal and repetitive gestures that 'algorithmic governmentality' tries to exploit today.

Tragedy and the Digital Environment 143

Conclusions

To conclude, what does tragedy know about the digital? It all comes down to questions of our own relations with non-human forces and entities, our own embeddedness into an environmental sphere that once bore the name 'cosmos', our own coping with the according agencies – in short: to questions of our own 'being ecological' (and thus our 'being not-protagonist'). Today, this question is indeed deeply grounded in a technological transformation that started at least with the general cybernatization after the Second World War, giving rise to a world of hyper-connected network environments. At the same time, the question has been raised by experiences like climate change and species extinction – phenomena which ultimately present us with the costs of our long-established desire to ignore our ecological embeddedness, i.e. of protagonist hubris. Then again, both these aspects come together in a contemporary condition which accordingly has been called 'ecotechnological', referring to a primal impossibility to divide natural and technological processes any longer and simultaneously taking into account today's role of new object cultures that are more active and automatic, not to mention 'smarter', more and more immersed in our environments, informing our infrastructures, processing our experiences and background, and operating in new micro-temporal regions (Hörl 2015: 3).

Against this background one could in fact easily draw a whole series of – sometimes quite surprising – correspondences between the environmental dependencies tragedy dealt with and the crises, the topics, but also everyday developments of the interconnected 'kosmo-polis' of our times. We could think of questions of climate engineering; we could also think of new forms of human-animal-hybrids, for instance the so-called 'chimeres', i.e. the mice with human pancreas which were generated in Japan in 2019 and were even given the name of the ancient Greek composite creatures: a particularly good example of the fact that 'cosmos' as a hybrid realm of gods, animals, landscapes and humans has indeed been rediscovered as a field of technical manipulation and exploitation (although we of course do not inhabit the classical mythological horizons today).

However, considering the worldwide state of emergency the year 2020 saw, due to a infinitesimally small virus that grew pandemic and is assumed to have sprung from another entanglement between human beings and animals (bats), I would like to close this chapter with a last remark on the seer and the shepherd from the tragedy of Oedipus. Their non-protagonist positions do, as I said before, intertwine in a way that is reminiscent of a Mobius strip. What keeps the two sides of this strip apart, however, is the fact that the blind seer is, other than the shepherd, related to the cosmic ubiquity of the light and the birds: both being important attributes of Apollo (the god of oracles), and both being able to reach each and every place on earth. In contrast, the shepherd is a figure that very strongly indicates the 'here and now' of actual bodies – after all he was an eyewitness of the happenings preceding the tragedy. If both of these figures are nevertheless so closely connected we can find traces of an – again: environmental – knowledge here; a knowledge of the effects and resonances even the smallest activity has on a cosmic level, and vice versa: a bit like an ancient version of the so-called butterfly effect.

Regarding the circumstances of the 2020 pandemic and especially the further enforcement of digital formats it caused – is there not a striking resemblance between this two-fold topology and the two poles that merged in the suddenly omnipresent digital 'home office' with all its worldwide Zoom meetings, being a most recent icon of machinic enslavement and control power? And does on the other hand the vast attack on public sphere in the traditional sense which was another effect of the Corona 'lockdowns' not in a strange way mirror the questioning of the protagonist's location in the tragedy of Oedipus? No wonder 2020 saw a lot of desperate 'oedipal' energy demonstrating in the streets, denying the mere existence of the virus itself and at the same time invoking older forms of public space that have been under attack by technological developments long before the pandemic started.

It is still an open question what will result from this in the future. But even beyond the Corona situation it seems we are just beginning to recognize the contours of a transformation which will certainly introduce further and even more radical forms of environmental governmentality. And it seems an important question whether new ways of critical practice will be found in this situation, ways that do not relapse into the exhausted forms of (protagonist) subjectivity. The knowledge that there is something like a tradition of a chorus which on its own part can be seen as an environment-making form might at least be a good starting point.

References

Annuß, E. (ed.) (2014), 'Volksfiguren', *Maske und Kothurn* 02/14, Wien: Böhlau.
Annuß, E., (ed.) (2017), *kollektiv auftreten*, Tübingen: Narr.
Benveniste, E. (1971), 'Active and Middle Voice in the Verb', in *Problems in General Linguistics*, 145–51, Coral Gables: University of Miami Press.
Bodenburg, J., K. Grabbe and N. Haitzinger (eds) (2016), *Chor-Figuren: Transdisziplinäre Beiträge,* Wien: Böhlau.

Deleuze, G., and F. Guattari (1987), *A Thousand Plateaus: Capitalism and Schizophrenia*, Minneapolis: University of Minnesota Press.

Diogenes Laertius, *Lives of Eminent Philosophers*, Book VII chapter 1: Zenon.

Enzelsberger, G., M. Meister and S. Schmitt (eds) (2012), 'Auftritt Chor. Formationen des Chorischen im Gegenwartstheater', *Maske und Kothurn* 01/12, Wien: Böhlau.

Foucault, M. (1977), *Discipline and Punish: The Birth of the Prison*, New York: Pantheon.

Foucault, M. (2003), *Society Must be Defended: Lectures at the Collège de France 1975–1976*, New York: Picador.

Foucault, M. (2008), *The Birth of Biopolitics: Lectures at the Collège de France 1978–1979*, London: Palgrave Macmillan.

Foucault, M. (2009), *Security, Territory, Population: Lectures at the Collège de France 1977–1978*, London: Palgrave Macmillan.

Foucault, M. (2014), *On the Government of the Living: Lectures at the Collège de France 1979–1980*, London: Palgrave Macmillan.

Haß, U. (2014), 'Die zwei Körper des Theaters. Protagonist und Chor', in Tatari, M. (ed.), *Orte des Unermesslichen: Theater nach der Geschichtsteleologie*, 139–59, Zürich and Berlin: Diaphanes.

Haß, U. (2021), *Kraftfeld Chor: Aischylos Sophokles Kleist Beckett Jelinek*, Berlin: Theater der Zeit.

Hörl, E. (2015), 'The Technological Condition', *Parrhesia: A Journal of Critical Philosophy* 22: 1–15, Melbourne: University of Melbourne. Online at https://www.parrhesiajournal.org/parrhesia22/parrhesia22_horl.pdf (accessed 29 March 2022).

Kirsch, S. (2020), *Chor-Denken: Sorge, Wahrheit, Technik*, Paderborn: Fink.

Rouvroy, A. (2013), 'The End(s) of Critique. Data Behaviourism versus Due Process', in M. Hildebrandt and K. de Vries (eds), *Privacy, Due Process and the Computational Turn*, 142–68, London: Routledge.

Simon, Gérard Simon (1988), *Le regard, l'être et l'apparence dans l'optique de l'antiquité*, Paris: Éditions du Seuil.

Vernant, J.-P., and P. Vidal-Naquet (1990), *Myth and Tragedy in Ancient Greece*, New York: Zone Books.

Part Three

Avatars, masks and cyborgs: Augmenting the reality

7

Digital masks for ancient Greek drama

Artificiality, constraint and metamorphosis

Giulia Filacanapa and Erica Magris

Introduction

Staging Greek drama today is a journey towards the sources of theatre: both a search and an enquiry. The structure of Greek tragedy in particular, resplendent with its striking themes, is a challenge which pushes directors to express, as George Rodosthenous puts it, 'a strong, well-researched vision of re-telling an old story for a contemporary audience' (2017: 7), and to engage with a lost, historically distant, but extremely influential and fascinating form of theatre. Attitudes towards this repertoire vary considerably from adaptation to actualization, either seeking to make it more familiar or, instead, stressing its distance and strangeness. Nevertheless, as observed by Georges Banu, modern staging tend to produce a 'weaving of times' where archaic and contemporary mix (Banu 2015: 9).

By looking at international showcases in recent years, we argue that this is particularly relevant to digital performance – 'all performance works where computer technologies play a *key* role rather than a subsidiary one in content, techniques, aesthetics, or delivery forms' as defined by Steve Dixon (2007: 3) – as Greek myth is a prism through which artists can explore the troubles of our time as well as the unprecedented perspectives opened by the digital revolution. Greek tragedy – as well as the Homeric poem *Odyssey* – offers themes, characters and situations which can function as a metaphor, a resonator or a trigger for digital content and devices.

Through Oedipus, for instance, artists can investigate the boundaries between known and unknown, sight and blindness, by creating interactive performances where the audience's perceptions are challenged. Presenting his *Oedipus reloaded* (2004), Klaus Obermaier describes the character as the first explorer who does not know where he is, who 'wanders lost in the network of high-tech data, blinded by images and information'. Videos are projected on a vast screen and on the performer's body, and also reflected by the water which covers the stage. This hypnotic and metamorphic environment questions 'the shifting boundaries between illusion and reality, between knowledge, belief and memory' (Obermaier 2004). For the experimental company Crew, 'Oedipus symbolizes modern man and his tragic fate. Oedipus is blind when he can see, and he only starts to see when he becomes blind. His personal tragedy is that he never succeeds in obtaining a central perspective on the world' (Crew 2008). In their performance O_REX (2008) one member of the audience wears a virtual reality headset and is immersed in a virtual world while all the others watch a different show (see also Poulou in Chapter 2 above). More recently, Theater of War Productions launched the online initiative *The Oedipus Project* in order to develop 'powerful, healing online conversations about the impact of the COVID-19 pandemic upon diverse communities throughout the United States', in the same way as Sophocles' tragedy about 'arrogant leadership, ignored prophecy, and a pestilence' was a 'powerful public health tool for helping Athenians communalize the trauma of the plague' (Theater of War 2019) which had ravaged the city at the time. During the spring 2020 lockdown, Elli Papakonstatinou, who had already created in 2019 an immersive opera on freedom and necessity inspired by Oedipus' myth, worked on *Antigone* with six performers shut in their homes by using videoconferencing technology. *Traces of Antigone*, first performed online and now touring in real theatres, is a digital 'theatre of seclusion' where the myth is key to investigating gender inequality and sexual violence (Papakonstatinou 2019).

A strong echo between the myth and our time is also found in the story of Prometheus: it is through this portmanteau figure that multiple works are able to investigate the contradictions of technological innovation, as in *Da Prometeo. Indomabile è la notte* by Oscar de Summa (2019) and the *Internet Trilogy* by Urland (2014–16), where the fire of the myth becomes the Web. The Dutch collective explains that 'just as fire means both progress and destruction, so the Internet contains both the utopian promise and the dystopian decline. Urland wants to go beyond good and evil, and that too is playing with fire' (Urland 2016). The company develops theatrical applications for a complex series of different devices – motion capture; 3D virtual reality; the robot Fanuc S-500; the hardware and software for musical production Ableton among others – in order to create a digital universe of characters, stories and environments. In these productions, we observe that technologies are central to the dramaturgy by shaping both the writing and the staging, as well as by creating a thematic connection between the myth and our world.

The encounter between archaic and ultra-contemporary elements is also at the core of our practice-based research *Masks and avatars*, held from 2015 to 2018 in order to understand digital augmentation in theatre from the actor's point of view. This research was part of the broader Labex Arts-H2H project *La scène augmentée* directed by Erica Magris with the collaboration of Giulia Filacanapa, Georges Gagneré and Cédric Plessiet (both of them Associate Professor at the Departement of Arts and Technology of the Image, Univ. Paris 8). The project aimed to investigate acting techniques and dramaturgical possibilities in an augmented stage by establishing an analogy between digital technology and practices inherited by the tradition of theatre mask. Our team of theatre historians, computer scientists, and artists (actors, directors, digital artists) designed and implemented a motion capture device for the real time animation of digital avatars on stage, and created several short performances. The device relies on the digital platform AKeNe, developed over several years by the Digital Images and Virtual Reality team (INRéV Univ. Paris 8) by using an existing video game engine, Unreal, in order to preview motion capture data in real-time. The architecture of AKeNe, therefore, modifies the game engine and makes it suitable to be used in theatre. In our initial experimentations, at least two actors are always involved: one is masked and the other (the 'mocaptor') animates the avatar thanks to a mocap suit. The latter is present in a 3D digital space, whose image is projected on a screen at the back of the stage.

During the workshop *Tragedy 2.0: an augmented actor and stage for Ancient Greek drama* coupled with the symposium *Ancient Drama & Digital Era* (Michael Cacoyannis Foundation, Athens, 1–7 October 2018), we sought to reflect on how our specific technological device, as well as our research frame, could constitute an instrument to question and analyze Greek drama in its own richness and complexity. Two groups were formed for the workshop, one directed by Giulia Filacanapa on Aristophane's *Lysistrata*, one directed by Guy Freixe on Aeschylus' *Agamemnon*, both specialists in masked theatre. Two performances were presented at the end of the week: *Lysistrata 2.0*[1] (Filacanapa and Magris 2022) and *Agamemnon*. Moreover, Andy Lavender, a digital theatre specialist, presented *Agamemnon Redux* inspired by Aeschylus, on which he had worked for several years during the previous stages of the *Masks and avatars* project.

The frame: Digital technologies as masks

In order to understand the relationship between mask and digital technologies at the base of our research, it is necessary to consider the theatrical meaning of the mask as an object but also as a concept. Theatre has always been the place of augmented reality, whether of space or of the actor's body. In this sense, the theatrical mask is to be considered as the instrument *par excellence* of the actor's augmentation and metamorphosis: an artificial extension of the human body which transforms it into a hybrid one characterized by specific acting codes. The return to the mask in Western theatre during the twentieth century is an attempt to overcome illusionism and realism, in order to rediscover the strangeness and the otherness which can arise on stage. 'The mask is the ideal head of the theatre', writes Edward Gordon Craig (Craig 1921), and Charles Dullin echoes this when he states that 'the use of the mask strangely coincides with the most beautiful, or at least the most refined, moments of theatre' (Dullin 1946). The mask returns to Western theatre practices as a means of transfiguration, but also, for the actor, as a tool of training and acting. Jacques Copeau used the mask to restore the body's expressive power, because thanks to it the actor no longer can count on his/her facial expressions (Freixe 2010: 115–157). In fact, these objects force the actor to develop new expressive means, and in this way the voice, the gestures and the body as a whole become elements as important and significant as the spoken word. Are these features exclusive to the mask as an object or can they be deployed through other scenic means, specific to our digital era? Here we will argue that these technological devices can be considered as masks.

From the cameras and screens used on stage in Guy Cassiers' and Katie Mitchell's shows, and Robert Lepage's technological sets to Marcel·lí Antunez Roca's exoskeletons and Crew's experienced virtual doubles (Feral 2018; Monteverdi 2018), the study of multiple variations of the actor's relationship to analogue and digital technologies has led us to formulate the hypothesis that the mask can help us to understand the actor's response to new technologies and augmented stages. Indeed, in all the experiences mentioned above, although very diverse, technology creates alterity (sometimes even duplicity), thanks to the three fundamental conditions specific to the mask: artificiality, constraint and metamorphosis. Technological devices determine unnatural postures and functional gestures, modifying the presence registers and scale of the actors' movements; the body, face and voice are thus transformed, in a process that involves not only the spectator's perspective, but also the actor and his/her techniques.

In our perspective, the mask-avatar device is thus a 'technological mask', a dramaturgical and acting tool which, on the one hand, has a set of specific technological features as well as acting codes, on the other hand, is open to stage different dramaturgies and characters. Our aim is to investigate the theoretical and creative bridges connecting new technologies and ancient tragedy, starting from its specific dramaturgy and its original staging. Three possible formal equivalences, which are at the very core of this theatre form, and which constitute a challenge to contemporary directors and audiences, emerge: the mask, the chorus and the space.

Greek drama and the mask-avatar device

The first bridge between our device and Greek drama is undoubtedly the mask. As Thanos Vovolis put it:

> It is impossible to imagine the ancient Greek theatre without the mask, whether it be tragedy, comedy or satyr play. The mask was an organic element in the form of theatre that originated in the cult of Dionysus and which was of such great importance in the social and political life of the city state of Athens – theatre as ritual, ceremony, entertainment, education, social, political and philosophical discourse. (Vovolis 2009: 9)

Nevertheless, since then, the West, unlike the East, has not developed an unbroken tradition of masked theatre, with the only exception being Commedia dell'arte. Moreover, as the mask nowadays is generally associated with improvisation, it appears often positioned in opposition to an existing text: if the mask is used in the training of actors in Europe, as mentioned before, it is essentially to free the student's bodily expression, and rarely to work on written words. Ancient theatre is thus unique in the West, as text and mask were inseparable.

The Greek word for theatre mask – *prosopon* – means both mask and face. Françoise Frontisi-Ducroux has clearly explained that, for Greek culture, there is no distinction between them. Both express and reveal; they are a 'projector or a mirror of an outward-oriented personality' (Frontisi-Ducroux 1995: 39). As far as the worn mask is concerned, it 'does not conceal the actor's face. Instead, it abolishes and replaces it' (Frontisi-Ducroux 1995: 40). Also, as the etymology of the word suggests, the face-to-face is inherent to Greek theatre and structures the relationships between the characters, between the characters with the chorus, as well as between them and the audience. Nevertheless, it is a face-to-face between the human and alterity: the mask is a powerful means of metamorphosis which makes possible that mythical characters and gods materialize in the theatre space and live their stories in front of the audience. The mask dehumanizes the human, changes its scale, its proportions, and arouses a tension between natural and artificial, fluidity and rigidity.

In our project, as we have explained, the digital avatar, as well as the motion capture device which brings it to life, is considered as a mask. Thus, we intend to explore how resorting to these two different forms of alterity – Greek masks and digital avatars – could possibly give a contemporary twist to mythical characters and create new, original encounters. It is essential for us to mask all the characters on stage by using masks related to the ancient Greek theatre. We chose the masks created by Ferdinando Falossi based on extensive philological research on iconographic sources, materials and ancient manufacturing techniques (Falossi 2022). They are whole masks that cover not only the actor's face but his/her entire head. In this way the realistic features of the actor's face are lost, and his/her vital essence is accessible only through tiny holes for the eyes and the mouth. As Falossi points out, 'the sight of the tragic hero is none other than the sight of the Human, without any connotation of personality' (Falossi 2022).

For this reason, his tragic masks seem very similar to neutral masks: static faces befitting the canons of classical, hieratic and inexpressive beauty; 'as in the paintings and statues, men and gods have the same face and countenance' (Falossi 2022). As far as the avatars are concerned, the technological tool imposes some limits. On the one hand, it is possible to choose among the set of figures offered by the Unreal engine. On the other hand, we can improve the quality by using faceless robots or models, on whom only the colour and texture of the surface are modifiable, and upon which it is only possible to put additional elements such as masks. The video game aesthetics of the first typology of figures available, and the mechanical, artificial and impersonal nature of the latter is considered as a creative constraint imposed by the system.

The space where the encounters between masked characters and digital avatars arise is also fundamental in our approach. As Ferdinando Falossi and Fernando Mastropasqua point out:

> The theatre, for the Greeks, seems to be located in that extreme limit of civil life beyond which the kingdom of the night begins; the darkened land of the dead that hides the souls of heroes, mythical ancestors, founders, and their knowledge inaccessible to humans. Darkness and light collide in front of that threshold where *the audience and the actors try to steal the secrets of an afterlife wisdom*. The theatrical place is at the edge, borderline, between life and death, between darkness and light, between the one and the multiple; a magic circle in front of a sacred forest, and between the two places, a threshold, a wall, a diaphragm destined to open. (Falossi and Mastropasqua 2014: 215)

Greek theatrical buildings embody this contradictory meaning: they are meant to organize the collective watching and listening, by defining two different areas, one for those who act and one for those who assist, but at the same time not closing off this temporary assembly to the outside world as they are open to the landscape and to passing everyday life. Its 'generative centre' – to use Fabrizio Cruciani's expression (Cruciani 1999: 74) – is the orchestra which is surrounded around 210 degrees by the *theatron* where the audience sit; the opposite side is closed by the *skené*, that assumes also a fictional meaning as it represents the interior from which the characters come in front of the audience.

Both the exterior of the *skené* and the open air of the theatre as a whole correspond to the exterior fictional location where the drama takes place: for the Greeks it is therefore impossible to have access to the inside, which is invisible and cannot be transposed by convention to the outside. In order to stage the plays created for this specific space to our smaller and completely closed modern theatres, directors often work on equivalences. They translate ancient features to modern ones which can express the threshold between visible and invisible (darkness and light, walls, doors, stairs) and suggest the dynamics between the *skené* and the orchestra. We hypothesize that in our device this double articulation can be transposed to the relationship between the two different spaces which compose it: the real one (the stage) and the virtual one (the 3D space on screen). The images are projected onto a background screen, designed as a window on another dimension, an interface, a threshold that could link the world of the stage to the virtual world.

The question of space – in particular of the orchestra – is entangled with the last imaginary bridge, the chorus. The chorus, as Roland Barthes suggests, 'is what is completely lost' (Barthes 1953: 21) today from Greek drama: this is because, as Evelyne Ertel points out, 'it has totally disappeared from our social life' (Ertel 2007). The chorus entered after the prologue and was always on stage observing the characters and commenting their situation, choices and actions, but also recalling the past and predicting the future. As Lucy Jackson explains, it is a window open towards other worlds (Jackson 2014, 2019). The members of the chorus danced and sang, and resembled each other by their costumes and masks: they formed a collective character which was both a citizens' representative and a guardian of the mythical past and of the religious origins of theatre. In our device, the 3D video projection visually opens to different times and spaces, and digital avatars can be replicated in order to constitute a multitude of performers, as well as various, simultaneous and mobile acting positions on stage and on screen can be adopted. Also, for the mocaptor, the device implies gestures and movements constraints which make its presence hieratic, unnatural.

The performances presented at the Michael Cacoyannis Foundation engaged with these theoretical hypotheses and opened up different understandings of the relationship between digital theatre and Greek drama. Let us now move on to the description and analysis of them.

Agamemnon Redux: Doubling the action line

Scholar and director Andy Lavender's dramaturgical adaptation of Aeschylus' tragedy is based on the principle of condensation. Aeschylus' verses are drastically reduced and simplified. Three scenes are retained – 'Chorus', 'Agamemnon's return', 'Cassandra' – corresponding to different times of the Atreides's tragic stories: first, the past, as the background of the Trojan war and Iphigenia's sacrifice are introduced by the old men chorus; then, the present of the king's arrival, in which, nevertheless, the encounter between him and Clytemnestra is entangled with omens of his imminent murder; finally, the future, which Cassandra sees in her visions and reveals in her monologue, associating it with the terrible slaughter of Thiestes' sons. As the dramaturgy exalts the manifold temporalities of Greek tragedy, the mask-avatars device is exploited to multiply the narrative levels by creating a cinematic storyline which unwinds simultaneously to the action on stage. The 3D world projected on the background, created by Tim White, embraces the video game aesthetics of Unreal.

As in *EXPLORER/Prometheus Ontketend* by Urland, the characters are urban warriors with dark leather jackets, whose bodies are realistic, but whose faces are strangely immobile and inexpressive, or, in some scenes, threatening androids. The landscape they live in is a sunny desert, where a luxurious palace rises up. The virtual cameras move around the space and the characters, which are seen from multiple, cinematographic, points of view. The atmosphere is far from ancient Greece, but evokes instead a gangster or science fiction game such as *Grand Theft Auto* or *Halo*. On the one hand, in Urland's production, the drama takes place in the virtual world and the role of the two 'mocaptors' on stage, who are dimly visible, is just to animate their avatars in the digital space. Showing their actions and movements provokes a distancing effect, which contrasts with the immersiveness of the 3D images and demystifies the technological device. On the other hand, in Lavender's production the action on stage and on screen are equally important and visible. The two performers wear black suits under the mocap ones, as well as Falossi's masks on their head. They speak and move slowly, their few gestures are controlled and hieratic and, at the same time, they play the characters on stage and the avatars in the digital space. Because of the slowness of the action, the audience can progressively understand the performativity of the device and technological connection between the two worlds. The spoken text also binds them together. However, the meanings that assume the same gestures and words differ in relation to each of them.

The digital images show a brutal, contemporary world which in some scenes collides ironically with the solemnity of the words and the posture, for example when the old man relates the Trojan War leaning on a stick, the screen shows a lonely man seated at a bar; or when Clytemnestra welcomes Agamemnon, he gets off a four-wheel drive. The two actions – on stage and on screen – contrast with one another and draw the audience's attention towards two completely different versions of the same story. By concentrating Aeschylus' original text, Andy Lavender creates the conditions for using the digital device in order to exalt the complex textures and meanings of Greek tragedy.

In the final scene, the two storylines begin to converge, focused on Cassandra's monologue, as the images show her visions. Their convergence culminates at the moment of Agamemnon's and Cassandra's slaughter by Clytemnestra: they happen at the same time, one acted on stage by the masked performers who play the prophetess and the queen, and one on the digital world by two avatars animated by the actors themselves. The stabbing gestures of the murderers, the suffering body of the victims are exactly the same, but they are embodied in different characters and times. The device creates an augmented dimension, which concentrates Cassandra's frightening premonitions, the obscene present and the accomplished catastrophe of the tragedy.

Agamemnon: The tragic chorus and the character's inner vision

The staging of *Agamemnon* by scholar, actor and director Guy Freixe also focuses on Cassandra. He intends to use the mocap to conduct a dramatic reflection on the explosion of Cassandra's consciousness when she is taken to Agamemnon's palace where she will be killed by Clytemnestra. Delirious, she foresees what is about to happen, while the chorus observes her and the coryphaeus questions her. In Freixe's staging, Cassandra is played by a live performer, while the chorus is both real and virtual, in this case animated by a single mocaptor. The 3D space is inspired by drawings and engravings by Edward Gordon Craig and Adolphe Appia, and is constructed with straight, simple lines, geometric volumes defining clear directions and acting areas. It is conceived as an extension of the stage: a dark space where heavy walls close a deep corridor leading to the invisible entrance to the palace, accessed by steps.

In the dimly lit stage, first the chorus enters, wearing Lecoq neutral masks. The group must act together and each actor must find the individualized gestures and movements of her character that, nevertheless, should be connected to those of the others by the same strength, intention and breathing. The masked chorus, supported by live music, gradually finds a state of blind anger that pushes it to rush to the captive – personification of the defeated enemy – at the rear, to grasp her and throw her into the centre of the stage. Cassandra is wearing a priestess' mask, with long wool air and bandages, its mouth and eyes frozen. The character comes to life through the body and the altered voice of the actress while she screams: 'Ah! Apollo! Apollo! What pain, Apollo! What pain!' (Aeschylus 2005: line 1075).

At this first invocation of Cassandra, the avatars' chorus appears on screen: a virtual but implacable army of white robots which invades the dark hall leading to the palace. The mocaptor – visible at the left front of the stage – must find a way to express her multiple virtual doubles while acting in harmony with the chorus and the character on stage. Moreover, in order to avoid an excessive standardization of the avatars, they are divided into different rows whose independent positions are decided in real time by two people from the control desk; also, a third person is in charge of the camera movement: the virtual scene is moving, the avatars approach, rise, grow, to the rhythm of Cassandra's visions, in a space that becomes a mental extension of the action. The chorus tries to understand the meaning of what Cassandra says and question the prophetess: 'Apollo? Loxias Apollo? Why him? He is no god in need of wailing women!' (Aeschylus 2005: line 1076). Guy Freixe entrusts the coryphaeus' words to an actor in the right front of the stage, outside the dramatic space, where she reads her lines at the microphone, behind a desk. Thus amplified and separated from the three different embodiments of the chorus – the masked characters, the mocaptor and the avatars – the voice seems to originate and resonate inside Cassandra's head. It strengthens at sound level the subjective, mental effect that the 3D space induces visually.

The dissociation of the different elements of the action – the result of an overall work of the actors on stage, the mocaptor, the three manipulators at the control desk, the coryphaeus and the musician – corresponds to the complexity of the dramaturgy and the staging of the ancient Greek theatre; but here, thanks to the digital device, this dissociation also assumes the contemporary meaning of an internal conflict: the fragmentation of a character's psychological integrity. Diving into the feelings of a victim, a woman conscious of her destiny, the emotion arises and the frozen face of Cassandra's mask seems to change expression and show her suffering, her helplessness and her anger.

Conclusions

The two performances we analysed – *Agamenmon redux* and *Agamemnon* – were created by two different directors in the frame of a common practice-based research on the theatrical potential of a specific motion capture device, itself conceived as a 'digital mask'. This digital mask had a pivotal role in dramaturgy and staging, by its constraints, its artificiality and its power of metamorphosis. This existing device, with its possibilities and its limits, was positioned as an instrument able to shed new light on Greek drama and its staging today. Three bridges between ancient Greek and digital theatre were identified – the mask, the chorus and the theatrical space – in order to establish theoretical and practical parallels between the texts, their original form and the features of a digitally augmented stage and actor. Following these experiences, through the three analytical paradigms of our research, several theoretical reflections arose.

First, the central role of the mask in Greek theatre is a very powerful connection between ancient drama and digital motion capture. Since the rigidity of the entire masks of tragedy and comedy corresponds to the mechanical nature of the avatars, the quality of the characters' presence on stage and on the screen appears particularly compatible. It produces a disorienting but at the same time plausible co-presence between different forms of alterity, which respond to each other in different ways. In the showcase by Guy Freixe, the relationship between the three figures of otherness on stage – Cassandra, the masked members of the chorus and the avatars ones – create a circuit of acquired expressiveness: the expressiveness of the actors' and avatars' bodies and their movement reverberate in the body and the text of the actress who in turn gives them meaning. The digital avatar and the mask produce the same emotional quality of the tension between reality and fiction, life and death, organic and artificial. If the 'mortal' actor plays with an image that cannot die, it is thus necessary to find the organic nature of inorganic material – and vice versa – and the use of masks on stage and in the digital universe reveals itself to be extremely compelling.

Secondly, as far as the chorus is concerned, our experiences proved us that using new technologies and in particular digital avatars, can be a way to reinvent the complex relationship which, in Greek theatre, exists between the characters, the audience and the chorus. In particular to find for the latter a new, contemporary role in mediating between the real – to which the assembly of the spectators belong – and the fictional worlds. The device opens different possibilities: the chorus' movement and chorality through the multiplication of avatars; the tension between the chorus' individual and collective features; proxemics and gesturality during the dialogues between the characters and the chorus.

Moreover, in most of the examples analyzed, the chorus itself is not present as a collective uniform character because of the use of different media and forms of embodiment. The screen tends to aggregate this decomposed chorus, thanks to the very complex and subtle dialogue that the various agents perform through real time. For tragedy, the augmented chorus becomes a mental projection of the character, thus a transfer through interiority, a vision shared by both the character and the audience. It also allows an effective representation of the character's condition; materializing her fears, desires, and passions. In this threefold relationship the masked actor on stage plays with the augmented chorus in a way that sometimes allows the device – how it functions, its potential and its limits – to be revealed.

Finally, the plurality of languages used in ancient Greek theatre (acting, poetry, music, dance) and their spatial articulation in two distinct spaces (the orchestra and the *skené*) allow the establishment of parallels with the dissociative effects produced by technology, not only between the stage and the screen, but also between the different agents involved. In Andy Lavender's *Agamemnon Redux*, the parallel, but organically connected by real time motion capture, storylines on stage and on screen reveal the complex temporal texture of myth in the tragedy, while in Guy Freixe's *Agamemnon* the separation of the chorus in four visible agents – the neutral masks, the mocaptor and the voice on stage, as well as the army of robots on screen – exteriorize the internal dissociation of Cassandra's character.

The real and virtual spaces are not only both in the audience's range of vision, but are also dramaturgically equivalent. Unlike in *EXPLORER/ Prometheus Ontketend* by Urland, where the virtual world projections are highly immersive and the actions on stage, which are functional to the avatars' animation and barely visible, creates a counterpoint to the story on screen, the digital space and the stage are intertwined in producing a fictional world (see also Poulou in Chapter 2 above). In a process similar to the one which involves the spectator of ancient theatre, the spectator of the mask-avatar device creates an imaginative connection between different elements and in particular between the scenic and virtual space. Through this bifurcated vision, it is possible to emphasize liminality and to embody the dialectics between visible and invisible, exterior and interior, essential in Greek drama.

These experiences thus showed an interesting direction for the contemporary staging of the Greek tragedy – certainly still to be explored – in which technology drives new dramaturgical interpretations by bringing this archaic universe closer to the imagination of contemporary audiences while preserving its alterity and distance. Thanks to new technology, the audience is invited to live a collective experience and to take part in this attempt to build a *polis* for the twenty-first century through theatre.

Note

1 *Lysistrata 2.0*, being a comedy, will not be studied in this article because it falls outside the scope of this volume.

References

Aeschylus (2005), *Agamemnon*, trans. G. Theodoridis, https://www.poetryintranslation.com/PITBR/Greek/Agamemnon.php (accessed 28 October 2020).

Banu, G. (2015), 'Avant-propos', in G. Banu (ed.), *Tragédie grecque. Défi de la scène contemporaine*, Etudes théâtrales 21.

Barthes, R. (1953), 'Pouvoirs de la tragédie antique', *Théâtre populaire* 2.

Craig, E. G. (1921), *Exhibition of Drawing and Models and other plays by Edward Gordon Craig*, catalogue of the exhibition at the City of Manchester Art Gallery, 23–25, republished in O. Aslan and D. Bablet, (eds) (1999), *Le masque du rite au théâtre*, 142–3, Paris: CNRS éditions [1985].

Crew (2008), 'O_Rex', production programme, http://www.crewonline.org/art/project/22 (accessed the 24 August 2020).

Cruciani, F. (1999), *Lo spazio del teatro*, Rome and Bari: Laterza [1992].

Dixon, S. (2007), *Digital performance*, Cambridge, MA: MIT Press.

Dullin, C. (1946), 'Considérations sur les acteurs japonais', in *Correspondance*, n° 16, mai 1930, published in *Souvenirs et notes de travail d'un acteur*, 61, Paris: éditions Odette Lieutier.

Ertel, E. (2007), 'La tragédie grecque et sa représentation moderne', in J.-C. Lallias and J.-J. Arnault (eds), *La tragédie grecque. Théâtre aujourd'hui*, (1), CNDP, [1992].

Falossi, F. (2022), 'Entre apparences et mystère', G. Filacanapa, G. Freixe and B. Le Guen (eds), *Le masque scénique dans l'Antiquité. Pratiques anciennes et contemporaines*, Montpellier: Deuxième Époque.

Falossi, F., and F. Mastropasqua (2014), *L'incanto della maschera. Origini e forme di una testa vuota*, Turin: Prinp.

Feral, J. (ed.) (2018), *Corps en scène, l'acteur face aux écrans*, collection 'Les Voies de l'acteur', Léverune: L'Entretemps.

Filacanapa, G., and E. Magris (2022), 'Masques et avatars numériques : premières expérimentations pour le drame antique', in G. Filacanapa, G. Freixe and L. G. Brigitte (eds), *Le masque scénique dans l'Antiquité. Pratiques anciennes et contemporaines*, op. cit.

Freixe, G. (2010), *Les utopies du masques*, collection 'Les Voies de l'acteur', Léverune: L'Entretemps.
Frontisi-Ducroux, F. (1995), *Du masque au visage. Aspects de l'identité en Grèce ancienne*, Paris: Flammarion.
Jackson, L. C. M. M. (2014), *Modern Interpretations of Greek Chorus*, educational video, National Theatre, https://www.nationaltheatre.org.uk/file/modern-interpretations-greek-chorus (accessed the 22/10/2020).
Jackson, L. C. M. M. (2019), *The Chorus of Drama in the Fourth Century BCE. Presence and Representation*, Oxford: Oxford University Press.
Monteverdi, A. M. (2018), *Memoria, maschera e macchina nel teatro di Robert Lepage*, Milan: Meltemi editore.
Obermaier, K. (2004), 'Oedipus reloaded' project programme, http://www.exile.at/oedipusreloaded/project_english.html (accessed 25 August 2020).
Papakonstatinou, E. (2019), 'Traces of Antigone' production programme, https://elli.site/projects/traces-of-antigone/ (accessed 22 October 2020).
Rodosthenous, G. (ed.) (2017), *Contemporary Adaptations of Greek Tragedy: Auteurship and Directorial Visions*, London: Bloomsbury Methuen Drama.
Theater of War (2019), 'The Oedipus Project' project presentation, https://theaterofwar.com/projects/the-oedipus-project (accessed 25 August 2020).
Urland (2016), 'De Internet Trilogie' project programme, https://urland.nl/en/project/de-internet-trilogie/#documentation (accessed 19 August 2020).
Urland (ed.), (2019), *De Internet Trilogie*, Amsterdam: Uitgeverij Karaat.
Vovolis, T. (2009), *Prosopon : The acoustical mask in Greek Tragedy and in Contemporary Theatre: Form, Function and Appearance of the Tragic Mask and its relation to the Actor, Text, Audience and Theatre Space*, Stockholm: Dramatiska institutet, book n. 5.

8

Cassandra in *PythiaDelphine21*

Oracles, cyborgs and the tragedy of Cassandra and temporalities within the digital

Julie Wilson-Bokowiec

Introduction

In 2016 a short residency in Athens and an opportunity to create a new interactive performance piece, to be premiered at the International Animart Festival in Delphi, provided the impetus to explore the synergies between ancient oracular practices and our own cyber-art performance. The piece that resulted, *PythiaDelphine21* (2016), centres on the real-time processing and diffusion of the voice through kinaesonic[1] means with the Bodycoder System. *PythiaDelphine21* was informed by a close reading of Cassandra in Aeschylus' *Oresteia*, the psychogeography of the sanctuary at Delphi, ancient accounts of the oracle, artefacts and the social-political circumstances we encountered in Greece during the making process.

This chapter explores further the trans-historical nature of mediation and the social-political frames it constructs, the spatiotemporal and the boundary busting abilities of oracles and cyborgs. Taking an interdisciplinary approach discourse draws on the writings of Luce Irigaray and Donna Haraway and expands the practice view to look at the Wooster Group's *To You, The Birdie! (Phèdre)* (2002), Le Fura del Baus' 2012 production of *Oresteia* and ODC Ensemble's Zoom production *Antigone Test* (2020). This writing takes us on a journey through landscapes: real and conceptual, theatrical, ontological and technological.

Contexts, architectures, landscapes

Athens in 2016 felt dangerously unstable. There were riots and a tangible sense of both rage and despondency. Government imposed austerity measures were biting and many people were suffering. Greece was also in the grip of a refugee crisis as a result of the war in Syria. When we arrived in February there were fears that the Macedonian border would be closed effectively trapping refugees inside Greece; this happened in March following a European Union/Turkey summit which also resulted in countries further up the Balkans closing their borders to refugees. For Greece this felt like a two-pronged attack aimed at destabilizing the country, and there was talk of impending military action. While in Athens we experienced rioting in Exarchia: a soundscape that found its way into *PythiaDelphine21*, as did the sounds of the central fish market which we recorded following conversations with our hosts who told us that islanders had, out of respect and health concerns, stopped eating fish because of the mass drowning of refugees in the Aegean. In Delphi, on the eve of our performance of *PythiaDelphine21*, the valley shook with the sudden and deafening sound of three Turkish fighter jets swooping in from the Gulf of Corinth, the hotel staff froze and quickly checked their mobile phones: perhaps Greece was now under attack! In ancient times the oracle at Delphi was consulted at moments of great social and political turmoil; 2016 felt like one of those moments.

At Delphi and Athens the ancient theatre buildings sit within larger sanctuary complexes. At Delphi the sanctuary established in the eighth century BCE operated as a sacred, social/political, cultural and psychophysical well-being/healing centre with its main activities focused around a cyclical calendar of festivals. The ruins of the amphitheatre seen today sits on the slope above the temple of Apollo where the Pythian oracle could be consulted initially once a year in the month of Byzios (February-March) but as the influence of Delphi spread during the sixth century access to the oracle was extended. The proximity of the two buildings meant that the vista from the audience' perspective must have included full or partial sight of the temple of Apollo immediately below and beyond, backed by mount Kirphis and the deep valley between containing the great 'sea of olives' (the sacred grove) stretching down to the Gulf of Corinth, to Itea and the beginning of the Sacred Way (the pilgrims' path from the sea to the sanctuary). The psychogeography of the sanctuary complex is significant because it embodies psychophysical engines that configure the audience experience of ancient Greek tragedy. Firstly, the physical proximity of the sacred: at Delphi this was Apollo and his human mouthpiece the Pythian oracle. Secondly, the sense of a literal immediate past and a transformational journey from the domestic to the liminal space of the sanctuary, signified by the sight of the *Sacred Way*. Thirdly, a visceral sense of the present seated within a landscape in which the prehistoric past; the origin myths of the founding of the ancient audiences cultural identity from which the older mytho-cult phenomena of snakes (pythons), eagles and the earthly totems of Gaia are very much alive. This is landscape as *flesh* – a place of visceral/bodily encounter with cultural identity. In such a landscape what lies beneath and beyond the present is a tangible past that also offers an intimation of a future. This fourth, fathomable/imaginable *future* dimension, falls in part to the performance action itself to expose, but it is also embodied within the landscape as a potential. This future is possible because 'the visible landscape has the other moments of time 'behind itself' precisely in that the future waits beyond the horizon, as well as *behind* every entity that I see, as an unseen 'other side' of the many visibles that surround me' (Abram 2017: 215). This way of perceiving the world is common among cultures where place and origin genealogies are attached to landscape. We find it fully embodied in the topology of Delphi and seeded, particularly in the expositions, of Aeschylus' *Agamemnon* and *Eumenides (The Oresteia)* as cultural scene setting that deepens, reminds and heightens what is visible and/or dramatically signified within the present and known landscape. Although the significance and aliveness of such ancient cultural orientations are lost to contemporary non-Greek audiences, and seated in an enclosed darkened theatre building we are dissociated from a rich psychogeographic context of nature/culture. Nevertheless the aesthetic trace of an enriched landscape is still present in the aliveness of past, present and future embedded in the performance aesthetic and theatre experience itself.

> The sensorial landscape (world of the play) ... not only opens onto that distant future waiting beyond the horizon (the promise of events to come) but also onto a near future, onto an immanent field of possibilities waiting behind every (word), behind every (action), behind each (idea, image, sound) from whence a (thought) may at any moment come crawling into our awareness. And this living terrain (of the performance) is supported not only by that more settled or sedimented past under the (cultural) ground, but by an immanent past resting inside each (vocalization), within each (movement), within each (lived idea, image and sound), within the very muscles and cells of our own bodies. (Abram 2017; Wilson-Bokowiec)[2]

The connection between ancient analogue forms embodied in myth linked to landscape/nature, drafted through the earliest forms of Greek tragedy, settled inside a generalized contemporary performance aesthetic are, I would suggest, reinvigorated by the specificities of digital mediation where past, present and an imagined/foreseen (and materialized) future become malleable and dynamic.

An arsenal of technologies: Temporalities, channelling and synchronicities

For digital theatre makers, dark and/or blank spaces and screen offer potentially empty/neutral environments in which to construct unique landscapes and architectures. Companies such as the Wooster Group have laid down layers of making practice in the same empty space (The Performance Garage) over a number of decades – in effect creating their own past. They have generated rituals, crafting practices and ways-of-being that are uniquely their own. They have forged material relationships and generated remnants and artefacts that have a tendency to resurface in a variety of works. These accumulations settle around the work as *flesh*, as a dimensional psychogeographic terrain, as available grounds for new work, as an ever evolving culture, one in which its origins are referenced and constantly honoured.

The Wooster Group's performance environment includes a huge arsenal of technologies with which they freely play with spatial and temporal forms, with disjunction and fragile synchronicities. At the same time the Wooster Group's performance terrain is never hermetically sealed; materials from the wider cultural sphere past and present are included in works. In *To You, The Birdie! (Phèdre)* (2002) randomly spliced video sequences (that change from performance to performance) from Martha Graham's *Voices of Desire: Phaedra*, Marx Brothers and Merce Cunningham pieces are diffused across live-feed monitors viewed by the actors (these are not visible to the audience) to inform actors movement choices, gestures, postures and aid the generation of acting impulses. The company refers to this as *channelling*, as a deliberate attempt to bring the spirit of the pre-existent into the space/place of performance and to use it as a means/strategy for choosing (or indeed thwarting) physical/vocal behaviours (Bogart 2012: 283; Cartelli 2019). The additional use of in-ear monitors worn by the actors allows Elizabeth LeCompte as director to feed actors instructions and suggestions during performances. This adds another layer of information to be channelled *on the fly* by the actors.

Emma Cole suggests that the effect is acting that 'made it clear that the performers were being controlled, puppet-like, by external forces as there was an almost methodical, robotic-like manner to their behaviour' (Cole 2020: 155). Where for Cole the effect is one of pervasive alienation, I see actor's choices in the moment of performance, the critical intensity and immediacy of their effort. I see a kind of disassociation in operation that separates and objectifies all the component parts of the work – its physical, visual, acoustic, time and space temporalities – making each distinctive aspect a potential subject for the audience's gaze and consideration of the audience.

Le Fura del Baus' 2012 production of Xenakis' *Oresteia* at the Suntori Hall in Tokyo with Takashi Matsudaira in the role of Kassandra/Athena fully engages the underlying mathematic, architectural and spatiotemporal dimensions of Xenakis' work within its visual production design. The production features video mapping and digital imagery (computer graphics, texts in Japanese and English, hieroglyphs and constellational representations), some interactive technologies are employed (sound to image triggering and manipulation), large mechanical stage devices and trans/neutral/non-binary costuming. This production is important in light of Xenakis' suggestion (within the programme notes for the 1967 partial staging which did not include the Kassandra section added in 1987 and La Déesse Athéna added in 1992) that the traditional forms of Kabuki and Noh Theatre offer a potential 'mediation ground' and solutions to the problems of staging ancient Greek plays in particular with regard to the treatment of the voice sung or spoken and the vocal poetry of ritual sonorities (Xenakis 1967).

Digital spaces and on-line environments

As well as physical spaces a range of digital and on-line environments is used for the making and presentation of new theatre work. Commercial platforms such as Zoom, StreamYard, CrowdCast and Facebook; on-line repositories of recorded media such as Vimeo, YouTube, Bandcamp etc.; and an ability to code, stream and co-opt such platforms, contents and features as a digital theatre space/place is an aesthetic/design choice that weaves the temporalities, tools, manners and prevalence of social media into the context of new theatre works.

Antigone Test by Elli Papakostantinou and ODC Ensemble, an interdisciplinary piece based on *Traces of Antigone* by playwright Christina Ouzounidis that premiered on Zoom on 18 May 2020. Described as 'a digital show created and performed on line in seclusion',[3] the work was rehearsed on line and performed live with each of the seven performers live streaming from their own domestic living space to a viewing audience spectating via the Zoom platform. The look and experience of the work was very much shaped by the front-end aesthetic and technical limitations of the Zoom platform. Elli Papakostantinou remarked that the work called for a 'low-tech craftswomanship'[4] approach to the platform limitations and use of resources available to each performer within their own domestic situations. For the geographically dispersed company separated in some cases by time zones, one of the problems they encountered was streaming latency that made synchronizing sound and images difficult.

Choric speaking and music making had to be presented in such a way that it incorporated latencies. Some sequences positively emphasized the dissociation between sound and images. Actors manipulated the inherent architecture of Zoom's fixed frame dimensions by moving to, from and across the camera view, they created paper cut-outs to re-frame mouths, eyes, body parts, blocked off and switched off to create notional exits that also served to direct the gaze of viewers toward active frames. The company worked hard to open the multi-frame 'depth of field' creating vistas into created spaces, domestic/home rooms and garden environments. However, for all the creative responses to the limitations of Zoom the overwhelming impression was of a performance caught in the cells and breakdown frames of a restrictive architecture that imposed its particular temporality of time processing lag and other random broadcast glitches on the work. Zoom's ubiquitous agency inextricably infiltrated the moral/cultural and spatiotemporal core of the action.

The Bodycoder System and *PythiaDelphine21*

Standing amidst the ruins of the sanctuary at Delphi in the present day it is clear that the amphitheatre is not simply a neutral container for dramatic action, but a sophisticated immersive environment, geographically sited and architecturally engineered for optimum sensual, psychological and cultural stimulation. New technologies (devices/hardware), digital environments (platforms) and their associated software/coding architectures can create equally resonant spaces of encounter. The Bodycoder System in its configuration for *PythiaDelphine21* attempts such a multiplicity of spatiotemporal, sensorial and cultural dimensionality. The performance schematic (see Fig. 8.1) offers a partial visualization of the field of encounter: in essence a map of the trans-historical connections, underlying digital architecture, hardware, bodies and the motifs of the social-political circumstances that marked its passage into the world.

Since its inception in 1995 the Bodycoder[5] has been described as a *system* in deference to its collection of human and nonhuman elements. These comprise of the bodies of a performer and a composer (a porous and fluid designation) computer hardware and various software programming environments, sensor hardware, radio/wireless elements, microphone(s), multichannel loudspeaker array, image projection (when visuals are incorporated) monitor(s), lighting and costume. Not a singular thing-in-itself like an instrument, tool or indeed an architecturally fixed platform, *system* is the correct noun for a complex whole formed from inter-related parts. System also suggests a network of underlying and interconnected principles, ways of being, methods and schemas. A stratification of elements laid down over the twenty-five years that the system has been evolving

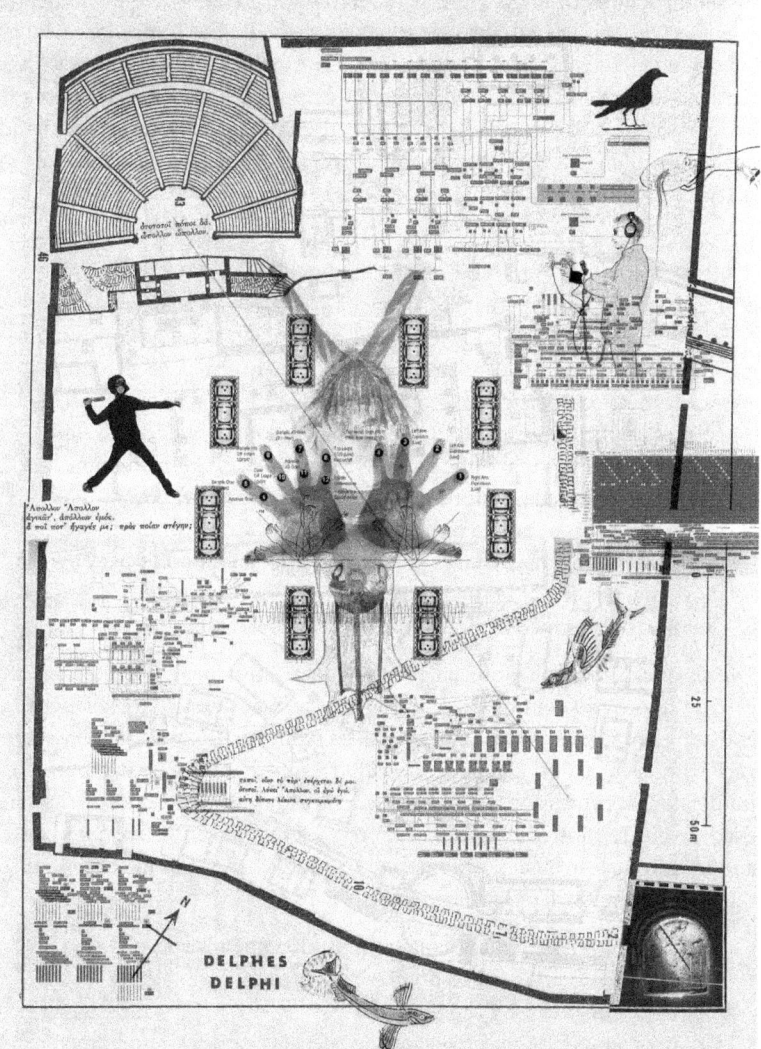

Fig. 8.1 Performance Schematic: *PythiaDelphine21*.

through practice. The hardware end of the Bodycoder system is our notional Performance Garage although unlike the Wooster Group's workspace, its presence is less bricks and mortar than code, computer and loudspeakers.

In *PythiaDelphine21* we utilize a multi-channel loudspeaker system to create a shape-shifting immersive sound environment in which both audience and performer are equally enveloped. In this space the sense and sensation of other (human and non-human) sonic presences are encountered. These are either related to the performer (as second order sonic identities) or hybrid independent others. Acoustic phenomena that enter and move within the space as live and automated processes mapped to implicit (utilitarian) as well as well as explicit (expressive) physical gestures. Literal sleight-of-hand operations alongside explicit gestural kinaesonic manipulation, giving rise to six types of perceivable phenomena:

1. A seen and heard mediation enacted by the performer – one-to-one real-time (gesture-to-sound) kinaesonic manipulation.
2. Auditory phenomena that seem to enter the acoustic field as independent entities.
3. Sound that is seen to be associated with the performers vocal gestures that is transformed electro-acoustically into other sound entities. These entities can be subjected to further re-mediation giving rise to:
4. Re-mediated live kinaesonic manipulation: a sample re-mediation mapped/controlled by another part of the performer's body.
5. Diffusion that is a sample re-mediation moved away from the body of performer to the loudspeaker system and into autonomous patterns that move independently in the space.
6. The simply amplified acoustic voice of the performer.

This palette of sonic phenomena and their associative forms of mediation are used to frame and contain dramatic actions and position characterful sonic entities. They also explicitly sonify qualities of interaction with unseen others variously shaped as dialogue, as choric intervention, as possession/immersion, as expressions of empowerment and control. In addition they are used to create dimensional atmospheres, suggesting unseen architectures, and to introduce acoustic scenography that indicates a shift in scene setting. Structurally the work operates on multiple levels:

- Technical/compositional/architectural substrate (unseen)
- Expressive/utilitarian kinaesonic live interaction (visibly embodied by the performer)
- Dramatic/emotional/electro-acoustic effects (heard/felt and immersive)
- Spatial diffusion soundscape (live, automated and signified)

- Temporal dimensionality (live, live sampled and re-articulated in the immediate future, and recorded in a past outside the piece).

Live sampling and the introduction of field recordings bring past temporalities and locations sonically into the performance space. These widen the spatiotemporal frame of the work and bring a lensed set of social-political resonances into moments of the piece. Live sampling of the acoustic and/or processed voice in performance brings the immediate past (seconds ago) into states of present temporality. Sampled sound is held in the present through the use of automated spatial diffusion that gives the sounds movement trajectories that echo, refract, and ripple within the space. These forward moving trajectories serve as platforms or sonic scenography across which other future voices enter, traverse and exit.

What is seen and unseen in our work is very important. The majority of the hardware and software technology used in our work is hidden from the audience. With the exception of data gloves and the radio microphone the rest of the performers' sensor array is concealed beneath a costume. There are several reasons for this: first, we try to avoid the inscriptive nature of technology – the banded and custom tools should not be what defines the work; and secondly it focuses the audience attention on the act of mediation rather than the means of mediation. The slight glimpses (gloves, microphone) signal the presence of the technological but it is minimized and fleeting. The Bodycoder aesthetic is completely different from that of the Wooster Group where technology is at the forefront of works such as *To You, The Birdie*. As we have seen quantity and presence of the technological/digital does not necessarily equate to ubiquitous inscription while something as basic and seemingly benevolent as Zoom can be impactful. Careful consideration of what is seen and unseen was clearly a concern for ancient oracular practice at Delphi.

Plutarch (45/50 to 120/125 CE), an ordained priest serving in both the Temple of Apollo Delphi and the sanctuary in Athens in the second century, suggests that certain unseen ecstatic techniques[6] were deployed that enabled the oracle to enter into an altered state, opening a connection to the unseen Other (Apollo). Such was the hidden nature of the transformation that the presence of the unseen other had to be verified for the supplicants. Plutarch describes the use of a goat in this process: if the goat trembled before the oracle, then Apollo was in the room. A certain amount of staging was also employed; the oracle sometimes appeared harnessed. The harness may have been a sign in the same way that data gloves and radio microphone is a sign that technology is deployed in our Bodycoder work. There is an undoubted mystery attached to those things that are hidden from view: the transformation of the oracle perhaps foreshadows the transformation of the actor in the ancient Greenroom. The layers of unseen sounds and images channelled by the actors in *To You, The Birdie* are deliciously mysterious and powerfully seductive.

In the loop: Cryptic utterances and intermediary control

At the height of Delphi's influence, supplicants, including rulers from across the ancient world from Greece, Persia and the Roman Empire, came to seek divine guidance on issues ranging from declarations of war and campaign tactics to domestic and personal problems. Plutarch writes that the Pythian oracle's responses to questions posed often required translation and interpretation by a presiding priest from near gibberish and/or cryptic utterances into a form that might hold some meaning for the supplicant. This remediation of information through a significantly male translator – a secondary processing loop (see Fig. 8.2) – changed the nature of what was uttered by the Pythia. The supplicant then had to fathom the meaning of the interpretation offered based on their own judgement and common sense. Clearly the role of the intermediary priest was one of immense power and influence since they were in a position to massage the message in order to satisfy and/or promote political/personal agendas, and to mitigate the dangers and impact of the raw and unadulterated voice of a divine Other.

Ultimately it was the biased and inauthentic nature of this intermediary control that sullied the reputation of the oracle and caused the demise of Delphi's influence in later antiquity. What is important, for this discourse, is the identification of the links in the mediation chain, these represent processing loops that transform the raw into information.

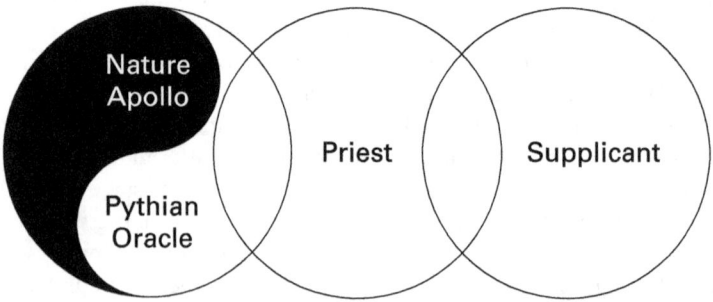

Fig. 8.2 Oracle mediation loop.

Luce Irigaray suggests that it is through the transformation of raw experience into information: the relationship of *matter* to *form* and the interval *between* the two that delivers a notion of place on the social/political/cultural spectrum. Irigaray proposes that 'each age assigns limits to this trilogy, be they *matter, form, interval* or *power, act, intermediate – interval*' (Irigaray 1991: 167). Because through limitation and the fixing of identities inside a notion of place the social/political/cultural spectrum becomes solidified around a narrow immobilising set of relational powers, principles and values. Limitation of interaction and mediation produces a social/political/cultural status quo. Call the first loop in the mediation chain (the Pythia's contact with Apollo/Nature) *experience/raw DATA* and we begin to understand how the policing of access to experience/raw data by a powerful elite is an archaic invention as well as a contemporary concern. Part of the characteristics of the current technology driven status quo is the squeezing of social interaction onto enclosed and restrictive communications platforms designed to mine/control data for the purpose of converting it into capital. Platforms such as Zoom, Facebook, Twitter etc. are by nature powerful and prescriptive.

In *PythiaDelphine21*, we place the audience in the gap between the performer and her dissociated voice(s) and other sonic entities diffused within the loudspeaker system. The audience is literally inside the field of disassociation. The one-to-one mapping of sound to human gesture anchors sound to the presence of the performer, even though it emanates from the loudspeaker system on the periphery of the performance space. The ancient Greeks rationalized this type of sonic phenomena in the myth of Echo disembodied, incarcerated in rock or condemned to reverberation and reflection. Such mythologies draw attention to a perceptual attenuation of an absent presence. Extreme processing of the acoustic voice often creates sounds that seem unrelated to the human voice, they are nevertheless all derived from the materiality of the voice. Automated movement patterns within the loudspeaker system gives sounds independent trajectories. Manipulating pitch produces shifts in vocal gender types.

The space is populated with characterful sonic entities, with glitch infestations, howler tones, clustering sonic-amphibians, and swirling flocks of synthetic granular flyers with their own spatiotemporal dimensions.[7] There is a strategic disconnect between what the audience sees and what they hear – only gesture (kinaesonic) provides a partial relational logic. The emphasis is on the sound world being created, on the act of mediation and the experience of being inside the loop with the performer: an experience that is perhaps akin to that of supplicants before the oracle. By removing from the sight of the audience much of the technology used to accomplish the extraordinary interactive electro-acoustic sound worlds associated with our work, we are deliberately creating an illusion of direct and inexplicable transformation. In this chosen act, a female performer is in complete control of the live processing of her own voice, and is experienced as the author of that extraordinary sound world. For the audience, our work in effect removes the priest/technology ring from the oracular mediation loop (Fig. 8.2).

Aeschylus, through Cassandra in *Agamemnon,* presents us with a similarly unrestrained female oracle. Cassandra extracted from her sacred/royal context, she is an oracle sprung from a conventional structure of mediation. Aeschylus uses Cassandra as a device whose function is to disrupt social/political, ethical/moral and spiritual norms, in this respect she might be considered a proto-cyborg: a boundary busting entity.

Of oracles and cyborgs: Transitions and perceptions

According to Donna Haraway, 'Cyborgs are about particular sorts of breaching boundaries that confuse a specific historical people's stories about what counts as distinct categories crucial to the culture's nature-technical evolutionary narratives' (Haraway 2000:127). Haraway's terminology is specific to and grounded in cyborg entities that became possible around the Second World War and just after, that are intimately involved in 'histories of militarisation, of specific research projects with ties to psychiatry and communications theory, behavioural research and psychopharmacological research, theories of information and information processing' (Haraway 2000: 128–9).

As such the Delphic oracle and the character of Cassandra do not fit within Haraway's definition; however, they do share a number of characteristics, and are equally capable of generating similar destabilizing effects. What is true, for both oracles and cyborgs, is that their boundary-breaching nature stems from an ability to inhabit transitory states and to embody levels of multiplicity that problematize simple and/or binary solutions. They are *different* by nature, skills and/or use of technologies and inhabit and/or unite different spatial and temporal dimensions. In their *difference from* the normative version of humanity, they represent a future evolutionary possibility and a potentially new way of viewing and experiencing the world. Therefore, oracles and cyborgs possess the ability to force a reassessment of notions of place/space, identity and temporality in a way that challenges social/political and cultural frames since they offer other ways of seeing and perceiving the world of things and ideas (see also Poulou's analysis in Chapter 2 above). It is through the articulation of other possibilities that oracles and cyborgs give birth to the new. This is perhaps why both cyborg entities and oracles are so tightly restrained – because the kind of new they represent is *different* from that legitimized within the status quo.

> The transition to a new age ... necessitates a new perception and a new conception of *time* and *space,* our *occupation of place,* and the different *envelopes known as identity.* (Irigaray 1991: 167)

Cassandra is an oracle torn from her sacred setting: there are no priests to mediate and interpret her words. Moreover, the gift of prophecy had been granted to her by Apollo in exchange for her (sexual) affection, and because she denied this, Apollo has laid a curse on her words: although she can see the future, no one will believe her.

This critical biographical information is given to the audience prior to the onset of Cassandra's prophetic visions. The play centres on the relationship between male and female, and Aeschylus is about to disrupt the rights and powers of gods and mortals and their powers to act upon each other. This can only be broached by a cyborg; a 'boundary breaching' character that sits in the liminal space between the mortal and divine and has the power to traverse past, present and future temporalities 'endlessly *passes through the envelope or envelopes* from one end to the other, postponing every deadline, revising every decision, undoing the very idea of repetition' (Irigaray 1991: 173).

Cassandra is in essence an *event horizon;* standing at the edge of the visible, known world she brings the future into the present temporality of the play. When prophetic visions descend upon Cassandra it is the chorus (mortal elders) the common people who witness and wrestle with the meaning and consequences of her words. The god Apollo does not speak to or through Cassandra, the words that both chorus and audience hear are not

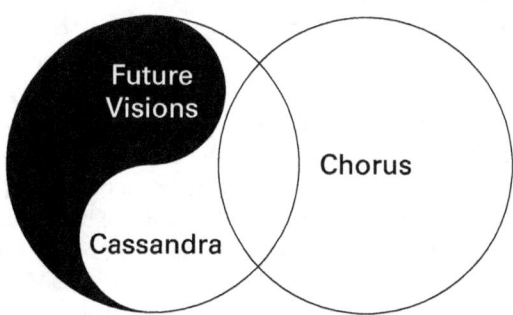

Fig. 8.3 Cassandra mediation loop.

interpreted by an intermediary priest, or come from the immutable authority of a God, what they hear is raw data, a literal report from the future in the moment of its transmission.

Disruption of the moral/ethical compass at the heart of the myth was perhaps quite radical at the time and it is clear I would suggest that Aeschylus worked hard within the text to strengthen the impact heightening the resonance for its intended audience. He employs text-based techniques (witty jokes and ironic banter) at key moments to suspend the course of Cassandra's prophecy:

> **Cassandra**
> Surely though, you must have missed the meaning of my prophecies.
> **Chorus**
> Aye, since I do not understand the scheme of him who is to do the deed.
> **Cassandra**
> And yet all too well I know the speech of Hellas.
> **Chorus**
> So too do the Pythian oracles; yet they are hard to understand.
> (Aeschylus 1926: 109–11)

The distance created by such interventions – a comic/ironic breathing space – ensures that the delivery of the moral/ethical polemic that follows is not subsumed by the seductive drive and passive reception of the dramatic narrative that is known to the audience.

What comes next is a description of the matrix of unfettered murder and revenge that viscerally exposes the moral/ethical problem at the core of the myth. This elevates the simple retelling of a popular myth onto a higher plane. The impact of this moment is enhanced by Cassandra's physical act of condemnation of Apollo by trampling the insignias of her prophetic office into the ground 'Thee at least I will destroy before I die myself. / To destruction with you! / And fallen there, thus do I avenge myself on you' (1926: 111). It cannot be underestimated how shocking this action might have been for the audiences of antiquity. This is followed by a visceral and self-affirming acceptance of a foreseen death 'I dare to die' (1926: 113). While the chorus attempts to ennoble her acceptance of death, Cassandra refuses the 'illusion' of nobility; instead, she describes the squalid nature of her ending in a house that reeks of blood-dripping slaughter that smells like breath from a charnel house, exclaiming that such is the end of all human fortune. Cassandra exits the stage knowing that she is walking toward death. A scream is heard from the palace (announcing the murder of Agamemnon) and the chorus empowered by their first-hand knowledge of what is happening (this is Cassandra's prophecy) deliver their opinions on the course of action to be taken. Aeschylus gives us a chorus of 'common people' expressing themselves as individuals, on the brink of taking matters into their own hands. This is revolutionary: an action that threatens to upset the status quo.

Ultimately Aeschylus does not follow through. Nevertheless, the possibility has been proposed and it inhabits the Oresteia as a background potential. The reason why Aeschylus' Cassandra is such a great disruptive device (and coincidentally why the Pythian oracle is heavily policed) is because she is *Other to / Different from*. By other/different and to/from I mean to emphasize the multi/trans dimensional nature of the identity/place/space occupied by the Cassandra device which also means that no human, divinity or time/space can claim the device (or place that it occupies) as its own (the device does not belong to and is not therefore partisan or subject to) but crucially she is akin (a kin) to all. Only a device/being (cyborg by its trans and boundary-breaching nature) that is *different* and independent, can bring about the kind of coexistent 'being-with' that marks the birth of a new order of existence, because:

> The link uniting or reuniting masculine and feminine must be both horizontal and vertical, terrestrial and celestial ... this link must forge an alliance between the divine and the mortal, in which a (sexual) encounter would be a celebration, and not a disguised or polemic form of the master-slave relationship. In this way it would no longer be a meeting within the shadow or orbit of a God (the Father) who alone lays down the law, or the immutable mouthpiece of a single sex. (Irigaray 1991: 174)

Xenakis places his Kassandra at the centre of his Oresteia opera and limits the figures of Agamemnon, Clytemnestra, Orestes and Electra. Perhaps Xenakis recognized the radical potential of Aeschylus' Cassandra; certainly his musical setting and choices go a long way to configuring in musical practice the multi/trans dimensional nature of the identity/place/space occupied by Kassandra in the Oresteia.

Exit in *wonderment* with a summary conclusion: Solidification of value and notions of place and space

In this chapter I have tried to highlight a number of connections between landscape, the spatiotemporal, the historical and the use of technology, focused around the synergies between ancient oracular practices and mediation. The physical proximity of oracular practice and the theatre can be observed in the sanctuary complexes of Delphi and Athens and the cultural importance of this close connection is evident in early Greek Tragedy particularly within Aeschylus' *Oresteia*. I have described the rich psychogeography of Delphi and have suggested how the spatiotemporal dimension of past, present and future are drafted into the act of performance. The spatiotemporal in music and applied computational mathematics (stochastic probability) is an important aspect of the work of Iannis Xenakis. Largely influenced by ancient Greek natural philosophy and Pythagorean principles Xenakis developed a new ontology of sound that is both trans-historical and bridges the gap between nature and culture. In particular, Xenakis offers a range of insights into the staging of contemporary versions of Greek tragedy and a specific re-framing of the oracle Kassandra within his *Oresteia*.

Oracular practice provides us with an ancient example of a primary mediation model: I have described this as a loop. Thinking through the mediation loop exposes the various mechanisms of socio-political control and identity positioning that is rested within it. Luce Irigaray formulates the solidification of value and notions of place and space within the limitations of such a mediation loop. Descriptions of oracular mediation at Delphi provide evidence of the restrained passage of information through the mediation loop. The policing of information, restraints and limitation on access to raw data together with the careful manipulation of what is seen and unseen within the field of encounter are significant and impactful staging choices that configure ancient oracular practice as well as the structuring of digital media encounters.

The careful negotiation of what is visible in digital performance can also thwart the inscriptive power of technology and add to the theatricality of the work. For example, the Wooster Group deploy technology to fracture and dissociate – to literally prise open mediation loops – particularly in *To You, The Birdie! (Phèdre)*. Mediatized disassociation creates gaps and intervals in which the socio-political becomes visible. *PythiaDelphine21* puts the audience inside a field of disassociation to experience the affects first hand and to draw attention to the act of intimate kinaesonic one-to-one mediation.

Identifying structural relational positions helps artists to expose, thwart and imagine different types of encounters and to posit revolutionary ideas, forms and personas that have the potential to overturn the status quo. An early example of this is the Cassandra device within the *Oresteia*: a character with the boundary-busting characteristics of a cyborg entity. Aeschylus' Cassandra operates outside the oracular mediation loop, offering a direct/

raw one-to-one experience of data/visions. The cyborgs' disruptive nature stems from their ability to inhabit transitory states and to embody levels of multiplicity that problematize simple and/or binary solutions. They are *different* by nature, skills and/or use of technologies and inhabit and/or unite different spatial and temporal dimensions.

Both oracles and cyborgs possess the ability to force a reassessment of notions of place/space, identity and temporality in a way that challenges social/political and cultural frames since they offer other ways of seeing and perceiving the world of things and ideas. Kassandra reimagined by Xenakis is a trans-gendering, trans-historical voice that traverses spatiotemporal dimensions. The Le Fura del Baus production of the *Oresteia* endows Kassandra with the totems of the origin myths associated with Delphi and the oracle: the python and the eagle/bird adding trans-species to her kindred persona. At the moment of primary experience, cyborgs and oracle commune with the stuff that defines their *difference from* and *kindred to*. They become a part of what Timothy Morton calls a 'spectral solidarity'[8] with Others. This new solidarity creates its own ontology of intermingled language(s), interrelational structures and types of resonances that inhabit a range of spatial and temporal dimensions.

In *PythiaDelphine21* kinaesonic interaction is deepened by the sense of there being another unseen presence working in symbiotic relationship with the distinctly tangible operations of the performer. The dimensionality of what is directly perceived and what is felt as present but remains veiled within the performance is important not just for the dramatic (a re-staging of the oracle) but because what is embodied is a language of interaction with an Other non-human technological presence. Bodycoder is a sympoiesis in which the digital and the human are dialogically weaving a relationship with each other through improvised, random, composed, automated, errors and dirty connections.

In closing, Irigaray repositions Descartes' notion of the 'first passion' of encounter – *wonder*, 'surprise and astonishment in the face of the unknowable' – to reconfigure the space of encounter between different Others. Again, weaving a perspective through/for *sexuate difference*, Irigaray foregrounds a general attitude through *difference* where integrity and autonomy of identity/being and subjectivity is preserved and observed on each side of the encounter. Further such a state of wonder is not filled with 'greed, possession, consummation, disgust ... it can not seize, possess or subdue such an object' (Irigaray 1991:171–2). *Wonder* holds the interval open between two, it also causes us to wonder at our own reaction – *wonder* has an outward as well as an introspective curve – that throws us back to self; a self without knowledge of the thing before it (see Fig. 8.4). From this position *difference* becomes both sense and sensation before knowledge.

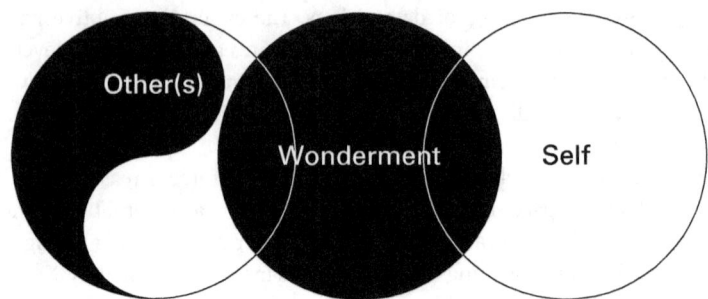

Fig. 8.4 Wonderment mediation/encounter loop.

The famous epitaph 'know thyself', inscribed on the wall approaching the temple of Apollo at Delphi, is both a warning and a reminder that as audience to the act of mediation/remediation the supplicant is part of the mediation loop. The supplicants' point of view from the perspective of their own desires and prejudice may influence their reading of the event/word/other: separations, gaps and intervals create spaces in which knowledge and understandings might slowly meet and begin to coalesce.

Notes

1. 'Kinaesonic' is a term for our practice in 1997, derived from the compound of two words: *kinaesthetic* meaning the movement principle of the body and *sonic* meaning sound/noise. The term 'kinaesonic' therefore refers to the physicalization or real-time mapping of sound to bodily movements. For a full explanation see: Wilson-Bokowiec and Bokowiec 2006: 47–58.
2. The words within brackets are my own, replacing Abram's to draw a connection between a sensorial landscape ontology described by Abram and performance ontology to expose the point at which contemporary performance intersects ancient Greek forms.
3. https://www.facebook.com/tracesofantigone/ (accessed 20 May 2020) and https://elli.site/odc-ensemble/ (accessed 21 May 2020). *Antigone Test* was made in lockdown during the global pandemic (Covid-19) in 2020.
4. Unpublished on-line conversation with the author 23/5/20.
5. More information at https://www.bodycoder.com (accessed June 2020).
6. The techniques and technologies are hotly contested and range from the imbibing of volcanic vapours to the ingestion of psychoactive organic substances; Haralampos Harissis offers a convincing argument for the use of *Nerium oleander* leaves (Harissis 2014: 353).

7   Description of sonic entities occurring in *Vox Circuit Trilogy*, taken from various reviews. See www.bodycoder.com
8   Timothy Morton's terminology: see Morton 2017.

References

Abram, D. (2017), *The Spell of the Sensuous: Perception and Language in the More-Than-Human World*, New York: Vintage Books.

Aeschylus (1926), *Aeschylus: [plays] in two volumes ; with an English introduction by Herbert Weir Smyth*, London: William Heinemann.

Bogart, A. (2012), *Conversations with Anne*, New York: Theatre Communications Group.

Cartelli, T. (2019), *Reenacting Shakespeare in the Shakespeare Aftermath : The Intermedial Turn and Turn to Embodiment*, New York: Palgrave Macmillan.

Cole, E. (2020), *Postdramatic Tragedies*, Oxford: Oxford University Press.

Haraway, D. J. (2000), *How Like A Leaf: An Interview with Thyrza Nichols Goodeve*, New York and London: Routledge.

Haraway, D. J. (2016), *Staying With The Trouble: Making Kin in the Chthulucene*, Durham, NC, and London: Duke University Press.

Harissis, H. V. (2014), 'A Bittersweet Story: The True Nature of the Laurel of the Oracle of Delphi', *Perspectives in Biology and Medicine* 57 (3): 351–360, Johns Hopkins University Press, doi: https://doi.org?10.1353/pbm.2014.0032.

Irigaray, L. (1991), *The Irigaray Reader*, ed. Margaret Whitford, Oxford: Blackwell.

Irigaray, L. (2005), *Between East & West: from Singularity to Community*, New Delhi: New Age Books.

Morton, T. (2017), *Humankind: Solidarity with Nonhuman People*, London and New York: Verso.

Wilson-Bokowiec, J., and M. Bokowiec (2006), 'Kinaesonics: The Intertwining Relationship of Body and Sound', *Contemporary Music Review. Special Issue: Bodily Instruments and Instrumental Bodies* 25 (1–2), London: Routledge Taylor & Francis.

Wolff, C. (2017), *Occasional Pieces: Writings and Interviews, 1952–2013*, Oxford: Oxford University Press.

Xenakis, I. (1967), 'Notice sur l'Orestie,' in *Sigma 3, Semaine de recherche et d'action culturelle, Bordeaux, 13-[19] Novembre 1967*, Bordeaux: Samie, 1967.

Xenakis, I. (1992), *Formalized Music: Thought and Mathematics in Composition*, rev. ed., Stuyvesant, NY: Pendragon Press.

9

Colonial convulsions

Akram Khan's *Xen(os)* and the digital Prometheus

Mario Telò

Introduction

In this chapter, I consider how the digital medium may not just disseminate but inhabit – in spite of itself – the aesthetics of Greek tragedy. To do so, I explore the convergence of three material domains with their political implications: the unremitting convulsions of the colonized soldier in *Xen*, the video solo performance of British Bangladeshi dancer Akram Khan, which is inspired by the Aeschylean *Prometheus Bound*;[1] overflowing form in the verbal texture of the ancient play; and a flux of unruly, continuous sensation that from within the digital pushes against the organization and transmission of discrete information, against the medium's constitutive discontinuity. In line with the theoretical approach adopted by other chapters of this volume (especially Chapter 7 by Filacanapa and Magris, and Chapter 8 by Wilson-Bokowiec), in what follows I will use my case study to discuss the possibility of a radical, anti-colonial micropolitics intermedially emerging from the synergies between ancient tragic form and digital formalisms.

Somatic infinitude and the digital an-archivic

To understand how the Prometheus of Akram Khan makes us rethink the condition of the colonized subject in the Aeschylean play, I will look for ways to connect the somatic infinitude of his kinetic spinning with modes of recalcitrant expansion, continuity, and infinitude in tragic language as well as in the digital medium per se. Through punctuation, word division, syntactical break, language exerts haptic violence, a kind of cutting that seeks to arrest the flowing continuum of resistant being. This partitioning (a literal Rancierean 'distribution of the sensible') parallels the discreteness of the digital – 'a data technology that uses ... discontinuous values to represent, store, and manage information' (Fazi 2019: 4). Privileging the discrete over the continuum, digital techno-formalization enforces, for Deleuze, a representational determinism that kills 'the lines of flight' of sensation (Deleuze 1992). Some studies in media theory have, however, looked at digital coding as a perpetual flux, with 'a pre-representational status that always breaks away from rational synthesis and logocentric descriptions' (Fazi 2019: 9). Another possibility for positing a continuous, restless sensation within electronic discrete formalization is by seeing the digital as an archival medium, 'embedded in architectures of software and in the political economy of social media platforms' (Ibrus and Ojamaa 2020: 66).

For Elizabeth Povinelli, 'the archive is a kind of Lacanian desire, always dissatisfied with its object ... the thrill of discovery quickly giving over to the anomie of lack, propelling the archivist into more and more collections' (2017: 150). The digital archive multiplies this desire, for 'the software itself depends on a vast network of state and capital infrastructures' (2017: 163), that is, on a swarm of archontic powers, which aim to archive (that is, immobilize) us, within their vulnerable systems of impression and recording while deluding us with the fantasy of free access and a sempiternal, always 'refreshed,' survival. In *Xen*, I want to argue, the whirling movements of Khan's Prometheus, a colonial soldier impersonated by a performer of Indian Kathak dance, destabilize the digital medium's archival aspiration by exposing its 'anomie of lack', and embracing this 'anomie' as a corporeal contortion, which besieges petrifying colonial power by persistently spinning around it.

This dizzying movement bodies forth the ever-endangered 'infinitude' of the colonial subject (Fanon 1967: 114–15), caught in a bodily spasm, in an unruly contortion between *life* and *death* – the two inseparable directions of the archive, digital or otherwise, with its constitutive (in)animation. In the Aeschylean *Prometheus*, poetic form is likewise caught in a circuit between two conations: a phonemic infinitude sprawling beyond syntactical partitioning, and language's cutting impetus, its urge to break a free, unsignifying flow of letters into discrete units of meaning. Aeschylean letters resemble digital data, the bytes similarly caught in a spiralling double bind, assembling into a discrete informational sequence, a recording unit, and yet flowing rebelliously, rejecting the discontinuity of electromagnetic signification.

This spiralling is reflected in the pirouettes of the soldier/performer that are placed before our eyes by *Xen's* video technology. What we can call the digital 'anarchivic' converges with the colonial soldier's spasms, which bring out the electric waves of an enraged *jouissance*, a swirling *thumos* unsettling archival enclosures and networks as well as colonial petrification. This anger, the manifestation of a continuous spiralling between *life* and *death*, conveys the affective infinitude that shatters the opposition between *bios* and *zoê* through which colonial, thanatopolitical sovereignty establishes who has the right to rights and who does not. The ultimate pay-off of this affective infinitude is not the notion of the tragic Prometheus, ancient or modern, as a cyber-subject, or an agent of nonhuman life force. It is, rather, an invitation to rethink the temporality of *dissensus*, to consider ways for theorizing an ever-continuing moment, for stretching *ad infinitum* the intensity of political rupture, for extending a disruptive point in time through ever-spinning circles.

'Fighting against time'

Xenos, the solo dancing performance digitally archived in *Xen*, is the last choreographic project of Akram Khan, the artist whom *The Guardian* called 'the master mover who redefined dance'. In the live performance, which premiered in Athens in 2019, Khan placed himself as a Promethean soldier on the battlefield of the First World War, standing for the millions of Indian soldiers enlisted in the British Army from 1914 to 1918. The performer moves amid manufactured objects (ropes) and the technology of a gramophone in a setting of primordial, burning, nonhuman desolation. Khan's declaration that he is 'fighting against time' can perhaps be understood to express an aspiration not just to overcome temporal perishability but to attain, kinetically, a sort of a-chronicity, or a non-linear chronic continuity – the (a)temporal dimension suggested by the materiality of the setting, the Promethean solitude of the performer, and the formal rigidity of the Aeschylean play itself. Siobahn Burke suggested that, while 'whirl[ing] in breath-takingly rapid circles' (2018), the performer 'seems to be cycling through memories of a bygone life' and asks 'Is there any escape? Any return to what came before?' As I will argue, looping around and through soil, a rope, and a gramophone to the point of exhaustion, the Promethean soldier in *Xen* experiences traumatic memory – the tragedy of a plural singularity – in an imaginary thin zone between *before* and *after* the beginning of life, a flickering space similar to the one where the digital medium dizzily spins, with its colonizing coercion disguised as global freedom.

Merging the two Greek prepositions *en* and *ex*, the title of this digital Prometheus (*Xen*) folds together *entrance* and *exit*, *insider* and *outsider*, *birth* and *death*, the boundaries that are constantly confounded in the whirling movements of Kathak dancing, which causes a solo male performer to *enter* and *exit* multiple roles, identities, and genders. In the film, the appearance of the Prometheus figure is visualized as an *exit* from an undifferentiated material expanse, a heap of dirt and dust under which he is buried. A fracture in the earth appears as a hand emerges, then a body – the undead – from a boundless mass. The reawakened body opens a breach for itself through spasms, the movements of a newborn or of a dying man, the almost indistinguishable agonies of beginning and ending life. With dirt adhering to his clothes and skin, the reborn or newborn subject touches the flesh of the earth, feels the viscosity of the continuum of life and death that is the soil. He is extracted from, yet still pulled into, a 'geological miasma' (Smithson 1996: 100).

Evoking the cinder of post-war destruction, the fragments of annihiled bodies turned into a mass of gritty matter, the archive of dirt figures the paradoxical entry-as-exit of the colonized soldier – *en*listed, taken or let *in*, afforded a deceitful sense of inclusion, just to be *ex*terminated. But it also tropes the opposite dynamic: the soldier's exit-as-entrance, an apparent sense of perverse, hyper-accelerated *ec-stasy* indistinguishable from *en*trapment in the stifling *en*tropy of a sadistic Symbolic, in 'the motionless, petrified world of colonization' (Fanon 1965: 61), a monolith or a granular accretion. As Karl Britto has observed, in reference to the Indochinese soldiers enlisted in the French army of the First World War 'the proper value of the soldier's body lies precisely in its capacity, through mutilation or death, to offer partial repayment for the successful passage of the colonized subject into the incorporeal realm of civilization' (2009: 149). The colonized soldier's entry as an outsider (a *xenos*) turns his body into that of a 'zombie'; his being *in*strumentalized as bare matter by the realm that, perched on the pedistal of self-styled incorporeality, calls itself civilization makes him undead, symbolically leaving the realm of the living just as the imperative of 'continu[ing] to serve [his] master' traps him in, prevents him from actually exiting.

When we tune in with our computer screens to watch the mutilated life gasping in *Xen*, the sudden fissure surrounding birth/rebirth that initiates the film appears like the trembling fault line of an earthquake, breaking the heap of war's own ruins and launching the tragic rhythm of life as death. This fissure corresponds to the breach, a wound or *trauma* that, according to Freud in *Beyond the Pleasure Principle* (1920), brings about life as an interruption of the blissful quiescence of undifferentiated inorganic matter. Life in Freud's schema 'begins as a rupture vis-à-vis itself, an interruption of inanimate by an animate that has somehow lain inert' (Wills 2016: 69). Life, therefore, amounts to 'an intractable inextricability of animate and inanimate,' with life instinct and death drive combined in what Derrida calls *lifedeath* (2020). In Freud's schema, the life instinct is at the service of the death drive in that its goal is to lead the human body to death at the right, ostensibly natural time, countering the death drive's precipitous rushing forward to the same goal, which is the 'before life,' a closing of the breach that is life.

When we click on the switch of our computer and on the 'play' (or 'rewind') button, making the show begin (again), we simultaneously open a breach in the mass of dust, turning on the machinic soldier, reduced to a robot more than a cyborg, thus activating the digital mechanism that sets him in motion for endless iterations of his gyrations, just like the colonial power serially enlists him for one war after another, without ever letting him breathe, or embrace again the primordial, breathless rest. As Judith Butler puts it, 'colonization is the deadening of sense, the establishment of the body in social death, as one that lives and breathes its potentiality as death' (2015: 189). While the digital automatism driving the choeregraphic swirls makes us complicitous in a surveillance system and in the violence that converts the colonized soldier into a zombie, it also displays its homology and subjection to the loop of *lifedeath*. Speaking of photography, Roland Barthes noted, '*Life/Death*: the paradigm is reduced to a simple click' (1981: 92). But, as Scott Curtis noticed, the idea of the cine loop is essential to 'any sequence of digitized movement that has been set to repeat.' As he puts it:

> Edison's Kinetoscope contained a looped filmed sequence that would repeat with every nickel. The content of the scenes filmed for these machines matched the form: a group of blacksmiths hammering rhythmically, a somersaulting dog, circular dances. (Curtis 2004: 241)

Khan's 'circular dance' can thus be seen as a metaphor of any cine loop, of the archival circuit of *lifedeath* that links together Edison's Kinetoscope and the techniques of the digital cyberspace.

A-chronic cyberspace and colonial thanatopower

The wasteland of Khan's Prometheus – a kind of a-chronic cyberspace in itself – entrusts his mutilated subjectivity to the energies, of birth and destruction alike, that spring forth from potential enfoldings, from movements toward or away from non-human objects, and from influences and affections stemming from them. In *Xen*, the Prometheus figure experiences his precarity relationally – through an inter-body encounter with a rope, the equivalent of the chains that appear as ankle-bells in the performed show and that imprison his immortal counterpart in the ancient play. Life reduced to purely digital existence aggravates the position of the colonial performer of Khan's *Xen*, his precarious search for a relational (pseudo-)

subjectivity. This search for him passes first and foremost through the encounter with a rope, an obvious sign of his constitutive enchainment to the Big Other of colonization. This object externalizes the foreigner's desire to bond and connect, but also the inevitable constriction of this desire in the grip of sovereign power. The soldier's contact with the tensile properties of the woven fibre delivers what Eve Sedgwick, reflecting on her dedication to crocheting at the time of her terminal illness, called 'the rub of reality' (2011: 71).

The outcome of this mutual influencing – of skin and fabric – is a bond or meta-bond in which the colonized soldier's subjectivity is cast as a web of interobjective affections and his human objectality is recognized in the very pliancy of the cord. Like the cord, the human body of the colonized subject can be pulled back – down into the earthen pile – or pulled apart in the very act of resistance. 'Life and death are knotted in a thread / the hanged man's rope, and the umbilical cord,' says Chilean artist Cecilia Vicuña (2009), whose textile art Julia Bryan-Wilson (2017) refers to as threads of protest, peaceful and enraged – what Khan's Prometheus also spins around, with his body reaching out to, and becoming the rope. He becomes the Lacanian Real, the excess of non-meaning, that the colonized, in a sense, always is, for 'the colonized ... has a designated place, but in that place [he] experiences a void of no identity' (Hudson 2013: 267). More importantly, the knot of *lifedeath*, an untying and re-tying, materialized by the solo performer as he spins and trembles, affords him a 'ge-ontic' power, similar to that of the earth itself, which trembles while giving birth to life through its own fracturing.

This spinning expresses *lifedeath* not as a cycle or a blurred confusion but as a source of *jouissance*, which also involves the perverse joy of material – fabric as well as bundles of electromagnetic energy and the metallic supports of digital archivization – in its own giddy fraying. Also evoking *lifedeath*, the gramophone, the sound object that acts as the rope's companion onstage, iteratively emits the impression of a live vocal event as disembodied sensory matter at once alive and dead. Its central aperture suggests another *xen* (that is, an *ex*- and an *en*-), an endless passage – *jouissant*, orgasmic (in the etymological, Greek sense of 'angry') – in and out of intensities. But as we feel, sympoietically, the synergic spinning of texture, flesh, and of the digital medium itself, we are also impelled to circle back to the motion of Aeschylean form, a preview of the (an-)archivic electromagnetic loop.

At the beginning of *Prometheus Bound*, tragic form fashions 'the inexplicable mass of rock' (Kafka 1971: 432) not just as the iconic object and place of Promethean torture, but also as a marker of deep time – still solid, if not unworn – and pure being. After the first couplet, where the setting is bookended by *chthôn* ('earth'), the first word, and *abroton ... erêmian* ('the deserted place with no mortals'), which closes the second line in a formal circling back, Prometheus appears as a two-syllable deictic direct object (*tonde* 'this man'):

> ... *tonde pros petrais*
> *hupsêlokrêmnois ton leôrgon ochmasai*
> *adamantinôn desmôn en arrêktois pedais*
>
> ... [it's your job] to nail this man to rocks,
> high-craggy ones, the criminal,
> in unbreakable chains of adamantine fetters
>
> (*Prometheus Bound*, 4–6)

In this exhortation, which the personified Kratos ('Might') addresses to Hephaestus, Prometheus's presence in language barely registers within the overdetermined thicket of nouns and adjectives clustered around the rock and the chains, the quasi-homophonic *petrais/pedais* at the end of almost consecutive lines. One gains the impression of metallic and stony matter seeking to incorporate the human body – an impression that persists when Hephaestus announces Prometheus's eternal punishment: 'You [=Prometheus] will guard this rock (*tênde ... petran*), standing (*orthostadên*), sleepless, without bending your knee' (31–2).

The immobility of Prometheus – 'sleepless,' always 'standing' (*orthostadên*), never flexing his limbs – assimilates him to the rock, as does the resonance in endings between the adverb *orthostad-ên*, effectively a modifier for Prometheus, the subject of the sentence, and *tên-de ... petran* ('this rock'), the objectifying object in the accusative. Although the punishment inflicts upon Prometheus a perennial insomnia, denies him any respite, exposing him to the petrifying frenzy of thanatopower, the formal texture of poetic form conjures a different condition, occupying the heart of the rock, undergoing what Jean-Luc Nancy calls 'the mineralogy of being,' an experience that is tantamount not to non-human being but to being as such (1994: 171). This is not the 'bare life' imposed by colonial biopolitics, but a radical wiping off of the Symbolic, a fantasy of deep, a-chronic time that arises in the undoing of poetic form. Fanon asserted that 'the colonized are denied their freedom and thus relegated ontologically to the status of things – things like stones ... They are forced violently into an unfree and in human "zone of nonbeing"' (1967: 8). As I will suggest, in the symbolism of ancient and modern *Prometheus*, pure being, or being as such, is aligned with a kind of de-petrifying rupture. As Fred Moten and Stefano Harney put it, 'blackness operates as the modality of life's constant escape and takes the form of flight';

it is located 'in the invention of escape, stealing away in the confines, in the form, of a break' (2011: 355). We can say that Prometheus stands for tragic form (verbal, kinaesthetic, digital) in the sense that he embodies the break of form – the potential break that form always is.

In the Aeschylean play, deep time is felt in the stretched-out length of adjectival compounds, aggregates of letters, which threaten the discreteness of language, the avatar of digital discontinuity. For example, in 109 (*nartheko-plêrôton de thêrômai puros*), where Prometheus describes the theft of fire that got him into trouble ('And I hunt for the fennel-stalk-filling [fountain] of fire'), half of the line is occupied by the compound *nartheko-plêrôton* ('fennel-stalk-filling'), whose length is further prolonged by the postpositive *de*. There is the effect of phonemic matter liable to disorganize itself into an undifferentiated sequence, eager to keep going beyond meaning, resistant to word breaks and to articulation into distinct semantic units. If we see meaning constructed by syntax as an archival consignation, a series of orderly graphemic aggregates, whereby order consists of multiple regular intervals, the compounds that appear to prolong the sprawling of letters resemble an uncontrolled gathering of signs that, by banning discontinuity, may explode meaning, turning it into ever-continuous gibberish. We can think of possible violations of the principle of discrete information in the digital realm as well: randomly overextended, tilted coding, hypertrophic accretions of symbols corresponding to the 'wrong' succession of electromagnetic signals.

In 20 (*pros-passaleusô tôid' ap-anthrôpôi pagôi*, 'I will nail [you] to this crag far from men'), in which Hephaestus verbally affixes Prometheus to the rock, the drawn-out verb *pros-passaleusô* ('I will nail [you]') is followed by the tetrasyllabic compound *ap-anthrôpôi* ('far from men'), which modifies 'crag'. While separating Prometheus from the human realm, de-deifying him and, in a sense, de-humanizing him, the prefix *ap-*, which works as a kind of alpha privative, is also the glimmer of the rebellious manifestation of a matter (or an ontopower) – mineral, verbal, or digital – that swallows the human, refusing to be colonized by it, to be contained in bound, controlled units. Building the interobjective relationship of human and rock, the juxtaposition of *pros-passaleusô* and *ap-anthrôpôi* furthers the formal impression of all-encompassing matter – stubbornly opposing its own fragmentation, its division into units of meaning, just like the heap of dirt which Khan comes out of.

The discontinuity enforced by verbal and digital language corresponds to the breach that is the beginning of life, the rupture of matter's 'protective shield,' as Freud puts it (1920: 27), a rupture that throws the colonized subject into a suffocating Symbolic, but also launches the raging loop that we see in the *jouissant* breathlessness of Aeschylean form and Khan's spinning kinaesthetics. When in 799 Prometheus deploys three bulky words (pentasyllabic, trisyllabic, and tetrasyllabic) to refer to the 'snake-fleeced, mortal-hating Gorgons,' the petrifying creatures the sight of whom will leave every mortal without 'breath' (*pnoas*), we are primed to think of the two word breaks in 799 as short inhalations:

> *drakontomalloi Gorgones brotostugeis*
> *has thnêtos oudeis eisidôn hexei pnoas.*
> snake-fleeced mortal-hating Gorgons,
> seeing whom no mortal man will keep his breath
> (*Prometheus Bound*, 799–800)

While rupturing the potential apnea of a petrifying burial with injections of *élan vital*, these inhalations simply prolong the breathlessness induced by the continual material growth of Promethean form. Besides the imperative of a continued versification, of an orderly repetition of structures of meaning, there is a different compulsion, a competing drive – the death drive simply called the drive by Lacan – which combats the breathlessness of verse-making, the endless reproduction of language (patriarchally driven just as much as reproduction tout court and, of course, the archive and war).

In *Prometheus Bound,* the long speeches of Prometheus and the characters who come to console (or threaten) him, are what keep the play going, while simultaneously making it static, petrifying it, that is, mimicking the calcifying, suffocating force of Zeus's paternal *logos*, the ancestor of the colonial power invisibly torturing Khan's performer. The dramaturgical conceit of the play, which forces the same, protagonistic actor to remain onstage (in some kind of subaltern posture) and deliver lines from the beginning to the end, enacts the phallologocentrism of the sovereign, who always 'enlists' its victim, paining his throat, potentially reducing him to silence through sadistic mimesis. But the emerging possibility of graphemes not entrapped in words, of characters spreading and spilling, going nowhere, refusing the destination of meaningful consignation creates the sense of the break of form. This break, which breaks the verbal distribution of the sensible, is the unruly continuity, Fanon's Real 'infinitude' (1967: 114–15), the expanding rage – an expression of the drive – that energizes the looping kinetics of Khan's solo Prometheus, his sensuously vertiginous, persistent siege of a system petrifying through partitions, distinctions, cutting intervals, through the very rupture that brings about life.

While reading the long Promethean compounds in our postdigital world, we cannot but imagine the possibility that, acquiring radical autonomy, they may turn into gibberish characters stubbornly glued together, into accumulations of motley symbols, impossible to parse, into viscous bundles of electromagnetic sensation. Transforming the viscous ongoingness of Aeschylean form, the movements of Khan figure the 'anomie' or the looping drive of the digital archive, the flux of continuous sensation that is repressed by its discrete logic. In a sense, this continuous kinetics does not just figure, but it also activates the 'digital anarchivic,' destabilizing the electromagnetic medium – in itself a colonizing structure – that brings the soldier to life, makes him visible.

Formal unboundness, colonial contraction

The Aeschylean play itself suggests synchronies and synergies of unstoppable bodily and formal kinetics, which foreshadow the digital anarchivic. In the parodos, the Chorus of Ocean's daughters enter, singing and dancing in iambic and choriambics, to console Prometheus, who has already been chained to the rock, petrified into his status of colonial (pseudo)subjectivity. While in kinaesthetic motion, the Chorus seems to stall verbal form, its contortions conveying the sense of a sprawling expansion in danger of paralyzing or petrifying *logos*, annihilating words into a viscous blob. In these lines, sung by the Chorus, compounds appear to visualize the eternity of Prometheus's punishment, his assimilation to the rock to which he has been affixed:

> ... *son demas eisidousai*
> *petrai **prosauainomenon***
> *taisd' **adamantodetoisi** lumais*
>
> ... we saw your body
> drying up by the rock,
> with the wounds of these adamantine bonds.
>
> (*Prometheus Bound*, 146–8)

The apparent lithification described here is precisely what makes graphic matter spin around, disorganize itself into a frenetic unboundness, with fading markers of semiotic distinction, with no intervals. While mimicking the oppressive immobility of the punishment, that is, the 'untameable' materiality of Zeus's chains, the triple compound (*a-damanto-detoisi* 'adamantine,' that is, 'untameably bound'), parallel to *pros-auainomenon*, arrests the logocentric flow. It releases the energy of a negative resistance, carried by the single yet letter *a* (the alpha privative), which has the power to break, to 'tame,' the chains of the signifier and of signification through anarchivic indistinction. This indistinction can be viewed, in fact, as the self-sabotaging consequence of colonial power's all-encompassing grip, of its archival manic greed, intolerant of its own partitions, of the logic of discontinuity that enforces it, in all its forms (digital or not). Modifying the word *demas* – the imprisoned body of Prometheus – the participle *pros-auainomenon* does not simply convey his eternal torture, but it also links recalcitrant poetic form with Promethean physicality, previewing Khan's spasmodic choreographic movements between life and death.

This syntactical agreement also creates a connection between Prometheus's apparently immobile body and the marine Chorus, the moving corporeal assemblage that is the most conspicuous *demas* in this lyric section. The formal expanse of *pros-auainomenon*, which comes to qualify or define this *demas*, codes kinaesthetics as a crazed accumulation, a looping swathe of material impulses (see the chiastic structure *petrai pros-auainomenon . . . a-damanto-detoisi lumais* at 147–8), an endlessly circulating stretch of unruly desire, just like the continuous undulation of the waves, on the verge of filling (or burying) intervals. There is a sense in which the graphic expansion conveying Prometheus's petrification paradoxically mobilizes him, diffusing the chorus's kinetic breathlessness, bringing forth an interruptive insistence, or an interruption through feverish continuation that is the aesthetico-political marker of this experimental play, a genuinely Promethean break of form.

When in his response, Prometheus voices the desire to be hauled down into Tartarus, he is not simply verbalizing a suicidal fantasy, or the wish to rejoin the *archai* of the Titanic world or of chaos itself – the shapeless mass that we may see reflected in the pile of detritus from which Khan's soldier emerges:

ei gar m' hupo gên nerthen th' Haidou
tou nekrodegmonos eis aperanton
Tartaron hêken desmois alutois

If only he [Zeus] had sent me down the earth,
underneath dead-accepting Hades,
into the boundless Tartarus, with unloosened bonds.
(Prometheus Bound, 153–5)

In the juxtaposition – only interrupted by the short preposition *eis* – between *nekro-degmonos* ('dead-accepting') and *a-peranton* ('boundless') we feel the force of an expressive form that longs to extend itself, to cover the whole graphic space with its own expansive convulsion. This is a desire pressing against 'bounds' (the *perata* negatively present in the word *a-peranton*), not just the chains hurting Prometheus's feet, or the signifiers entrapping his tongue in the play's suffocating verbal cascade. These 'bounds' are also the apparent breaks, the inhalations that prevent a word such as *nekro-degmonos* from spilling over, from being precisely *a-peranton*.

When later on Prometheus includes writing in the catalogue of his benefactions to humankind – *grammatôn te suntheseis / mnêmên hapantôn, mousomêtor' erganên* ('combinations of letters, memory of everything, the Muses' mother, effective' 460–1) – he presents it as a *sun-thesis* of letters, but, followed by the maternal compound *mousomêtor*', this '*com*bination' or '*con*signation' seems to jeopardize a priori any principle of mnemic distinction, of (paternal) semiotic cutting, conjuring an image of pre-linguistic maternal fusion, of phonemes affectively cemented together. Yet this intimate continuum is far from evoking an asfixiating mother. Rather, the formal lack of breath, a kind of strained breath in itself, or a *thumos*, that is generated in the somatics of the Chorus, Khan, and of tragic form can be reclaimed as an emancipatory, and anti-colonial gesture, which evokes Fanon's idea of the colonized's contracted 'in-finitude' (almost a translation of *a-peranton*).

The fantasy of occupying an undifferentiated, chaosmic space – a zone of unrepresentability reminiscent of the Levinasian concept of ethical infinity – may thus implicate not non-being, but a kind of persistent being, the continued intensity of a *thumos* ('breath' as well as 'rage') not confined to the moment, but pressing with no relief against the divisory cutting of every distribution of the sensible. The digital space that allows Khan to move before our eyes exemplifies this hierarchical partition, but it is also a potential chaotic or chaosmic formation permeated by a material desire that flows through all interstices, subjecting every division to a loop of appearance and disappearance.

When Io arrives onstage launching frenzied balletic convulsions that make her seem the most direct ancestor of Khan's performer, tragic form seems to be shaken, just like a digital surface, by electric, or electromagnetic, jolts. The word breaks that, in the play, pierce the sprawling formal matter are like the sting of the gadfly on Io, the girl turned into a cow – another victim of Zeus's colonial violence – whose manic appearance unsettles the static non-plot of the play. In this line delivered by Io in the midst of her dizzying lyric fit, bodily spasms ripple through rhytmic and formal contortions, just like seismic rifts or electric waves:

he he, oistrêlatôi de deimati deilaian

Ah ah, [me] wretched with fear driven by the gadfly ...

(*Prometheus Bound*, 580)

As Sarah Nooter puts it, 'the grating persistence of the [bug's] music is temporally limitless' (2017: 62). The interjection *he he*, which vocalizes the pain of the insect's sting, turns into sound the breaks in Io's skin/hide, rending the expanse of formal matter like the breach in the earth's entombment of Khan. But as though in response, the *e* sound stretches into the triple alliterative sequence *de deimati deilaian* that ends the line as matter strives to reconstitute its punctured protective shell, its violated impermeability. The push-and-pull between the vivifying puncture and the sprawling recalcitrance of formal matter manifests the *jouissance* of *lifedeath*, but also the loop of formal contraction and expansion. There is a dissensual dimension to the verbal fragmentation provoked by Io's frenzy – a 'queer' repudiation of 'speech, song, and language' (Olsen 2020) or a cyborgic becoming. Caused by a sadistic power deceptively taking on a minoritarian disguise, this fragmentation brings to mind the words of Fanon on his condition as colonized (pseudo)subject, 'I am being *dissected* under white eyes, the only real eyes ... they ... *cut away slices* of my reality' (1967: 116).

The dissection undergone by Io as she swirls – a quasi-electrocution that 'cuts away' pieces of her body – is, after all, an extreme version of the discrete logic of verbal, and digital, language, another manifestation, in spite of her apparently excessive, deterritorialized appearance, of what Fanon calls colonial contraction (1967, 114–15). The phonemic continuity engendered by the triple alliterative sequence *de deimati deilaian* thus marks a rebellion against a marking, a formal and somatic breaching – not through reparation, but through a faint yet relentless motion toward the full being and duration of infinitude, the onset of a sprawling wave that stretches out the body, yielding an unyielding, electro-magnetic *orgê*, an expansive *thumos*, a raging breathlessness as a *jouissant* demand for a deep, unbroken breath.

The gadfly's sting looks ahead to the eagle's poking of Prometheus's liver – an image of the dissection that life is for the colonial subject, like Khan's performer, who is exposed to discrete electric shocks every time he is digitally brought to life and light breaches out from within the screen's metallic darkness. The eagle transforms Zeus's punishment into torture, but, along with a breaking of *bios* or *zoê*, there is a breaking out of colonized life, which, like the rapacious bird, never stops poking, prodding, awakening, 'enlisting' its subject. In his prophecy of Prometheus's future destiny, Hermes announces that, after having been enveloped and held tight in a kind of embrace by a rock, Prometheus, 'after a long stretch of time (*macron* . . . *mêkos* . . . *chronou*' (1020), will come back to life, that is, will be reborn into a painful loop, launched by a cruel dissection of flesh at the behest of Zeus's animal emissary:

diartamêsei sômatos mega rhakos
aklêtos herpôn daitaleus panêmeros
kelainobrôton d' hêpar ekthoinêsetai

[Zeus's eagle] will render your body a big rag,
the uninvited banqueter, crawling all day long;
your blackened-from-gnawing liver he will eat away.

(*Prometheus Bound*, 1023–5)

Line 1025 comprises two other pentasyllabic compounds, the adjective *kelaino-brôton* ('blackened-from-gnawing') and the verb *ek-thoinêsetai* ('[he] will eat away'), which besiege *hêpar*, the word for 'liver'. The two intervals that prevent these three words from forming a thick mass of letters correspond to the bodily tear inflicted by the eagle's beak – what, two lines earlier, is called *rhakos*, a 'rag,' literally a 'rupture'. The gap eaten out of Prometheus's body is homologous to the brief gap between the dual punishments of growth and consumption, the space where we find near-contiguity between the two rhythms in the loop of *lifedeath*: on the one hand, a deadening or inanimating filling-in of tissue tending toward matter's closed-off impermeability; on the other, the enlivening or animating carving-out of tissue tending toward life's gaping vulnerability.

For Bernard Stiegler, 'Prometheus's liver, consumed by day and restored by night, is the Titan's clock ... It is the ceaseless process of différance in which time is constituted with that one coup of technicity that is the mark of mortality' (1998: 203). Prometheus's liver is the organ, physical and formal, of his mortality because it is what produces Symbolic life, what, in other words, separates the words *kelaino-brôton* and *ek-thoinêsetai*, causing the fundamental dissection, or *distinctio verborum*, that obstructs a phonemic infinitude, a *différance* liberated from the oppression of signifying chains. A digital Prometheus, the body of Khan's soldier is enlisted to experience the technologies of colonial-as-virtual life, not just the gadfly's sting morphed into electric shocks, but also the kingly eagle's sadistic play of expansion and contraction turned into the loop of 'on' and 'off', a digital *lifedeath*. Yet, in the unruly temporal expansion, in the impression of sprawling duration that is created by the all-encompassing force of his *kinêsis* we can feel the claim of infinitude, the possibility that the word for 'liver' in 1025 may no longer separate or be separated, but become part of an anarchivic phonemic aggregate, or a non-finite expressivity – an image not of incorporeality, but of full corporeal integrity, of brimful, unbroken being.

In *Xen*, the infinitude reclaimed by Fanon for colonized subjectivity amounts to an eternal immanence, an attempt to turn somatic and technological looping into the intense insistence of a dilated and diluted temporality, just as an exhausting phonetic continuity casts the colonized subject's raging endurance as a spiraling overexposure, a self-expansion beyond time or an hyper-presence, which dislodges spectators/readers from their safe position, making them breathless too, assimilating the colonizer to the colonized.

Prometheus's durational punctuality

Akram Khan's digital and dancing Prometheus does not only show the dissensual potential of the Aeschylean play's apparently static aesthetics, but it invites us to rethink, in these times of global crisis, current theorizations of *dissensus*. Jacques Rancière has seen dance as a primary expression of dissensual aesthetics, of how sensation can open emancipatory lines of flight within the *consensus* – the maintenance of the political status quo – that is enforced by representation, with its constitutive division between subject and object, those who have part and those who have no part. In his discussion of the spectacular balletic performance of Loïe Fuller at the Folies Bergère of 1893, he observes the bodily excess, the self-extension into forms of *dis*appearance that, for Rancière, marks her performance. 'Whirling in space,' turning the body into a line, Loïe Fuller exemplifies the notion of *dis-sensus* as *dis*-incorporation, *dis*-identification, the moment in which a system exits from itself (2013: 94). But the idea of disappearance also evokes the distinctive temporality of *dissensus*, which, for Rancière, 'is always of the moment and provisional' (2011: 51).

Seeking to combat the discontinuity of digital semiosis and unleash the unruly continuum of virtual sensation, Khan's convulsions translate the dissensual force of Aeschylean form, a *dis*identification that occurs through the constant threat of no *distinctio verborum*, no distribution of the verbal sensible. But tending toward an unbroken infinitude in time through breathless, continuous kinesis, the body of the colonized soldier also contests the temporality of Rancierean *dissensus* – a constant starting over, at different times, of rupturing moments. Speaking about the surge of demonstrations, of peaceful *dissensus* on the streets provoked by the assassination of George Floyd, Angela Davis has voiced the need for prolonging the intensity of the moment, for thinking of 'how we act in the aftermath' (2020). With a 'fluidity of role switching and the intensity and continuity of character portrayal,' and 'no "gaps" for the spectator' (Shah 1998: 7), the tradition of Kathak choreography alters the distribution of the sensible – 'leading spectators to experience the heights of that which is neither actually seen not is directly seeable' (1998: 12). Yet it goes beyond the temporal limits of Rancierean *dissensus*, generating multiple points of disruption folded into ongoingness. Akram Khan's digital choreography offers an apparently contradictory model of intensive temporality that does not get lost in the moment; it is a kind of durational punctuality, which expands a spasm of disidentification through a body gesturing frantically toward a beyond, prospectively swarming around the aftermath, and encircling the future with its looping energy. This colonized Prometheus is 'a swelling wave' – another phrase used by Rancière for Fuller – which makes a tragic urge for never contracted *thumos*, lingering yet mobile, percolate through the narrow, electrified interstices of Aeschylean form.

Note

1 https://www.youtube.com/watch?v=FLI7fMiqLMU (accessed 22 June 2022)

References

Barthes, R. (1981), *Camera Lucida*, transl. R. Howard, New York: Hill and Wang.
Britto, K. A. (2009), 'L'esprit de corps: French Civilization and the Death of the Colonized Soldier', in E. Mudimbe-Boyi (ed.), *Empire Lost*, 145–61, Lanham, MD: Rowman & Littlefield.
Bryan-Wilson, J. (2017), *Fray*, Chicago: University of Chicago Press.
Burke, S. (2018), 'In *XENOS*, A Dancer Turns Troubled Warrior', *New York Times* November 1.
Butler, J. (2015), *Senses of the Subject*, New York: Fordham University Press.
Curtis, S. (2004), 'Still/Moving: Digital Imaging and Medical Hermeneutics', in L. Rabinovitz and A. Geil (eds), *Memory Bytes*, 218–54, Durham, NC: Duke University Press.
Davis, A. (2020), 'Race at a Boiling Time: The Fire This Time', https://www.youtube.com/watch?v=3I22E2Sezi8 (accessed 2 April 2022).
Deleuze, G. (1992), 'Postscript on the Societies of Control', *October*, 59: 3–7.
Derrida, J. (2020), *Life Death*, trans. P.-A. Brault and M. Naas, Chicago: University of Chicago Press.
Fanon, F. (1965), *The Wretched of the Earth*, trans. R. Philcox, New York: Grove Press.
Fanon, F. (1967), *Black Skin, White Masks*, trans. R. Philcox, New York: Grove Press.
Fazi, M. B. (2019), 'Digital Aesthetics: The Discrete and the Continuous', *Theory, Culture & Society*, 36 (1): 3–26.
Freud, S. (1920), *Beyond the Pleasure Principle*, in *The standard edition of the*

complete psychological works of Sigmund Freud 18: 1–64, London: Hogarth Press.

Hudson, P. (2013), 'The State and the Colonial Unconscious', *Social Dynamics*, 39 (2): 263–77.

Ibrus, I., and M. Ojamaa (2020), 'The Creativity of Digital (Audiovisual) Archives', *Theory, Culture & Society*, 37 (3): 49–70.

Kafka, F. (1971), *The Complete Stories*, trans. E. Muir and J. Stern, New York: Schocken Books.

Moten, F., and S. Harney (2011), 'Blackness and Governance', in P. T. Clough and C. Willse (eds), *Beyond Biopolitics*, 351–61, Durham, NC: Duke University Press.

Nancy, J.-L. (1994), *The Birth to Presence*, trans. B. Holmes, Palo Alto, CA: Stanford University Press.

Nooter, S. (2017), *The Mortal Voice in the Tragedies of Aeschylus*, Cambridge: Cambridge University Press.

Olsen, S. (2020), *Solo Dance in Archaic and Classical Greek Literature*, Cambridge: Cambridge University Press.

Povinelli, E. (2017), *Geontologies*, Durham, NC: Duke University Press.

Rancière, J. (2011), *Dissensus*, trans. S. Corcoran, London: Bloomsbury.

Rancière, J. (2013), *Aisthesis*, trans. Z. Paul, London: Bloomsbury.

Sedgwick, E. K. (2011), *The Weather in Proust*, Durham, NC: Duke University Press.

Shah, P. (1998), 'Transcending Gender in the Performance of Kathak', *Dance Research Journal* 30 (2): 2–17.

Smithson, R. (1996), *The Collected Writings*, Berkeley: University of California Press.

Stiegler, B. (1998), *Technics and Time, 1*, trans. R. Beardsworth and G. Collins, Palo Alto, CA: Stanford University Press.

Vicuña, C. (2009), *The Precarious*, Hanover, NH: University of New Hampshire Press.

Wills, D. (2016), *Inanimation*, Minneapolis: University of Minnesota Press.

POSTLUDE

Pre- and post-human(-ist) confluences in Greek tragedy

The complete eradication of the live actor from the tragic stage

Paul Monaghan

Introduction

From theatre's apparent beginnings in the late Archaic Age of Ancient Greece to the twenty-first century, the living body of the human actor has been seen as the central and defining feature of the medium, the source of theatre's uniqueness as well as its limitations. Whether viewed as semiotically or phenomenally heavy, whether experienced as an iconic sign of the world that exists continuously with and contiguously alongside of the performance space or as an intrusion of hard-core reality into the comfortable conventions of bourgeois modern drama, what is distinct about the body of the live actor is that it is obdurately *of* and *in* this world. The corporeality of the live actor, however, has impelled innovators, from Maurice Maeterlinck and the French and Russian Symbolists in the late nineteenth century to twenty-first-century creators of digital performance, to call for the complete eradication of the human actor from the stage; tendencies towards this end can be seen, for example, in the work of Heiner Goebbels, Romeo Castellucci (see Castellucci 2007), Kris Verdonck and Hirata Oriza. Such a desire, sometimes made with some rhetorical exaggeration, is particularly striking when applied to Greek tragedy, a genre that seeks to reveal fundamental truths about what it is to be human in a world in which only partially identifiable forces limit human understanding and agency.

In this Postlude I focus on a series of attempts to minimize, depersonalize and eventually to eradicate the live human actor in the performance of Greek tragedy. I locate the origins of this attempt in the ontological ambiguity of the masked actor at the very foundation of tragedy in ancient Greece. The Modernist and later use of puppets and the depersonalization of the actor in various kinds of postdramatic productions of Greek tragedy have taken up this ontological ambiguity, but it is the use of avatars, virtual actants and complex, layered juxtapositions of contemporary digital media that have taken questions regarding the presence of the live actor in performances of Greek tragedy to a whole new level. In this historical context, the modern subject and its counterpart, the modern dramatic character, can be seen to have been an aberrant interloper in productions of Greek tragedy. The chapter asks to what extent such depersonalized and virtual performances, which in retrospect we can see have been driven by an increasing awareness of our 'posthuman' situation, serve the foundational aim of the tragic genre.

Ancient Greek tragedy and 'being human'

From ancient Greek epic, as well as from its earlier Mesopotamian and Anatolian predecessors, Greek tragedy inherited a central concern with what it means to be human. In particular, epic and tragedy are concerned with human suffering, mortality, and the tragic limitations to our understanding and agency in a world filled with capricious forces, understood in Greece to be immanent and ever-active divinities of various theogonic generations, continuously yet unpredictably robbing human beings of sufficient knowledge with which to make critical decisions and the autonomous agency needed to limit the moral remainder of those decisions. Being human, in epic and tragedy, means being in a world where agency is shared between humans and more powerful forces, where the boundary between human, animal, and something beyond both is porous. As Vernant and Vidal-Naquet put it, '[s]ince the origin of action lies both in man himself and outside him, the same character appears now as an agent, the cause and source of his actions, and now as acted upon, engulfed in a force that is beyond him and sweeps him away....' (1990: 77).

This 'ambiguity of tragic action' is perfectly expressed by the ghost of Darius in Aeschylus' *Persians* who says, 'when a mortal himself works for his own downfall, a god comes to abet him' (line 742). Neither the sovereign modern subject, 'a bounded, unique, more or less integrated motivational and cognitive universe, a dynamic centre of awareness, emotion, judgment, and action' (Geertz 1983: 59), nor its theatrical equivalent, the modern dramatic character possessing the individual agency to make decisions and act in the world according to their own will (a concept that does not exist in the ancient Greek language (Vernant & Vidal-Naquet 1990: 49–84)), is anywhere to be found in Greek tragedy (see also Monaghan 2016b).

Moreover, Greek tragedy expressed this sense of 'being human' using a hybrid medium combing an artificial entity (the chorus) that moved and voiced together as a collective with, at different times, both more than and less than ordinary human insight into the mysterious patterns inherent in and governing human life; the piercing music of the aulos; individuated actors and their speaking and singing bodies; and most importantly, masks that effectively removed the actor's face and body and replaced it with the face of a long-dead Bronze-Age/'Homeric' semi-divine being from the historico-mythical age of heroes. Debates over the purpose and/or effect of the Greek tragic mask have raged long and hard; many agree, however, that the mask did not offer the spectator an image of himself – at least not directly and in the manner of modern drama – but rather brought an otherworldly and metaphysical perspective into the performance space (Monaghan 2008).

As Calame argues, the frontal gaze of the Greek tragic mask was 'a gaze which offers the spectator an image of the different, of that which lies beyond himself' (1995: 111). The effect, as Wiles argues, may have been that the Bronze-Age personae who populated tragedy were understood to be *actually* present as hologram-like living beings in the here-and-now of the performance space, re-enacting events that happened in the distant past (2007: 245). The Greek tragic mask, argues Wiles (following Frontisti-Ducroux), abolished the actor's being and gave voice and presence to long-dead *personnages* for 'ritual-centred viewing' (2007: 247–60), that is, for the purposes of a direct gnosis of those beings. The mask, in this view, offered the spectator something akin to the Hindu meaning of 'avatar', that is, a 'descent' into human form of a non- or super-human being. The physical space of the performance was thereby transformed into a metaphysical space in which gods, heroes, and ordinary mortals explored how the age of heroes related to life-as-we-know-it in the fifth and fourth centuries BCE.

Greek tragedy and (digital) puppets

After calling for the eradication of live actors from the stage, and inspired by Greek tragedy, Maeterlinck wrote numerous Symbolist plays 'for puppets', or at least for puppet-like actors. Puppets were seen as a useful alternative due to what Piris calls their 'ontological ambiguity'; while materially an object, in performance the puppet appears to the spectator as a subject endowed with consciousness (2015: 37), an appealing solution to Symbolists caught in a 'constant dialectic ... between material manifestation and spiritual signification' (Heller 1985: 152). Similarly, Maurice Bouchor's work with marionettes from 1888 to 1892 at the Petit Theatre de Marionettes in Paris was inspired by a desire 'to make known to the public those great ancient Greek, Latin and Indian dramatic texts' (Lecucq 2009). Much later, classicist, director and puppeteer Peter Arnott used marionettes in his *Oresteia* (1974), *Antigone* (1977), *Oedipus the King* (1977), *Hippolytus* (1981), *Medea* (1988) and *Bacchae* (1989). Believing that the 'sense of a dimly perceived controlling force [of Arnott manipulating the marionettes from above] is precisely right for Greek tragedy', Arnott also claimed that 'the puppet is exactly like the [Greek tragic] mask – a mask which has grown arms and legs' (Cowan 1980: 52).

A similar call to eradicate the live actors from the stage and replace them with puppets is strongly, but somewhat misleadingly, linked to Edward Gordon Craig. Craig famously stated in his 'The Actor and the Übermarionette'[1] that 'The actor must go, and in his place comes the inanimate figure – the *Übermarionette*' (Bablet 1966: 104ff). Craig was inspired by Greek and other masked acting traditions; in his *Daybook I* (3 February 1909), he wrote, 'I wish to remove *The Actor* with his *Personality* but to leave *the Chorus of Masked figures*' (original emphasis; cited in Bablet 1966: 110). What Craig wanted, however, was not the eradication of the live actor, but the eradication of the ego-filled realist modern actor. The Übermarionette, described as 'the actor plus fire, minus egoism; the fire of the gods and demons, without the smoke and steam of mortality' (Craig 1925: 37), would go beyond 'flesh and blood' life to express the 'death-like beauty' of the Greek masked tragic actor (Craig 1925: 36; Bablet 1966: 109).

An actor who is beyond 'flesh and blood' suggests the digital in its various manifestations. A 2012 adaption of *Antigone* took the use of puppets into the digital age, although the digital in this production was confined to an aggressive electronic sound track, moving lights and text projections. Co-directed by Ulrike Quade and Nicole Beutler, the adaptation featured mostly mute Bunraku puppets, specially made in Japan by Kazunori Watanabe for this project, interacting with human dancing bodies within a densely layered posthuman environment. The production focused on issues of agency and responsibility, on the question, 'Are our actions truly free?'[2] According to Gruber, the performers manipulating the three puppets are at first identified with the three 'characters' in this adaptation, Antigone, Ismene and Polyneices, but as the performance progressed this quasi-organic unity between actor and character is disrupted by the performers constantly changing roles and becoming, at various moments, other substances both animate and inanimate (2016: 130). According to Gruber, this postdramatic and posthuman strategy 'throws into crisis the relationship of fate and individual responsibility' in the tragedy by creating 'a rather rhizomatic network of agency' (2016: 130), a theme expanded upon by Stalpaert (2015) in her analysis of the 'posthuman' characteristics of this performance. Stalpaert foregrounds the 'composite body' of Antigone in the production, and her strategy of resistance 'in which agency is not generated by human deeds or corporeal, targeted actions. Rather, it operates in a "distributed agency" of "vibrant matter"' (2015: 19, drawing on Bennett 2010).

Digital avatars and Greek tragedy

Towards the end of the century, postdramatic productions of Greek tragedy became heavily digital (see Monaghan 2016a). Eckersall notes that both robots (autonomous machines) and virtual figures (mostly projections) 'have become increasingly visible in live performance, functioning more as actors than simply as objects, props, or décor'. The use of robotic and virtual figures in such productions is intended 'to replicate, augment, and/or replace human actors in performance', and indeed in many such performances 'human and non-human actors are virtually indistinguishable' (2015: 123). What makes these figures particularly interesting for this chapter is that their use, in what Eckersall et al. (2017) define as 'new media dramaturgy', constitutes 'the beginning of an understanding of new modes of subjectivity ... a machinic assemblage of "human and non-human flows ..."' (Eckersall 2015: 124, citing Maurizzio Lazzarato).

Giulia Filacanapa and Erica Magris' chapter in this volume explores tragedy as fully digital performance, defined by Dixon as 'all performance works where computer technologies play a *key* role rather than a subsidiary one in content, techniques, aesthetics, or delivery forms' (2007: 3, cited by Filacanapa and Magris on page 149 of this volume). Their examples include the Belgian company Crew's *O_Rex* (2007–08);[3] Dutch company Urland's *The Internet Trilogy*, consisting of three events based on the Prometheus story (from 2014 to 2016);[4] and the German artist Klaus Obermaier's *Oedipus reloaded* (2004), described by Obermaier as featuring an Oedipus who 'wanders lost in the network of high-tech data, blinded by images and information'. The latter production focused on 'the shifting boundaries between illusion and reality, between knowledge, belief and memory'.[5] (For a fuller description and analyses of these productions, see Chapter 7 above). Jan Fabre's *Prometheus-Landscape II* (2011) and *Mount Olympus: To Glorify the Cult of Tragedy* (2016, ongoing) situate highly physicalized human actors inside a harrowing digital landscape. In Romeo Castelucci's radical *Orestea* (1995–96, 2015), humans, animals, and objects are equally enmeshed within a nightmarish digital world that dismembers and incinerates Aeschylus' tragedy.

Examples of tragedy performed in virtual reality are increasingly common. Canada's Avatar Repertory Theatre, for example, staged a completely virtual production of *Oedipus Rex* in 2009–10, when the technology to do such a thing was far more limited than it is now. Prepared and directed by Judith Adele and advised by Dr Jack Turner, the show was performed in Second Life by actors manipulating avatars from their own homes or offices in the UK, Australia and the US.[6] Images of the virtual production show how much time and effort went into the scenography of the work. The script drew from five existing translations to create a simplified text that for the most part followed the Sophoclean original. But long speeches (for example choral songs and messenger speeches) were shortened and intercut with responses from other characters, and the messenger's account of the death of Jocasta and self-blinding of Oedipus was seen happening inside the palace as well as sparsely reported outside by the Messenger.

At the University of Pittsburgh at Greenburg, Stephen Schrum and Elliot Sheedy created a Virtual Reality (Second Life) production of *Prometheus Bound* (2010–11) in which the driving research question was whether a VR production could achieve the aims of Artaud's 'theatre of cruelty' (Schrum 2012). Especially pertinent for this chapter was the question of whether a VR production of Greek tragedy, in which the screen and underlying technology mediate the relationship between the user, the avatar, and the audience, would be able to 'overwhelm the senses of the user' (2012: 212) and also, presumably, the spectators. Schrum makes the valid point that users of VR become fully immersed in that world (referred to as 'telepresence'), keenly experience the 'co-presence' of their fellow users and feel the whole virtual world as being fully real (2012: 212–13). I would add here that digital recordings of live performances are increasingly experienced as perfectly immersive with a strong sense of physical 'presence', especially with more recent technologies and when one is used to 'seeing through' such recordings to the physical realities of live performance. Nevertheless, Schrum admits that the eventual performance of *Prometheus Bound* in December 2011, as both a VR production and a live event in which spectators watched the actors manipulating avatars and the mechanics of the creation of the VR world in real time and motion, did not fully succeed in manifesting Artaud's theatre of cruelty, in part because of limitations in technology available at that time (2012: 219). Both these productions, however, demonstrate the potential for VR Greek tragedy for the purposes of both research and deep experience.

I noted above Filacanapa and Magris' chapter in this volume. What is particularly interesting for this chapter is Filacanapa and Magris' research project *Masks and Avatars*, in which they established 'an analogy between digital technology and practices inherited by the tradition of the theatre mask' (page 151). The mask, they argue, should be considered 'as the instrument *par excellence* of the actor's augmentation and metamorphosis: an artificial extension of the human body which transforms it into a hybrid body characterized by specific acting codes' (page 152). Filacanapa and Magris identify the three fundamental properties of the mask as 'artificiality, constraint and metamorphosis', and suggest that contemporary technology creates the alterity that corresponds to the Greek tragic mask (page 149). Moreover, they suggest, the multiplicity of actants in layered digital performance, including live motion capture, projections, live actors, avatars, participating technicians and so on, produces a dissociative effect in the spectator that takes on meaning in relation to the experience of living in a world of forces far more powerful and less knowable than our own individual subjectivity and agency (page 158). This is most likely exactly what the Greek tragic mask achieved when worn by actors in ancient Greek tragic performances.

The posthuman in Greek tragedy

Why have so many practitioners over the last 130 years sought to depersonalize, mask, technologize, diminish or eradicate the live human actor from productions of Greek tragedy or from other productions inspired by tragedy? As I have suggested in this chapter, the answer, I believe, is multiple, but perhaps the most significant is a recent awareness of what is referred to as our 'posthuman' condition. After some centuries of belief in a concept of 'being human' based in the agency of the purposeful, autonomous, and bounded 'modern subject' (see Geertz 1983: 59), an individuated centre of awareness who is 'the proprietor of his own person or capacities' and therefore in possession of 'freedom from the will of others' (Macpherson 1962: 3, cited in Hayles 1999: 3) – and the modern subject's theatrical counterpart, the modern dramatic character – the relatively recent 'non-human' or 'posthuman' turn suggests a new understanding of what it means to be '(post-) human' that is surprisingly close to the ancient conception described at the beginning of this chapter (see also Telo and Mueller 2020; Mueller 2016). As Katherine Hayles articulates the concept in her groundbreaking *How We Became Posthuman*, the posthuman subject 'is an amalgam, a collection of heterogenous components, a material-information entity whose boundaries undergo continuous construction and reconstruction' (1999: 3).

Possessing a 'distributed cognition located in disparate parts that may be in only tenuous communication with each other' (1999: 3–4), the posthuman subject, she argues, does not need to be 'a literal cyborg' (an organic-machinic amalgam), although this has been the focus of much later posthuman analysis; the defining characteristics of the posthuman 'involve the construction of subjectivity, not the presence of nonbiological components' (1999: 4). While the humanist modern subject – white and male, for the most part – makes his own decisions from a state of closed-circuit homeostatic stability (1999: 8), the posthuman subject, aware that she/he/they is subject to indeterminant flows and energies in the environment, 'begins to envisage herself or himself as a posthuman collectivity, an "I" transformed into a "we" of autonomous agents operating together to make a self' (1999: 6). Or perhaps not quite so autonomous; the posthuman, argues Gane, 'is a condition of uncertainty ... in which the essence of things is far from clear' (2006: 432). Being open to flows and energies, to patterns and randomness, contingencies and unpredictability (Hayles 1999: 285) 'radically destabilizes the ontological foundations of what counts as human' (1999: 24). The ontological ambiguity of the puppet and digital avatars embody just this 'condition of uncertainty'. As Victor Molina (1998) writes, in raising questions about subjecthood and objecthood, the puppet reveals 'that man's body is not a space that ensures the indisputability of his I, but right where man (and together with him, anthropocentrism) finds himself contested' (1998: 176, cited in Williams 2015: 27).

Braidotti suggests that a posthuman awareness brings about 'a displacement of the lines of demarcation between structural differences, or ontological categories' such as 'organic and inorganic, the born and the manufactured, flesh and metal, electronic circuitry and organic nervous systems' (2013: 89–90). While the modern subject conceived himself as possessing individuated will and agency – or rather, while 'that fraction of humanity who had the wealth, power and leisure to conceptualize themselves as autonomous beings exercising their will through individual agency and choice' (Hayles 1999: 286) – the posthuman subject 'envisages the conscious mind as a small subsystem running its program of self-construction and self-assurance while remaining ignorant of the actual dynamics of complex systems' (1999: 286). A more accurate description of (pre-human-ist) tragic protagonists like Aeschylus' Eteocles, Sophocles' Oedipus, or Euripides' Pentheus could hardly be imagined. Their *hamartia* (error, or lack of full awareness, but definitely *not* tragic flaw) in regard to the 'chaotic, unpredictable nature of complex dynamics' (1999: 291) in which they exist is poignantly tragic when misapprehension leads to thinking and decision-making – 'distributed between human and nonhuman agents' (1999: 289) – that has such dire consequences for both others and for themselves.

Later analyses of the posthuman subject draw attention to the continuum on which the human being exists along with animals, objects and machines – or at least technological modification (Chesi & Spiegel 2020: 2). It is here that 'the posthuman' becomes enmeshed with 'the digital', since digital technology has become the prevalent form of the enhancement (or substitution) of the organic (Eckersall et al. 2017: 5). What lies at the centre of the posthuman, in current thinking, is not only the notion that human beings are no longer seen as 'the most important things in the universe' (Gane 2006: 432), but also that other organic and non-organic substances impact human agency. As Jane Bennett (2010) argues in her key formulation of the posthuman, things and non-human bodies are 'vibrant', that is, they possess 'vitality ... the capacity of things – edibles, commodities, storms, metals – not only to impede or block the will and designs of humans but also to act as quasi agents or forces with trajectories, propensities, or tendencies of their own' (2010: viii). One might describe the gods in their many manifestations in Greek myth, epic and tragedy in just these terms.[7] Indeed, Bennet draws consistently on Spinoza's notion of *conatus*, a drive in each individual being or thing to preserve its own essential being (2010: 20–3), an anti-teleological response to Aristotle's notion that each substance or phenomenon strives to transform its innate potential (*dynamis*), which is constitutive of its essential nature (*phusis*), into its *telos* or state of actuality (*energeia*). In seeking to elaborate the notion of vibrant matter, Bennett also draws on the Homeric notion of ψυχή (*psuche*, an impersonal life force), Aristotle's concept of ἐντελέχεια (*entelecheia*, the force which drives potentiality towards actuality), and φύσις (*phusis*, essential nature) (2010: 75, 118). The posthuman, in other words, is also the pre-human(-ist). Where Latour (1993) argues that 'we have never been modern', Hayles suggests that 'we have always been posthuman' (1999: 291).

The future: Greek tragedy without humans

The resonances between the tragic protagonist and the posthuman subject may be at least a partial explanation for the explosion of interest in Greek myth and tragedy over the last 50 years (Hall et al. 2004, 9–46). In this chapter I have provided a brief sketch of productions and adaptations of Greek tragedy, and theatre inspired by Greek tragedy, over the past 130 years that strive to depersonalize the actor or to remove the live actor from the tragic stage altogether. I have argued that the core motivation for this drive is a reawakened awareness of the ontological ambiguity of (masked) tragic personae, of the world assumed and communicated in Greek tragedy, and of the posthuman world as we increasingly experience it. The question then arises, where to next?

I am yet to find a Greek tragedy performed by robots, perhaps because the expense involved would far exceed the budget of theatre companies or universities. But the ontological ambiguity of the Greek masked actor, the puppet, the personae and digital environments of certain postdramatic productions of tragedy, and the use of avatars and VR would be taken a step further by such a move. As noted in the previous section, Eckersall argues that the increasing use of virtual figures (mostly projections) and robots (autonomous machines) 'to replicate, augment, and/or replace human actors in performance' (2015: 123) constitutes 'the beginning of an understanding of new modes of subjectivity' (2015: 124). Belgian artist Kris Verdonck, for example, in his *DANCER # 1*, 2008, 'built dynamic sculptural robots, intended to work as uncanny performative 'figures,' as a commentary on existence' (2015: 125). His work with robots and projections, says Eckersall, creates 'an imaginative space for the viewer to think about the uncanny experience of being human and connected to a world' (2015: 130).

Japanese artist Hirata Oriza's 'robot theatre' features both human actors and non-human actors called 'actroids', designed by his collaborator, Ishiguro Hiroshi, to appear and behave as like as possible to a human being and to possess 'an ability to perform with apparent ease of rapport and sense of agency' (Eckersall 2015: 128). An actroid, Eckersall notes, is a 'somewhat liminal and transgressive figure; a machine that seems to be able to deal with existential concerns such as empathizing with [a] dying girl and, even more radical, dealing with phantasmic forces beyond the perceptible world' (2015: 129). The idea of Greek tragedy as robot theatre is tantalizing, as is a tragic theatre without any human figures whatsoever, whether real or virtual or even robotic. Heiner Goebbels' *Stifter's Dinge* (Stifter's Things), for example, for most of the show has no human figures at all. Certainly, this is not a production or adaptation of a Greek tragedy, but a 2018 review described Goebbels' creation with 'non-human protagonists with a visceral life' as 'philosophy made tangible'.[8] Again, tantalizing.

There has perhaps never been a time when our experience of being (post) human is so close to that of the fifth-century BCE tragedians. Michael Maffesoli argues that the 'philosophical foundation of the modern West: free will, the decisions of individuals or social groups acting together to make history' (2008: 326) is increasingly seen by many as an illusion. Similarly, Lehmann notes that our world is one in which 'political conflicts increasingly elude intuitive perception and cognition', and in which 'almost any form has come to seem more suitable for articulating reality than the action of a causal logic with its inherent attribution of events to the decisions of individuals' (2006: 175, 180). Felski suggests that what makes tragedy 'so resonant to modern theory is its gesturing towards what lies beyond the limits of human understanding' (2008: 1, 3). Terry Eagleton (2008) similarly argues that 'late modernity has recreated in its own way some of the conditions which gave birth to this scapegoat song in classical antiquity' (2008). He points to, amongst other factors,

> the fragility of the once-sovereign subject, its exposure to enigmatic, impenetrable forces, its lack of agency and quickened sense of mortality, the inevitable conflict of goods in a pluralistic culture, the complex density of a social order in which human damage spreads like typhoid. (2008: 340–1)

To communicate such an experience of being (post-)human in the world today, perhaps the most potent productions/adaptations of Greek tragedy now and in the near future will be those that explore the posthuman shifting boundaries between human and non-human, immersing depersonalized live and virtual actors or inanimate actants in a postdramatic, new media 'scenic poem' (Lehman 2006: 110ff) consisting of projections, avatars, robotic figures, technological masking and so on.

Alternatively, a few people will come together in a room; one will have the text of a Greek tragedy in hand and will begin to read it to the others. They will listen intently, making their own connections to the world in which they live.

Notes

1 'The Actor and the Übermarionette' was written in 1907 but published in the second edition of his journal, *Mask*, in 1908 and later in his 1911 *On the Art of the Theatre*.
2 Promotional material for the production when it appeared at the 2015 Incanti International Puppet Festival in Turin, Italy (see https://archivio.festivalincanti.it/en/history/211-2015b/performances-2015.html accessed 26 September 2021).
3 See https://crew.brussels/en/productions/o-rex (accessed 30 September, 2021). See also Stalpaert 2015.
4 See https://urland.nl/en/project/de-internet-trilogie/ (accessed 30 September 2021).
5 See http://www.exile.at/oedipusreloaded/project_english.html (accessed 30 September 2021).
6 Personal communication (25 January 2017).
7 Drawing on Latour's term 'actant' (2004: 237), Bennett describes things and bodies possessing vitality as 'a source of action that can either be human or

non-human; it is that which has efficacy, can *do* things, has sufficient coherence to make a difference, produce effects, alter the course of events' (2010: viii).

8 See https://www.heinergoebbels.com/en/archive/texts/reviews/read/1363 (accessed 30 September 2021).

References

Bablet, D. (1966), *Edward Gordon Craig*, trans. Daphne Woodward, London: Heinemann.
Bennett, J. (2010), *Vibrant Matter: A Political Ecology of Things*, Durham, NC: Duke University Press.
Braidotti, R. (2013), *The Posthuman*, Cambridge: Polity Press.
Calame, C. (1995), *The Craft of Poetic Speech in Ancient Greece*, trans. Janice Orion, Ithaca: Cornell University Press.
Castellucci, R. (2007), 'Agamemnon: Excerpted from Romeo Castellucci's *Oresteia* (Una Commedia Organica?)', trans. J. P. Cermatori, *Theater* 37 (3), pp. 49–71.
Chesi, G. M. and F. Spiegel, eds. (2020), *Classical Literature and Posthumanism*, London: Bloomsbury.
Cowan, S. (1980), 'Peter Arnott's Marionettes and *The Bacchae*', *Theater* 11 (3), pp. 49–54.
Craig, E. G. (1925), *On the Art of the Theatre*, London: Heinemann.
Dixon, S. (2007), *Digital Performance: A History of New Media in Theater, Dance, Performance Art, and Installation*, Cambridge, MA: MIT Press.
Eagleton, T. (2008), 'Commentary', in R. Felski (ed.), *Rethinking Tragedy*, Baltimore, MD: Johns Hopkins University Press, pp. 337–46.
Eckersall, P. (2015), 'Towards a Dramaturgy of Robots and Object-Figures', *TDR: The Drama Review* 59 (3), pp. 123–31.
Eckersall, P., H. Grehan and E. Scheer (2017), *New Media Dramaturgy: Performance, Media and New-materialism*, London: Palgrave Macmillan.
Felski, R. (2008), *Rethinking Tragedy*, Baltimore, MD: Johns Hopkins University Press.
Gane, N. (2006), 'Posthuman', *Theory, Culture & Society* 23 (2–3), pp. 431–4.
Geertz, C. (1983), '"From the Native's Point of View": On the Nature of Anthropological Understanding', in *Local Knowledge: Further Essays in Interpretive Anthropology*, New York: Basic Books, pp. 55–72.
Goldhill, S. (2007), *How To Stage Greek Tragedy Today*, Chicago: University of Chicago Press.
Gruber, C. (2016), 'The Other Antigones: Performing Deconstructed Legacies', in C. Gruber, K. Pewny, S. Leenknegt and L. Van de Dries (eds), *Occupy*

Antigone: Tradition, Transition and Transformation in Performance, Tübingen: Narr Franke Attempto Verlag, pp. 123–36.
Hall, E., F. Macintosh and A. Wrigley (eds) (2004), *Dionysus Since 69: Greek Tragedy at the Dawn of the Third Millennium*. Oxford: Oxford University Press.
Hayles, N. K. (1999), *How We Became Posthuman: Virtual Bodies in Cybernetics, Literature and Informatics*, Chicago: University of Chicago Press.
Heller, R. (1985), 'Concerning Symbolism and the Structure of Surface', *Art Journal* 45 (2), pp.146–53.
Latour, B. (1993), *We Have Never Been Modern*, trans. C. Porter, Cambridge, MA: Harvard University Press.
Latour, B. (2004), *Politics of Nature; How to Bring the Sciences into Democracy*, trans. C. Porter, Cambridge, MA: Harvard University Press.
Lecucq, E. (2009), 'Maurice Bouchor', trans. A. Nguyen, in *World Encyclopedia of Puppetry Arts*. UNIMA. Available at https://wepa.unima.org/en/maurice-bouchor/ (accessed 25 September 2021).
Lehmann, H.-T. (2006), *The Postdramatic Theatre*, trans. K. Jürs-Munby, London: Routledge.
Macpherson, C. B. (1962), *The Political Theory of Possessive Individualism: Hobbes to Locke*, Oxford: Oxford University Press.
Maffesoli, M. (2008), 'The Return of the Tragic in Postmodern Societies', trans. R. Felski, A. Megill and M. Gaddis Rose, in R. Felski (ed.), *Rethinking Tragedy*, Baltimore, MD: Johns Hopkins University Press, pp. 319–36.
Molina, V. (1999), 'Artificial Creatures', in *Escenes de l'Imaginari*, Barcelona: Ed. Institut del Teatre, Centre de Cultura Contemporània de Barcelona.
Monaghan, P. (2008), 'Mask, Word, Body and Metaphysics in the performance of Greek Tragedy', *Didaskalia* 7 (1).
Monaghan, P. (2016a), 'Aeschylus as Postdramatic Analogue: "A Thing Both Cool and Fiery"', in S. E. Constantinidis, ed. *The Reception of Aeschylus' Plays through Shifting Models and Frontiers*, Leiden: Brill, pp. 250–79.
Monaghan, P. (2016b), 'Tragedy Without Character: Dood Paard's Postdramatic "Cool"', in P. Monaghan and J. Montgomery Griffiths (eds), *Close Relations: Spaces of Greek and Roman Theatre*, Newcastle upon Tyne: Cambridge Scholars Publishing, pp. 197–223.
Mueller, M. (2016), *Objects as Actors: Props and the Poetics of Performance in Greek Tragedy*, Chicago: University of Chicago Press.
Piris, P. (2015), 'The Co-Presence and Ontological Ambiguity of the Puppet', in D. N. Posner, C. Orenstein and J. Bell (eds), *The Routledge Companion to Puppetry and Material Performance*, London: Routledge, pp. 30–42.
Schrum, S. and E. Sheedy (2012), 'Building a Virtual Reality Model of Artaud's Theatre of Cruelty', *Metaverse Creativity* 2 (2), pp. 205–21.
Stalpaert, C. (2015), 'CREW's O_REX (2007) and Nicole Beutler's *Antigone* (2012): Composite Bodies of Resistance', *Performance Research* 20 (2), pp. 18–23.

Telò, M., and M. Mueller (eds) (2020), *The Materialities of Greek Tragedy: Objects and Affect in Aeschylus, Sophocles, and Euripides*, London: Bloomsbury.

Vernant, J.-P., and P. Vidal-Naquet (1990), *Myth and Tragedy in Ancient Greece*, New York: Zone Books.

Wiles, D. (2007), *Mask and Performance in Greek Tragedy: From Ancient Festival to Modern Experimentation*, Cambridge: Cambridge University Press.

Williams, M. (2015), 'The Death of "The Puppet"?' in D. N. Posner, C. Orenstein and J. Bell (eds), *The Routledge Companion to Puppetry and Material Performance*, London: Routledge, pp. 18–29.

IN MEMORIAM – MICHAEL CACOYANNIS

Technological triumph and Greek tragedy
Digitizing Michael Cacoyannis' Trojan *Trilogy*

Marianne McDonald

Introduction

Visual performance is the acme of production. Sometimes, however, print or audio transmission is preferred, such as e-books or iBooks for an iPad or cell phones. In addition, there is a classical discussion list (CLASSICS-L), so that conversations take place on the classics and performances in the social context of the digital medium. There are many books on technology and performance in the theatre (see for example Burgess 2014; Olizewski et al. 2018; Warren 2018). However, this does not take into consideration all the other technological avenues of transmission – film, television or radio; mobile phones and other devices that also make performance possible.

Computers play a role, not only being able to play films and performances, but to digitalize data, and keep track of the multiple uses of words in the ancient manuscripts. I married the computer with Greek texts and brought the idea to Irvine where they were receptive, particularly with the offer of the initial endowment, which people claimed was the largest for a project in the humanities up to that time. That was the birth of the *Thesaurus Linguae Graecae*. For a while it had a branch in Greece, and both Melina Mercouri and Dora Bakoyannis were enthusiastic about it. Thus, a highly technological arena was spotlighted by a doyenne of the world of theatre and film performance and by another with more than a foot in the world of foreign affairs and cultural politics. But it has outlasted this splash of glorification and is now widely used by classicists throughout the world to better engage with the shades and textures of the meaning of words in those ancient texts.

The TLG allowed me, for example, to computerize *Terms for Happiness in Euripides* (McDonald 1978). It could locate all the occurrences in Euripides' manuscripts of the same terms, which then provided the basis for my commentary. The terms I chose were μάκαρ, ὄλβιος, εὐδαίμων, and εὐτυχής. The first term had a connotation of divine happiness, the second of wealth, the third happy inside (inhabited by a good *daimon*) and the last lucky. All of them, coupled with morality, are recipes for a good happy life.

This example of modern-day technological reconstruction of a distant yet still powerful actuality would not have surprised the Greeks I was studying and building a database around. They were technologically-minded themselves, and based on their needs and aims innovated as opportunity and circumstances both offered and allowed. In fifth-century Athens, the democratic Greeks were masters of the sea and of their land. Their drama and the settings for that drama showed a technological prowess that in many ways has not been surpassed. Their theatres, for example, were built into hills so that the topography contributed not only to the acoustics of what was being performed but also to the clarity of sightlines between the *orchestra* and the *theatron* – both very important because, while theatre was entertainment, it was also a way for the polis to educate its citizens. Athens and Epidaurus had theatres that also had spectacular views of the countryside, the effect of which must have been awe at the actors in this setting as well as a deepened wonder at the land itself. Modern Delphi uses its stadium beneath Parnassus to achieve these effects in modern times.

The actors wore masks and this allowed the same actor to take various roles. There is an excellent article which points out the nuances between the same voices yet different mask (Pavlovskis 1977). For instance, Ajax and Teucer sharing the same voice 'besides accenting their resemblance as brothers – for although Teucer is a lesser man, their characters are not unlike – this overlap emphasizes how Teucer identifies himself with his brother's interests after his death' (1977: 116). So even before modern technology the use of different masks with limited actors could add additional commentary. The Greeks had their own technological touches, then.

In this homage to Michael Cacoyannis, I shall concentrate on film and how it allows many liberties the Greek stage did not – for instance, change of location. There are also close-ups, and then the camera moving back – what is termed 'dollying-out' – would provide another nuance. Then there is depth of field, by which those marvellous views at Athens and Epidaurus come under even greater control of the director. Film, I should note, also delivers a type of immortality, as long as one can replay the film, in contrast to staged drama, which is necessarily unique in each one of its performances.

Michael Cacoyannis' Trojan *Trilogy*

One of the most famous directors of Greece (born in Cyprus), Michael Cacoyannis provides a gold mine in his Trojan *Trilogy* for effects provided by technology: *Electra* (1961), *The Trojan Women* (1971) and *Iphigenia at Aulis* (1977).[1] These films appeared in roughly the same chronological order as Euripides' plays did in *his* ouevre. More substantively, both the films and the plays all have an antiwar message with powerful criticism of the oppression of man by man.

Euripides and Cacoyannis also both disregard the chronological sequence of the narrative of the Trojan War: the sacrifice of Iphigenia, the last part of their trilogy, takes place before the war; *Trojan Women* dramatizes the plight of the women of the city after the taking of Troy; and *Electra* stages the catastrophe involved in the murder of Queen Clytemnestra and Aegisthus after these two tyrants, now rulers of Greece, had killed Agamemnon upon his return from the war. In all three films, Cacoyannis's leading actress, Irene Papas, was gifted with an emotional eloquence in her facial expressions that could tell more than any words. And these films covered close to twenty years of her life. Age, it would seem, is another actor – or is it perhaps a mask?

In the first film, Papas (as Electra) is a young girl facing adult decisions – love as well as revenge and murder; in the second, she is a femme fatale (Helen); and the third shows her as a mother (Clytemnestra), who in the final frame of the film guarantees vengeance for the sacrifice of her daughter Iphigenia: the film seems to stand still as the wind blows her hair across her eyes, eyes filled with hate. This last frame predicts Aeschylus's *Oresteia*, and we know that Agamemnon will pay for sacrificing his daughter simply so he could return victorious from the Trojan War. His death is foreseen in Clytemnestra's eyes, and we know it will come at her hands. All this is the result of technology showing us through facial expressions both the present and the future. The ancient mask, on the other hand, was unchanging and incapable of this sort of volatile emotional commentary.

Cacoyannis and Theodorakis have humanized the ancient Greek drama, and unfolded the Greek landscape before our eyes with the sun and moon adding their commentary. The camera allows the spectator to see revealing close-ups and can, in a moment, show the panorama of the setting. Thanks are due to the British cameraman Walter Lassally whose genius was apparent in the first two films; *Iphigenia* featured George Arvanitis as the gifted cameraman, adding his special Greek talent. The composer Mikis Theodorakis (one of the greatest composers Greece has ever had, if not the world) added his special genius to all three of these Cacoyannis films.

Electra

A prologue to the *Electra* reenacts the murder of Agamemnon, and also focuses on both Clytemnestra and Aegisthus gloating over this crime. The cinematic stage is set. The palace and the countryside with its cottage are well presented in the cinema in a way that would be impossible in the ancient theatre. The palace where Electra was detained (before being exiled to the countryside to marry a peasant, and so be no threat to the present rulers) was a prison and Lassally's camera captures its forbidding aspect. In the film, the countryside is hardly lugubrious exile, but is welcoming, with spaciousness, dances and lyrical song, particularly as provided by Mikis Theodorakis. His work replaces the songs and dances of the ancient Greek chorus. Then, the panning across the Greek landscape is a technological gift a fixed theatre cannot offer.

Cacoyannis's *Electra* uses facial expressions available through the casting of particular actors to make Orestes and Electra into hero and heroine. This would not be possible with the Greek mask. The murder of Clytemnestra and Aegisthus is still repulsive, but by the time it happens it is welcomed, even though Aegisthus was more loathed than Clytemnestra. Electra will not mate with the peasant she is forced to marry, but he is still kind to her. Aegisthus comes to taunt her when she visits the grave of Agamemnon. Electra fears for her life. Aegisthus is dressed in finery and Electra in peasant clothing. When Orestes tries to find his sister they are both cautious and then joyous when the tutor helps them identify each other, another effect of the close-up. Pylades, Orestes' companion, becomes a love interest in his expression of happiness when Electra reveals she has rejected any advance from her peasant husband. Greek tragedy is transformed into pastoral romance through the technology of cinema.

Orestes and Electra plot to kill the rulers. First, Orestes goes to a wine festival that Aegisthus is hosting. He and Pylades join in a dance, keeping Agamemnon's sword hidden until it is needed to kill Aegisthus. This was the very sword used to kill Agamemnon. The film makes this visual parallel possible: striking close-ups of the sword are intercut with the narrative. Then there is the sound of music: dance music plays against Orestes' clashing his sword on his shield after he has successfully killed Aegisthus. A joyous march follows as the body of Aegisthus is presented to Electra, who is faced with the Aegisthus who is characterized as Clytemnestra's 'pretty boy'. Electra says she will entice her mother to her house by suggesting she has a child. Orestes and she will be waiting.

The scene switches to morning. The cinema allows effects such as sunrise and the Greek countryside. Clytemnestra is plastered with makeup – the tight focus hardly allows us to miss it – and is lavishly dressed. She and Electra debate outside as Clytemnestra tries to justify herself: She claims she killed Agamemnon first because of the sacrifice Iphigenia so that he could have his victory at Troy. The second reason given is the fact that Agamemnon was importing Cassandra as his mistress. Lastly she says she embodies the curse on the house of Atreus. Electra beckons her to enter the house. Clytemnestra hesitates, but she complains that Aegisthus is waiting for her so she has no time to waste. Clytemnestra enters the house, where instead of Electra's baby, she meets her death. Screams are heard inside. Theodorakis punctuates this with the cries of clarinet, with percussion provided by wood blocks striking each other as in a climactic scene in Japanese Noh plays. This is the technology of music on modern or foreign instruments.

The peasant women outside scream and fall to the ground. Intercut imagery provides more commentary. We see an eagle chasing small birds: those in power abusing those who are more vulnerable. The setting shifts to the inside of the house. Clytemnestra falls, her hand covered by rings (close-up), grabs Electra's dress. As Orestes falters, Electra urges him on and helps by holding the sword with him. Cacoyannis is faithful to the Greek tragedy rule that violence is not shown on stage; he doesn't show the deathblow, but conveys it by Clytemnestra's scream. Both children suddenly realize the enormity of their crime in slaying their own mother. The people gather outside with none of the rejoicing that followed Aegisthus's death. The murder of a parent is never justified. All realize this is just another death in the house of Atreus, fulfilling the family curse, but it is still a curse. Electra and Orestes in killing Aegisthus and their mother realize they are no better than the criminals they slew.

Orestes leaves and starts up a hill with Pylades. Electra goes in a different direction. Orestes waves to Pylades to follow Electra, so he follows her. Both Orestes and Electra seem to be alone and isolated in their mutual crime. The visuals give added commentary, here showing duty vs a love interest. Cacoyannis through his filming Euripides' version has humanized the story, focusing on the human tragedy, rather than the fulfilment of a curse. He has also humanized the characters much more than Euripides, who cast them in a darker light. High and low angle shots show who has the power and who doesn't, and offers more commentary by the camera.

This film is in black and white, and both become symbolic in this story. The Greek landscape seems another character in this moving film, a feat only achieved by technology directed by the human hand.

The Trojan Women

The next film, *The Trojan Women*, shows an Irene Papas who has matured. She is seen as a figurehead, an excuse for a war that was inevitable given Troy's riches. Cacoyannis says in his prologue that he wanted to convey Euripides' 'timeless indictment of the horror and futility of all wars'. In each of these three films a victor becomes the victim, illustrating that the murder of another creates a debt that demands to be paid, and often with the life of the murderer.

Cacoyannis's prologue features a four-note leitmotif by Theodorakis at the beginning, which shows Troy burning and the Greeks leaving with prisoners and booty. It recurs later when the chorus recounts the taking of Troy, and finally the total destruction of the city at the end, with women and children led off to slavery fleeing the city in flames. Here, the city's destruction and its dire consequences are the fate of the city and the taking of its citizens as prisoners.

The prologue gives some of the facts, such as the war lasting ten years. We see men leaving loaded with booty and leading their new slaves. This will be echoed at the end of the film. In the prologue it is said the Greeks knew about the wealth of Troy so that 'when Helen, queen of Sparta, fled with Paris, deserting Menelaus for a Trojan's love, they were ready'. The four chords return and the prologue says 'Oh, fools, men who lay a city waste, so soon to die themselves'. Then Hecuba is seen lying before the gates, realizing her loss. Here is a real contrast with Helen as given to us by the camera. Then the film proper begins. It is in English, whereas the other two are in Greek with subtitles for distribution in countries that don't understand Greek. (Cacoyannis uses the translation by the renowned American classicist Edith Hamilton.) This film features a star-studded cast. Irene Papas plays Helen, Katherine Hepburn plays Hecuba, Genevieve Bujold plays Cassandra and Vanessa Redgrave plays Andromache: one American, one Englishwoman, one French and one Greek. This leads to an almost comical mixture of accents, another feature of modern technology. The audience, however, overlooks these discrepancies and accepts the conventions that the medium offers. Comedy leaves as tragedy seeps in.

The prisoners see to whom they are assigned. Close-ups show the agony in the faces of the chosen. Hecuba suspects Polyxena has been sacrificed at Achilles's tomb, and in the 'chorus' that follows, Andromache discovers her body. Soon, she will discover that her son Astyanax will also die. The camera shows Andromache lying on the ground with a high angle shot, emphasizing her helplessness. A close-up of Helen's beautiful eyes looking out of the cabin where she is held follows this shot of Andromache in despair. Helen gets water to bathe whereas the prisoners hardly get enough to drink. The camera indirectly shows the cause of this present tragedy (at least in the Greeks' minds, since they blame the war on Helen). Cacoyannis has the Greeks milling about, admitting 'Greeks don't go to war for gold, they find a cause. That's what Helen is – a cause.' Nevertheless, everyone is clear about why this war was fought. Not over a woman, but out of greed. Andromache pushes

Astyanax into the crowd of women for protection. From a low camera angle, they are seen flapping uselessly like birds. Again the cinema gives this perspective.

Another technological touch is playing the same music that was played as the Greeks were hauling off booty at the beginning. Even the music makes the real cause of the war clear. Cassandra appears with torches and the camera weaves to keep time with her frenzied movements. She is told she is destined for Agamemnon's bed. She says she will be his death. Hecuba is seen from a low angle shot mounting some stairs, then faces the camera: 'Count no man happy, however fortunate, before he dies.' A chorus follows recounting the taking of Troy; the camera shows the faces of women individually and close up as each delivers her line. Once again the Greek chorus is transformed by technology. The camera likewise contrasts the mobility of the Greeks versus the immobility of their prisoners. We see they are trapped and cannot escape. Also, Theodorakis's drums add to the solemnity, adding elements from Noh drama, so suitable for Greek tragedy. This is the most ritualistic of these three films by Cacoyannis on Greek drama, and drums contribute to this.

Through Cacoyannis's use of technology we share the victim's perspective, a powerful truth brought to bear through technological tools. The scene between Menelaus and Helen emphasizes her sexuality. She declares she was kidnapped, and taken against her will. Hecuba sneers at her, calling on Menelaus to kill her, but the camera makes clear that Helen has won him over, in spite of his protestations to the contrary. Helen grabs a knife from a guard, as if she were going to use it on herself. Menelaus takes it away from her and tells his men to take her to the ship. Menelaus says he will let the Greeks kill her in Greece, but his actions and the way he looks at Helen makes it clear that she has won. The camera shows this nonverbal victory, a tragic turn for those who wanted Helen punished for her adultery.

By cutting to the ship, Cacoyannis affirms Helen's victory. Another cut is to the scene where Astyanax is pushed off a cliff, a fatal consequence of this war and the mad cruelty of the conquerors. Cut again, and the billowing crash of the sail parallels the crash of Astyanax's fall, all technological devices to enhance the tragedy. Hecuba is left to bury Astyanax on his heroic father's – Hector's – shield. Astyanax's sacrifice is comparable to Iphigenia's, which we shall see, below, in the third film by Cacoyannis to be discussed. Both are innocents in contrast to their brutal murderers. Behind Astyanax's funeral, the same Byzantine chant that accompanied Cassandra's departure plays, drawing a musical parallel between these two innocent victims. Cacoyannis's camera allows us to see Cassandra leaving in a chariot and making her prophesies to anyone – no one! – who can hear her. We see her blink repeatedly in the final still, suggesting her madness. The camera is as powerful as she is in involving us in a truth that a stage rendition could not. Breaking up Cassandra's prophecies implies she has transcendence over time. So does the camera share this transcendence?

The city is set on fire, an effect that could only be achieved in the cinema. This film began at daybreak and ends in evening, another cinematic feat underlining mortality. The women are herded away like cattle. The credits roll over their departure. Dust is seen blowing and women's weeping is heard. Over the screen we read: 'We who have made this film dedicate it to all those who fearlessly oppose the oppression of man by man.' Cacoyannis technologically rewrites Euripides. At times he also alters Edith Hamilton's translation. He eliminates the gods from the prologue, and also their appearance at the end of Euripides' play.

Cacoyannis dashes all hope, even the hope that the Greeks will be punished, as Euripides' gods tell us. Cacoyannis's Hecuba does not believe one should trust the gods. Perhaps the new technology of cinema is all that should be trusted. The only hope that Cacoyannis gives is that we can see our mistakes vividly and clearly, and perhaps learn from them.

Iphigenia at Aulis

The final film in Cacoyannis's trilogy is *Iphigenia at Aulis*. Here the victim is also a heroine and shows herself above all the sordid men about to conduct a brutal war for gold. It is typical of Euripides that the protagonist is a heroine. And she is typical of the great women in Greek tragedy, so many more of them than in Shakespeare or most other writers.

The prologue tells us about an expedition to Troy to take vengeance for Menelaus's wife having been stolen. We are told there are a thousand ships about to set sail from Aulis to Troy, but also that they are forcibly becalmed. Shots panning across the harbour convey the absolute stillness. Some shots are low angle making the ships appear monstrous yet immobile. Calchas and his monks – Bernard Knox called them Hare Krishna priests[2] – appear. Flute music accompanies them, which suggests they are like Buddhist monks. Agamemnon commands his men to kill flocks of animals around the fields, but they are warned to avoid the sacred deer. Nevertheless they shoot it also.

One close-up of a ship shows a gargoyle that resembles a devil. The camera pauses on the still ocean and the title *Iphigenia* appears. The brutal slaughter has prefigured what will happen at Troy, but Iphigenia is here also obviously the sacred deer. That evening, the soldiers are aimlessly milling about. Calchas announces that they will have the winds if they give the gods the sacrifice they demand. Agamemnon agrees before he knows what that is; in private, Calchas tells Agamemnon that the gods demand his oldest daughter Iphigenia as the sacrifice. Agamemnon smashes the tablet on which the request is written. He leaves to the cheering of his men, who sing a song of victorious conquest.

Agamemnon is seduced by his men and power, just as Menelaus was seduced by Helen. Back in Mycenae, we see Iphigenia waving her arms at her mother as she stands on a hill. Her white dress flows in the wind and she resembles an angel. The scene shifts to the palace. Cacoyannis is able to suggest that these edifices are timeless, and he films in a way that does not show that many are ruins. Clytemnestra tells Iphigenia she is betrothed to Achilles, the great hero, and that therefore they both will go to Aulis for the wedding. This is the pretext Agamemnon is using to lure her to Aulis. Agamemnon tells her mother to stay at home. But we know Clytemnestra: she goes to Argos in spite of his order to stay in Mycenae.

At Aulis, Achilles is seen lying naked on the beach and the wind blows over the sand. We hear drums that seem to irritate Agamemnon. As Knox said of this in his review of the film, 'The native are restless tonight, Carruthers.'[3] The arrival of horses and carriages shows that the family has arrived. While the play does not show horses in the staging area because of space limitation, the technology of film removes these barriers.

In this film, Clytemnestra is seen as a loving mother, with the young Orestes and her daughter Iphigenia. The camera shows that her relationship with Agamemnon is cold and formal by comparison with the warm relationship she has with her children. When it turns evening, the moon is full, and that was mark the time of the sacrifice: it will take place in daylight, the very next day. When they arrive, Iphigenia wants to greet her father. There is a musical theme for Iphigenia which we heard back in Argos, but which plays here, and will play as she goes off to die. The music intensifies the drama. He weeps when he sees Iphigenia, and explains to her that he realizes they will soon be parted (one explanation, the marriage). He also says he will make a sacrifice, and she asks to be by his side. The irony is almost unbearable. She exemplifies *philia*, her allegiance to honour and principles, those that the army and Agamemnon seem to dismiss.

The truth comes out. Achilles tells Clytemnestra that he will protect Iphigenia, but in fact he is as weak as Agamemnon before the army. Clytemnestra confronts Agamemnon, pouring her hatred on him – not only for this, but now beause he is sacrificing his own daughter for a whore, Helen, who (seduced also by Troy's gold) ran off with Paris when she left Menelaus's home. Clytemnestra threatens Agamemnon with vengeance on his return. In a sense she threatens him with Aeschylus's *Agamemnon*. Iphigenia runs, but is trapped by the army in the forest like the defenceless deer they slaughtered earlier. Then later, she asks Agamemnon to kiss her. He does and explains that though he loves her, he is helpless before the army. Clytemnestra takes Iphigenia in her arms and sings what seems like a Greek folk song, pleading that the sun should hide, so that death might be lost from view. Cacoyannis began his play in sunlight and it ends in a sunset, which we see on the screen.

Calchas whispers to Odysseus that they should not delay because the wind is rising. This scene is included to show the corruption of all the players. Iphigenia's sacrifice was not needed but was just a power play, just as the sack of Troy was not to avenge a husband but to sack it for its treasures. The cinema of Cacoyannis rewrites myths, and shows the vulgar truth in its full corrosive splendour. Achilles is prepared to die for Iphigenia, as is her mother, but when the soldiers come for her, she walks freely to her death. She will die with honour for Greece. Her marriage will be to death as she puts on a wedding veil, and her father adds a wreath. She walks up a hill to Calchas who grabs her as the wind is rising, blowing black smoke. Calchas looks like a black bird of prey. A lament plays on the Greek *Baglamas* (a form of Bouzouki, only pitched higher) as the ships sail away. We see the wind blowing Clytemnestra's hair across her eyes filled with hate as she sails back to Argos and Mycenae. We know what will happen in the future.

Notes

1 See Cacoyannis's '*Electra*: All in the Family', 'Victor/Victim: A Dialectic: Cacoyannis's *The Trojan Women*' and 'Cacoyannis and Euripides' *Iphigenia at Aulis*: A New Heroism' in McDonald 1983: 129–319.
2 Knox 1979: 352–3. Professor Knox was quite irreverent and found many effects by Cacoyannis out of place (such as the Hare Krishna priests in their white robes and barefoot with shaved heads: he says they only need 'a begging bowl and a mantra or two'). Knox judges that he has created a new genre, 'the souvlaki Western'. I appreciate Knox's humor, but I have much more respect for Cacoyannis's modernizing than he did.
3 McDonald 1990: 69–84.

References

Burgess, Kieran (2014), *Technical Theatre and Production Design: In Immersive Theatre: Examining the Use of Theatrical Technologies in Creating an Immersive Micro-scene*, 2nd edn, Great Britain: the author, 2014.

Knox, Bernard (1979), *Word and Action*, Baltimore, MD and London: Johns Hopkins University Press.

McDonald, Marianne (1978), *Terms for Happiness in Euripides*, Göttingen: Vandenhoeck & Ruprecht.

McDonald, Marianne (1983), *Euripides in Cinema: The Heart Made Visible*, Philadelphia: Centrum.

McDonald, Marianne (1990), 'Iphigenia's *Philia*: Motivation in Euripides's *Iphigenia at Aulis*: A New Heroism', *Quaderni Urbinati di Cultura Classica* Nuova Serie 34.

Olizewski Alex, and Daniel Fine with Daniel Roth (2018). *Digital Media, Projection Design & Technology for Theatre*, New York and London: Routledge.

Pavlovskis, Zoja (1977), 'The Voice of the Actor in Greek Tragedy', *Classical World*, pp. 113–23.

Warren, Jason (2018), *Creating Worlds: How to Make Immersive Theatre*, London: Nick Hern Books.

Index

Aeschylus
   Agamemnon 151, 165, 174–6, 177, 221
   Choephori 75, 77, 103, 104, 108
   Oresteia 52, 65, 68, 101–2, 165, 178, 215; *see also* Lavaudant, Georges; Mitchell, Katie
   Persians 134, 200
   Prometheus 22
   Seven against Thebes 134
   Suppliant Women 133
Agamemnon Redux (2018), *see* Lavender, Andy
Age of Rage (2021) 2
Alcestis, *see* Euripides
Alexis Una Tragedia Greca (2010) 67, 75
Antigone 29, 53, 75, 202
Antigone
   Arnott, 1977 202
   De Fusco, 2012 16, 67
   Quade and Beutler, 2012 202–3
   Sophocles 133–4
   van Hove, 2015 53, 58
Antigone Test (2020) 163, 167–8, 180 n.3
Arnott, Peter 8, 202
audience
   and architecture 30–1, 41–3, 45, 75, 77–8, 83, 131–2, 155, 173–4
   as chorus 74–5, 100–11, 117–18, 120, 155
   digital 2, 7, 21, 29, 70–1
   engagement 1, 42, 45, 73–5, 77, 103, 105–7, 117
   perception 1, 65–6, 68, 70, 140, 178
   and technology 21, 30–1, 46–7, 73, 82–3, 102, 110, 150, 160, 167–8, 173–4, 204
augmented reality 1, 3, 11, 70, 77, 93, 119, 151–2, 159

Bacchae (2010) 119–22
   see also Euripides
Bacchae, The
   Euripides 20, 114–29
   Spiropoulos, Georgia (2010) 119–22
   Zé Celso (2016) 115–19
   ZT Hollandia (2002) 67
Brecht, Bertolt 45–6, 50

Cacoyannis, Michael 22, 213–14, 222 n.2
   Trojan *Trilogy* 214–22
Cassandra 149–81, 217, 218–20
   see also Aeschylus, *Agamemnon*
Cassiers, Guy 67, 152
Castellucci, Romeo 51, 65, 67, 74–5, 94 n.1
Celso Martiz Corrêa, José, *see* Zé Celso
chorus
   augmented 114–28, 160
   communality 19–20, 99–112
   digital 20, 49–50, 91–2, 100–12, 115, 119, 127, 157–60, 219
   function 100, 104–7, 109–10, 153, 155, 175–6, 200–1
   movement 54, 124, 159
   tragic 131–5, 139–40, 157–8
   voices 20, 74–5, 114–15, 116–17, 119–27
   see also audience, as chorus
communality 20, 99–107, 109–12, 150
Craig, Edward Gordon 41, 152, 157
   übermarionette 202, 209 n.1
cyborgs 21, 73–4, 174–5, 177–9, 186, 205

Index

Dadaists 44
digital
  body 64, 74, 92
  scenery 49, 56, 57–8, 83–94,
    94 n.3, 170–1, 204
  see also audience, digital; chorus,
    digital
  director 1–3, 7–8, 13–15, 51–2, 54,
    64–6, 74, 99–101
  dramaturgy 7, 12–13, 15, 93, 152–3,
    158–9
  new media 65–6, 69, 71, 94 n.2,
    203
  rhizomatic 75–8
  sonic 56–7, 74–5, 117

ekkyklema 41, 52, 55–7, 58
Electra, *see* Euripides
Euripides 213, 215
  Alcestis 67, 68
  Bacchae 20, 114–29
  Electra 215–17
  Hippolytus 81, 88, 95 n.10
  Iphigenia at Aulis 220–2
  Medea 81, 84, 86–8
  Phaedra 90
  Suppliants 134
  The Trojan Women 217–20
EXPLORER/*Prometheus*
  Ontketend (2015) 73–4, 156,
    160

Fabre, Jan 56, 203
Futurism 43–4, 56

Hippolytus, *see* Euripides
hypermediality 15–16, 75–6

intermediality 15–16, 18, 44, 46, 75–7,
  86, 102–11
intertextuality 18–19, 77, 86
Iphigenia at Aulis, *see* Euripides;
  Mitchell, Katie
Iphigenia in Between (2004), *see*
  Svich, Caridad

Kapsali, Maria 17
Khan, Akram 22, 182–97

Labex Arts-H2H 151
Lavaudant, Georges 100–2, 107–12
Lavender, Andy 151, 156–7, 160
Le Fura del Baus 163, 167, 179
Lehmann, Hans-Thies 94 n.2, 208
Lepage, Robert 48, 74, 152
light 10, 42, 71, 74, 75, 76, 119, 168
L'Orestie (1999), *see* Lavaudant,
  Georges

masks 21, 83, 151–4, 159–61, 200–1,
  205, 214–16
  virtual 119–21, 127, 149–61
  vocal 120–1, 127
Medea, *see* Euripides
Medea, *The* (2005) 84–7
  see also Scheib, Jay
Medea Electronique 67
Mitchell, Katie 56, 58, 94 n.1, 152
  Iphigenia at Aulis 57
  The Oresteia 53–4, 55–6, 67,
    101–7, 110–12
Motus, *see* Alexis Una Tragedia
  Greca
multimediality 15–16, 43–4, 48, 70,
  82–4, 87, 90, 93, 102–6, 111

Obermaier, Klaus 149–50, 203
ODC Ensemble 70, 163, 167–8
  see also Antigone Test (2020)
Oresteia, *see* Aeschylus; Castellucci,
  Romeo; Le Fura del Baus
Oresteia, *The* (1999), *see* Mitchell,
  Katie)

Papakonstatinou, Elli 150, 167
  see also Antigone Test (2020);
    ODC Ensemble
Persona Theatre Company 81, 90–3
Phaedra, *see* Euripides
Phaedra I– (2019), *see* Persona
  Theatre Company

Piscator, Erwin 44–6, 48–54
postdigital 18, 27–35, 190–1
posthuman 1, 18, 82, 200, 202, 205–9
Poulou, Angeliki 13, 19, 57, 101–2, 104
PythiaDelphine21 163–4, 168–70, 173, 178–9

rhizome 15–16, 75–8, 202
Rodosthenous, George 1, 106, 149

Sampatakakis, George 114
Scheib, Jay 84–7
scenic writing 64–5
scenography 7, 19, 49, 56–7, 83–5, 90, 94 n.3, 170–1, 204
  see also digital scenery; light; sound
Sidiripoulou, Avra 10–11, 19, 95 n.13
sound
  acoustic scenography 170–1
  kinaesonic 163, 170, 173, 178–9, 180 n.1
  see also dramaturgy, sonic; chorus, voices
Spiropoulos, Georgia 119–22
Suppliants, *see* Euripides

To You, the Birdie! (2002) 87–90, 166, 171–2, 178
  see also Wooster Group

Traces of Antigone (2019),
  see Papakonstatinou, Elli
Trojan Women, The, *see* Euripides

Übermarionette, *see* Craig, Edward Gordon
Urland and Crew
  EXPLORER/Prometheus Ontketend (2015) 73–4, 156, 160
  Internet Trilogy (2014–2016) 150, 203

van Hove, Ivo 2, 53–4, 58, 67, 94 n.1
  see also Age of Rage (2021); *Antigone* (2015)
virtual reality 21, 73, 150–1, 203–4

war 45–50, 103, 104, 164, 185, 190
  Balkan War 103, 110
  First World War 45, 184–5
  Second World War 49–50, 107, 143, 174
  Trojan War 56, 103, 104, 156–7, 215, 217–18
  Vietnam War 46
Warlikowski, Kzryztof 67, 68, 72, 73
Wooster Group 48, 54, 81–2, 87–90, 163, 166, 170–1, 178

Xen(os) (2018), *see* Khan, Akram

Zé Celso 115–19

www.ingramcontent.com/pod-product-compliance
Lightning Source LLC
Chambersburg PA
CBHW062216300426
44115CB00012BA/2091